Moral Inertia

Moral Inertia

Ideas for Social Action

❋ ❋ ❋

Mary Maxwell

University Press of Colorado

The University Press of Colorado is a cooperative publishing enterprise
supported, in part, by Adams State College, Colorado State University, Fort
Lewis College, Mesa State College, Metropolitan State College of Denver,
University of Colorado, University of Northern Colorado, University of
Southern Colorado, and Western State College.

The paper used in this publication meets the minimum requirements of the
American National Standard for Information Sciences—Permanence of Paper
for Printed Library Materials.
ANSI Z39.48–1984

∞

Library of Congress Cataloging-in-Publication Data

Maxwell, Mary.
    Moral inertia: ideas for social action / Mary Maxwell.
    p. cm.
    Includes bibliographical references and index.
    ISBN 0-87081-196-7 (hard: alk. paper). — ISBN 0-87081-197-5
(pbk.: alk. paper)
    1. Social ethics. 2. Social action. I. Title.
HM216.M313 1991
303.3'72—dc20   90-25456
                                                  CIP

For K.J.W., "the saint,"
and for Al Ain

Contents

Preface

Like the stripper from Kansas City who "went about as fer as she could go," I feel that I have gone about as far as I can go, in this book, in discussing and analyzing morality. This volume contains nine theoretical essays and eight book reviews covering numerous aspects of morality. Topics of the books under review include government secrecy; biblical ideas about economic stewardship; the protection of the environment and socially responsible investing; the ethics of hunger; war crimes and torture; greed, materialism, and the contemporary cultural emphasis on success; individualism versus community; racism; the settlement of conflicting interests; and the problem of military bureaucracy in democratic nations. (Is there much left to talk about?) The theoretical essays wax abstract about these matters, and they look into the meaning and role of morality in society.

Finding a title that succinctly conveyed the contents of this book was, of course, impossible. For a while the title *Social Morality* was used, but of course that phrase is redundant — how can morality be anything but social? (It's hard to think what a hermit would have to be moral about!) *The Structure of Morality* was also considered but sounded a bit dry and, worse, risked association with the structuralist school. The title *Morality and Power* made it to the finals, since it conjured up the fundamental rivalry between morality and power *and* hinted that morality is a form of power (two themes of this book). *Moral Inertia* squeaked in, however, because it identified a specific problem to be grappled with in this book and yet was broad enough to cover a multitude of sins. Going on the worry that book browsers might find the informational content of the title *Moral Inertia* a bit on the low side, the unambiguous subtitle "Ideas for Social Action" was appended.

In a preface, one is supposed to justify one's publication, explain why one wrote it, where it fits in the market, and so forth. I wrote several of the reviews for *The Age Monthly Review*, the literary supplement to Melbourne's daily newspaper, *The Age*. If you do not live in Melbourne (alas, even if you do), it is a fair guess that you have not seen these essays. The books they cover are absolute gems; need I say more to justify their inclusion? The theoretical essays came about at various times when I was struggling to account, in my own mind, for the state of contemporary morality. There seems to be a lot of brutality or at least noncaring around. Is this normal? Should one adjust oneself to it? Or should one adjust *it* — by doing something about it?

I have followed every lead I could find on the subject, especially in psychology, sociology, political science, philosophy, theology, and sociobiology. Hence, this book's place in the market may be that of a catalog of ideas about morality in society. As well, it is an attempt to draw as many connections as possible between these ideas and to force simultaneous consideration of such things as *morality, power, values,* and *choices.*

Acknowledgments

It is a happy task to thank the many friends and colleagues who have had some involvement with this book. I first thank Paul Carter, editor of *The Age Monthly Review,* and his predecessors, Jennifer Byrne and Robert Haupt, for publishing my reviews. Other publishing encouragement came from Sanford Thatcher, Luther Wilson, and the late Jean Dubos. I am grateful to scholars who have directed me to the works of others. These include Jack Beckstrom, Helen Fisher, Robert Kosky, Charmaine McEachern, Peter Mayer, and Nita Pigo-Cronin. I apologize to anyone whom I have absentmindedly omitted from this list, as bibliographical leads are always vital to me.

I received help on an early version of Chapter 15 from Andrew Linklater and Evelyn Menconi. For the chapter on cruelty (Chapter 8), Norman Maxwell-Clark gave me a lecture on the Rum Corps (his "bicentennial project"), and Carmel O'Laughlin persuaded me of the role of silence in abetting domestic violence. On Chapter 11, concerning power, I was aided by three sets of comments: one from Robert Carneiro, one from my friend Albert Somit, and one from an anonymous reader, later revealed to be the self-same Albert Somit (different comments). On the same chapter, I was saved by Helen Pringle from a misattribution and was assisted by the ever-reliable Colin Horne, emeritus professor of English at Adelaide University, in tracking down the verse concerning the beheading of Charles the First. Mine humble thanks to all of the above.

Eva Etzioni-Halevy reminded me, through a generous and geographically complicated correspondence, to provide definitions — something that I may now have overdone. Gene Gallagher whipped through the whole manuscript making excellent suggestions. Peter Grantham encouraged me to change some lists into narrative form. Max Stackhouse replied to my occasional theological questions with answers of inspiring erudition. What a privilege it is to partake of university life! I thank these persons for their colleagueship.

Additionally, I am grateful to librarians Ninette Ellis, Barbara Hennessy, and Valerie Gondek for years' worth of service with a smile and to Terry Lane, Jane Figgis, and Jill Kitson of Australian Broadcasting Corporation for inviting me to speak on their radio programs about subjects in this book. I must needs thank editor Jody Berman for prescribing manuscript medicine over the phone from Colorado and Ahmed Abdul Kareem for technical assistance kindly rendered. I have had many excellent typists, each of whose first language was other than English — to wit, Polish, Arabic, Tagalog, Hindi, and Dutch. I salute them all. I especially thank computer whizzes Tony Santos and Marijke Lammers.

I suppose one does not usually thank bookshops in a preface, but I'd hate to think where I would be without a certain four bookshops in Harvard Square (all within cooee of the late Bailey's). On the homely front I am eager to thank my brother, Kevin, for showing me the wonders of on-line research; my sister, Anne, and sister-in-law, Elsie, for providing hospitality "overseas," and my husband, George, for making a writing desk for me of just the right height. That last item probably did the most to put me in touch with my muse.

The many helpers listed above no doubt constitute only the tip of the iceberg in terms of influencing me in the present work. Since the subject matter is morality, the submerged portion of the iceberg must necessarily be my mother, my father, and my early teachers. Although it is customary in a preface to say "the aforementioned persons cannot be held responsible" — and I do so say — I make an exception for my late parents. I'm sure they would be happy to take all the blame — or the credit — for my interest in "right and wrong."

Grateful acknowledgment is made for permission to reprint the following. A portion of Chapter 13 appeared as "Durkheim, Remoralization, and the Inevitability of Justice" in *Revue Internationale de Sociologie* in early 1991. *The Age Monthly Review* published Chapter 12, "The Genetics of Racism," in December 1983; Chapter 16, "Nuclear Democracy," in January 1986; and Chapter 2, "The Trickle-up of Trust," in October 1989. *Zygon, Journal of Religion and Science,* published Chapter 7, "Moral Inertia: Contributing Factors," in March 1991. For Chapter 10, "American Moral Problems," Doubleday, a division of Bantam, Doubleday, Dell Publishing Group, Inc., gave permission to excerpt quotes from Bill Moyers's interviews from his book *A World of Ideas.* The Lerner and Loewe song, "With a Little Bit of Luck" (copyright [renewed] Alan Jay Lerner, Frederick Loewe, Chappell & Co., all rights reserved), was used by permission.

"The Elusive Butterfly of Power" was presented as a paper to the American Political Science Association in Atlanta on August 31, 1989. "Three Major Components of Morality" was presented as a paper to the first annual Human Behavior and Evolution Society Conference in Evanston, Illinois, on August 24, 1989, and appeared in different form in my book *Morality among Nations.*

MARY MAXWELL

Moral Inertia

Introduction

✳ ✳ ✳

We witness horrific things happening in the world all the time, yet do little to stop them. It sometimes seems as though we are watching a film over whose outcome we have no control, rather than participating in reality. Indeed, we *are* watching a film, since many of these things appear on the television news. Surely, though, the script is not fixed as it would be in a film — it is open-ended. We *could* influence the characters and the events. Why do we, often, not do so?

I intend the phrase *moral inertia* in the title of this book to convey primarily the notion of moral inaction. In the science of physics, one meaning of the word *inertia* is "the tendency of a body at rest to stay at rest." In common parlance, too, inertia is generally associated with inaction or torpor. By *moral inertia* I mean the tendency of people to remain morally at rest, or unperturbed, in the face of social evils. Such evils may include cruelty perpetrated on individuals or on whole nations, decisions taken that needlessly cause degradation of the biosphere, forms of communication that massively stifle truth, and so forth.

It is my plan in this book of essays to approach this phenomenon of moral inertia from as many angles as possible. Three chapters are specifically concerned with the failings of what I shall term the human moral system, namely, 1, " 'Design Errors' in the Human Moral System"; 7, "Moral Inertia: Contributing Factors"; and 8, "Is Cruelty Okay?" Each of these chapters sets up general models for analysis while three others deal with explanations of various specific instances of moral inertia, to wit, 10, "American Moral Problems"; 12, "The Genetics of Racism"; and 16, "Nuclear Democracy."

As it happens, the term *inertia* in physics means not only the tendency of a body at rest to remain at rest but also the

1

tendency of a body in motion to remain in motion! Thus, the title of this book, *Moral Inertia,* also appropriately indicates the fact that besides the large amount of human moral *inaction* in the world, there is a large amount of moral *action.* In fact, I take moral action to be the norm and moral inaction as the puzzling phenomenon. I consider moral inaction to be the problem to be addressed against a background expectation that people do act morally (or do at least consult moral principle) when they need to solve social problems.

Since I have, in a previous book, *Morality among Nations,* developed at some length the biological theory of morality, I shall discuss it only briefly here in three chapters, namely, 5, "Natural Law, Social Contract, and Sociobiological Theory"; 9, "Three Major Components of Morality"; and 14, "What Has Mortality to Do With Morality?" It is particularly in those essays that I define morality, but in fact the definition arrived at with the help of biology is really about the same as that commonly used by philosophers, anthropologists, and, for that matter, laypeople.

So as not to keep the reader waiting to find out what I mean, roughly, by *morality,* let me state here some of its aspects. Most basically, morality concerns the notion of right and wrong. At an individual-to-individual level, morality is a "felt" distinction: one knows, for example, that a partner has wronged one by not keeping a promise. At a broader social level, rights and wrongs are coded into rules, and felt distinctions give way to more objective ideas. Society as a whole then enforces these rules, rather than individuals enforcing them on one another. The seeming objectivity of right and wrong often causes people to believe in the permanence of morality and in its ultimate enforcement by a supernatural power. At the same time, however, people do seem to recognize the fact that moral beliefs get modified over time.

I personally look upon morality as a very fluid thing. Morality is "what people agree on" with reference to their manner of living together. For selfish individuals to cooperate, some regulations obviously would need to be set up. In an ideal mode, such as in social contract theory, each person contributes to the initial plans for social regulation. In actuality, though, that seldom happens: people enter a society in which the rules already exist. Nevertheless, they come to agree, more or less, on those rules. As is well known, of course, the rules often favor some members over others. (Thus a group could even "agree upon" a morality that condones slavery. Presumably the slaves do not agree, but so long as power is sufficiently organized against them their objection will not count.)

A belief in "fluidity" of morality may seem to carry the danger, first of all, that there will be no stable basis for moral judgment over time and place and, second, that morality might disappear altogether. I am persuaded that the risk of these things coming about is close to nil. There *is* a stable basis for moral judgment. Note that in the above scheme, morality is built on felt distinctions — individuals know when they are wronged; they have emotional reactions to unfairness (and thus will eventually do something about unfair social arrangements). Note, too, that in the above scheme, morality is something agreed upon: societies proclaim openly the ethics they hold. If questioned, they can come up with principles on which they base their rules. These principles are often flouted in the extreme, but the commonly observed need of people to justify their actions, even hypocritically, is itself testimony to our deep need to act according to right and wrong. Morality is, in short, a wonderfully stable phenomenon not because right and wrong exist "out there" but because sensitivity to right and wrong exists in *us.*

Among the chapters in this book that support the premise that public concern with morality is "par for the course" are 4, "Christianity: The Voluntary Society"; and 13, "The Inevitability of Justice." Two other chapters that acknowledge contemporary difficulties but suggest ways of getting morality back on track are 2, "The Trickle-up of Trust," and 3, "Ten Commandments of Interethnic Relations." In general, those four chapters buttress the second definition of moral inertia: the idea that moral action once set in motion is likely to remain in motion. They suggest, also, that complex institutions of society are really only social arrangements writ large and, as such, are just as subjectable to morality as are interpersonal dealings. Several of the authors call attention to the fact that even the most seemingly abstract political and economic issues of today are perfectly within the scope of ordinary people's moral judgment and that moral sensibility should, naturally, be brought to bear on public decisions that affect our lives.

A logical way to organize this book might have been to divide the moral inertia "mark one" chapters (regarding inaction) from the moral inertia "mark twos" (regarding action). Instead, it was thought better to organize this book by some criteria of palatability. Short chapters are alternated with long ones; optimistic chapters are alternated with pessimistic ones. As well, essays that review other author's books are alternated with chapters that are original (well, relatively original) with me. Hence, the book-review essays appear as the even-numbered chapters of this volume. The reader who perseveres directly in order through the seventeen chapters will enjoy at least a minor advantage of continuity, since I occasionally make reference to earlier points.

The reader who leapfrogs, backtracks, or generally gets into a spin may, however, be said to be entering into the true spirit of the research. A final suggestion, O Reader: if at any point you feel that the discussion lacks flesh and blood, or has become too academic, you could flip directly to Chapter 8, "Is Cruelty Okay?", which is in many ways the heart of the matter.

CHAPTER 1

"Design Errors"
in the Human Moral System

✳ ✳ ✳

They're always throwing goodness at you,
But with a little bit of luck a man can duck.
— Lerner and Loewe, *My Fair Lady*

Do not do unto others as you would have them do unto you.
Their tastes may not be the same.
— George Bernard Shaw

Things are in the saddle and are riding us.
— Ralph Waldo Emerson

What would constitute a perfect moral system for the human race? What combination of personal traits, social structure, belief systems, rules, or other factors would perfection entail? That is, of course, an impossible question to answer. If one were assigned to design "from scratch" an ideal moral system, one could hardly foresee how the parts would work together. For instance, what effects would certain personal traits have on rules? What effects would certain rules have on social structure? Beyond that practical difficulty, in any case, is the fact that the very notion of a perfect moral system is notoriously amiss. It implies that there is some shared idea of a perfect human life or a perfectly desirable society. But there is no such accepted idea, and as twentieth-century dystopians have depicted, efforts to perfect the human race lead to force rather than choice and usually guarantee "equality" only at the price of a dull, gray sameness (Passmore, 1970).

I propose, in this chapter, to steer clear of the notion of a perfect moral system and yet to identify flaws in the system we actually have. I call these flaws *design errors* while appreciating that the human moral system was never really "designed." (My belief, as will be argued in later chapters, is that the human moral system first evolved by natural selection and was subsequently developed by cultures in line with particular environmental and social needs. There never was a blueprint for its operation.) Thus, in saying that the present system has design errors, I merely mean that it has characteristics that impede its proper functioning. By the proper functioning of our moral system, here, I mean its ability to do the things that most people implicitly assume morality can do — such as guide the individual's behavior in keeping with society's wishes and offer a store of ethical principle from which cases can be adjudicated.

Of the seven design errors I shall nominate, four have been present since the earliest days of human society. I label these four the option of deviance, demographic limitations, tribalism, and the arbitrariness of values. They persist today because they involve psychological features of the human being. Another three design errors came to be troublesome only in the modern period of human history. I call them the diffusion of responsibility, the moral immunity of officeholders and group persons, and (with apologies for this cumbersome label) the coexistence of voluntarism and structuralism. These three arise not so much from the individual psyche as from features of the social organization of mass society. The list of seven is not meant to be exhaustive; it is just someplace to start.

My purpose in picking out these design errors of the human moral system is to make some headway in explaining contemporary moral problems. As with other, different approaches in later chapters, my attempt is always to get away from the vague assumption that moral problems, or social evils, exist because people are bad. People may very well be "as bad as anything," but that strikes me as an unsatisfactory explanation, and it recommends no corrective other than the impossible corrective of changing people's nature. Following a brief outline of the seven design errors, I shall consider whether these errors are correctable.

The Option of Deviance

The first, most obvious design error in the human moral system is simply the option of deviance: individuals can opt to deviate from the rules of society. Social animals of other species appear to perform altruistic acts rather blindly. For example, wolves that hunt in groups automatically refrain from nourishing themselves at the expense of their fellows. But in the case of humans, a conscious choice must be made. As Jean-Jacques Rousseau pointed out in his parable of the deer hunt, a member of the human hunting party may choose to abandon his post temporarily in order to catch a rabbit for himself. If he does so, the group may fail to catch the deer (1984, p. 111).

Humans can cynically calculate the wages of virtue and the profit of sin. An individual may notice that at the outer extremes of immoral or antisocial behavior there is a lucrative niche for anyone who can forgo his scruples. Pirates, highwaymen, and drug dealers occupy such niches. The society has to pour considerable energy into protecting itself from these entrepreneurs. There may well have been human societies in the past that collapsed because of the selfish endeavors of a few individuals who exempted themselves from the moral rules (and some say this is happening today also). I thus identify the option of deviance as a design error. It is maladaptive for society as a whole because it can undermine the whole social system. At the same time, I acknowledge that freedom of moral choice is considered to be one of the glories of human life and that freedom is *adaptive,* in that it makes our societies more flexible than those of automatonlike ants.

Demographic Limitations

Another design error consists of the fact that the human moral system works well only for a specific size of population, namely, the small size that existed at the time when morality first evolved. Judging by the hunter-gatherer societies that still exist, the maximum population of the earliest societies may have been about fifty to one hundred members. An important feature of the early moral system was that everyone knew everyone else: part of the mechanism for enforcing reciprocal altruism (we must assume) was frequent face-to-face contact. In very large groups, this is not possible: it is more tempting to cheat when the chances of getting away with it are great. Likewise, there is less inclination to perform a generous act if the act will go unnoticed. Some of the major religions, which came about at a time of great population increase, responded to this problem by teaching that there is a God who watches every individual's action.

The problem of "the tragedy of the commons," to use Garrett Hardin's phrase, should be mentioned in this discussion of demographic limitations. An individual can easily be socially trained to avoid doing something that would blatantly hurt a neighbor or hurt society in general. But it is hard to get one person to avoid an act that damages the group, if that person's share in causing the damage is only 1/1,000, and each of the other 999 wrongdoers is also sharing such a tiny portion of the blame. The typical example is that of grazing sheep on common land. It will help each farmer a lot if he can put on one extra sheep and will only slightly hurt the land, so a farmer's moral inclination is to do it. But since everyone feels the same way, the commons get overgrazed and eventually this is to the disadvantage of all (Hardin, 1968). The design error here is that there is no "natural" feature of our moral system to deal with this. Admittedly, this lack is sometimes overcome by insight and by such conscious effort as making laws on behalf of the whole community's welfare.

Tribalism

A major design error of human morality — given the fact that human groups now interact frequently — is its tribal orientation. The moral requirement to treat other people honestly, fairly, or with respect is usually limited to members of one's own group. Even advanced civilizations that espouse a universalistic morality tend to take it for granted that persons who can be designated as enemies are worthy of no consideration. P. Hesse's studies of children (1987) show that ideas about "enemies" develop early in life, although, of course, a child needs to be taught who the enemy is.

Arthur Keith (1948), Robert Bigelow (1969), and Richard Alexander (1979) have developed the idea that "group morality" is a special evolved trait that helps members to concentrate on the needs of their own group in the face of outside threat. The virtues of loyalty, patriotism, and self-sacrifice are thus among the most sacred in this scheme of morality, and the greatest sins are treason or even criticism of one's group. As I have argued elsewhere (Maxwell, 1990), it is important to see the function of group morality as distinct from the function of everyday social morality, which has to do mainly with individuals monitoring the fairness of transactions between themselves and their fellows rather than between groups.

Similar or even identical moral concepts and moral terminology happen to be employed in *both* areas of morality, yet their incompatibility often goes unnoticed. Within "standard" morality, killing other human beings is commonly listed as the foremost crime, yet killing a member of an enemy group (or sometimes even aliens in the domestic group) is praiseworthy. I list tribalism as a design error in the human moral system largely because of the way in which the *contradiction* between the two kinds of morality tends to pervert standard morality. Our group-morality mode of thinking can even get in the way of our evaluating historical facts. For instance, as John E. Mack points out, "Every nation, no matter how bloody and cruel its beginnings, sees its origins in a glorious era of heroes who vanquished less worthy foes" (1989, p. 386). Tribalism and nationalistic tendencies thus impair one of the principal components of the human moral system — evaluation, or judgment.

The Arbitrariness of Values

Another design error in the moral system has to do with the fact that the individual human mind works on a relatively "open plan." Whereas other animals have their behavioral routine largely given to them by inheritance, humans have to learn cultural values to guide their behavioral choices. For a nonhuman animal, a *value* is ordinarily a fixed quality in the environment. In the case of a very primitive animal, such as the woodmite, the values in the environment may be those of warmth and moisture. The sensorimotor equipment of that creature will have evolved to steer it toward heat and water or away from cold or dry places. In higher animals the needs are much more complex, but even here the brain will contain a guidance system referent to external values. The limbic system of a mammal, by producing feelings of pain or pleasure, can induce it to do the necessary things — for example, to hide from predators or to seek a mate. In general, the relationship between an evolved creature's brain and the values of the surrounding environment is a steady one and a logical or "healthy" one.

The first problem for humans is that values in the environment are harder to identify. Consider the case of food. Our taste buds may lead us to particular foods whose nutritional value has been tampered with by food processing. That is, the physiological signal for nutritional value is there (the taste), but the real value is not there. The second problem is that humans invent arbitrary values. Even such a basic biological value as reproduction can be arbitrarily altered. We find that humans may seek high fertility in one century and scorn it in another. Sometimes this reflects a sensible tracking of values in the environment, such as cutting down on reproduction when resources are scarce. At other times it is based strictly on some cultural or religious premise, such as the belief that God favors celibacy.

I list the arbitrariness of values as a design error in the human *moral* system because society's moral rules are proclaimed to be based on values. These values may be in tune with objectively real values in the environment or may be quite dysfunctional for society in some biological sense. Furthermore, it is in the very nature of religion, ideology, and other types of creative moral systems to be able to persuade people of the value of certain things. Value talk itself evokes a certain reverence. Then, once established, such values tend to be impervious to criticism and may take on dogmatic aspects that allow them to live past their time. In short, because values are arbitrary, and because a society's definition of good behavior is tied to its stated values, people may be led to "good" behavior that is arbitrary and in the long run maladaptive from some objective point of view. An example would be the contemporary ethos of desiring "the latest model," which leads to wasteful consumption.

The four aspects of the human moral system that I have discussed so far — the option of deviance, demographic limitations, tribalism, and the arbitrariness of values — have been potentially troublesome at least since the time that small nomadic groups of humans began to settle into large communities. The three that I shall now list have to do with the limitations of our evolved moral system in the face of very recent historical changes, particularly the change to "mass society." For the most part they have to do with the inability of individuals to regard themselves as moral agents in a situation where the values and the rules are unclear, the locus of decision-making is concealed, and the sense of moral responsibility is hazy.

The Diffusion of Responsibility

The problem of the diffusion of responsibility bears some resemblance to the earlier-mentioned design error of demographic limitations. The human moral system, particularly in its emotional underpinning, is set up for social interactions that occur at face-to-face level. People can feel responsible for their actions when they see the immediate consequences. Through reason and the extrapolation of moral principle they can also learn that certain behaviors are right and wrong even if their consequences occur far away or at a much delayed time. However, as I said, when any one person's share of responsibility for the consequences constitutes only a small fraction of the total responsibility — or is very time-removed from the ultimate outcome — it may be hard to arouse guilt in that person.

In modern times, the diffusion of responsibility is a more complicated problem. It is not always clear whose actions are causing what consequences, particularly in regard to economic relationships. For example, I may learn that U.S. fruit-canning companies are paying starvation wages to pineapple pickers in the Philippines. Does this mean that I should remove my participation from this marketing network by not buying canned pineapples? Or should I take some other action with the company to express my protest as a customer? Or approach my democratic government to legislate an ethical code for its multinational industries? Or do nothing?

The recognizing of "right" and "wrong" has traditionally implied some appropriate action, such as punishing the wrongdoers. In circumstances where no such action is possible or identifiable, people cannot act, and thus the general moral sensibility of a society may decline. Routine connections will no longer be made between the perception of wrong and social action to correct it. Hence a mood of *amorality* or irresponsibility may set in. It is especially because of this that I see our lack of a mechanism to deal with diffusion of responsibility as a flaw in the moral system.

The Moral Immunity of Officeholders and Group Persons

This design error — moral immunity — includes two separate but related problems. The first is that nations and corporations are frequently considered to be "persons," yet they are not held to the same moral standards as real persons. Second, their officeholders enjoy a certain immunity from moral criticism. If one asks who the actor is in a certain situation, the answer may be "the nation" or "the corporation," as if that body or entity had a mind and a will — as it arguably does. Yet neither of these group persons is expected to have a conscience or to act in other moral ways like individual human beings. This is very strange indeed, that the biggest actors who most affect human well-being are not held to moral standards.

In the case of the nation, its exemption from moral responsibility may have to do with the tribalist psychology whereby one's own group is always assumed to be right and good. Since we need our nation's protection, especially in the face of the enemy (the cultural barbarian, the economic or political rival), it is imperative that ours be considered a good nation. If it does things that some critics could call bad, there is usually an excuse available. The excuse could be self-defense, or that the nation inadvertently caused some harm while trying to do a greater good, or that its hand was forced by the logic of geopolitical strategy.

In the case of the corporation, its freedom from moral responsibility despite its ability to affect human welfare is probably based on the fact that it is being allowed to fill its appointed role. That role in capitalist society is to organize some part of the economy, such as manufacturing or finance. A corporation does its job well when it succeeds in making a profit, providing jobs, rationalizing the market, and so on. How then could we ask it to do anything else? Caring for the health of the poor, for example, or making the city beautiful, is hardly its proper mission. Hence, it has been thought, corporate action that directly or indirectly harms the health of the poor or ruins the architectural skyline cannot be morally reprehensible. It may be bad, but it is just a sociological fact of life, not a *sin*. Only in the last ten years or so has there been some change in this philosophy such that corporations may be thought accountable for their effects on society (see, for example, Shue, 1980, p. 112).

Second, there is our custom of not charging officeholders with personal responsibility for their official acts. In general it seems that their actions are not seen as those of individual human beings. Thomas Nagel notes, "The great modern crimes are public crimes. . . . [These] are committed by individuals who play roles in political, military and economic institutions. Yet unless the offender has the originality of Hitler, Stalin, or Amin, the crimes don't seem to be fully attributable to the individual himself" (1978, p. 75). Public agents, Nagel says, seem to have a "slippery moral surface" (1978, p. 75). Nevertheless, it appears that public attitudes toward moral immunity are sometimes rather selective. Nagel notes the case of an official who was "secretary of defense under Nixon during the completely illegal bombing of Cambodia which went on *after* the Vietnam peace agreements were signed. He then became attorney general and was widely acclaimed for resigning that office rather than comply with Nixon's request that he fire Archibald Cox for demanding the White House tapes" (1978, pp. 75–76).

One famous case in which eminent jurists determined that individuals were responsible for their actions even while acting under official orders was, of course, the Nuremberg judgments in 1945. (This case was also exceptional for its implication that one nation should stand in judgment of another in "domestic" matters [Luban, 1986, p. 11] and has not set precedent in international law.)

Nevertheless, it *has* become more common in the last decade or so for nations to hold their own deposed leaders accountable for crimes — such as the Gang of Four in China, the colonels in Greece, and the Emperor Bokassa in the Central African Republic. Even the movement to impeach President Nixon for the relative peccadillo of Watergate increased the American public's awareness of legal methods for dealing with its elected officials (and led to the use of the suffix "-gate" to mean a political abuse in which somebody got caught).

The Coexistence of Voluntarism and Structuralism

The final design error to be listed here is a reflection of the preceding two. By *voluntarism* I mean the ordinary belief of people that they are voluntary, responsible moral agents as has always been the standard arrangement in the human moral system. By *structuralism* I mean the fact that people in mass society perceive events as caused not so much by voluntary action or personal direction as by forces, structures, or inexorable trends (Lukes, 1977, p. 6). Thus, as mentioned above, things that the corporation or nation may do are seen as coming about not by anyone's will but by the momentum of the system that already exists. Consequences are to be explained by internal dynamics and logics, *rather than by human choices.*

It is the coexistence of the two attitudes — voluntarism and structuralism — that constitutes a design error in the moral system. More specifically, the problem is that the inconsistency between the two has not been appreciated. The moral system, both as biologically evolved and as culturally developed, has always been a major coordinator of human social life. It must normally be *total* in its scope. It must take all social actions into its brief for consideration of their rightness or wrongness and must have mechanisms for nudging *all* actors into line. In the modern situation, whole sections of social activity are exempt from moral consideration. This exemption allows social problems to develop that threaten the future of particular societies or the species as a whole. This state of affairs also weakens the moral sphere, which begins to be thought of as a trivial component of social life.

In sum, the coexistence of voluntarism and structuralism is troublesome. Voluntarism's persisting reputation as an important part of human life masks the fact that ever-larger proportions of activity have been removed from voluntary control and even from moral scrutiny.

Correctability?

Having listed seven design errors in the human moral system, it now seems requisite to inquire into their correctability. Is the human moral system hopelessly flawed by these errors? Are they bound to bring about the collapse of society? I believe that, of the first four errors listed, two are relatively nonlethal. The danger of one of these — the *option of deviance* — is easily counteracted by the vigilance of society; morality is nothing if not the ability of the group to control deviants. The other one — the *arbitrariness of values* — will have less and less force in the future, I ween, because moral language will come in for increasing inspection and criticism.

The remaining two, tribalism and demographic limitations, involve a real conflict of interest that is experienced by many people, perhaps the majority of people. Because of the *tribalism* design error, people can wish to observe standard morality, such as the rule to treat others humanely, and yet be very much caught up in a system of group competition that dictates ferocity instead. Because of the *demographic limitations* factor, one can not so easily act for the benefit of, say, millions of neighbors as one can for the benefit of local neighbors with whom one has set up mutual obligations. Any correction of these two design errors will require some actual realigning of people's interests (as is coming about anyway due to the so-called shrinking of the planet) and will, I assume, require much moral persuasion.

I see the three remaining design errors as largely correctable. The diffusion of responsibility, the moral immunity of officeholders and group persons, and the coexistence of voluntarism and structuralism are all associated with mass society. Yet mere *size of population* is not the cause of these design errors in the human moral system. Rather, it is the insufficient development of ethics in the modern period, or just *clouded thinking*, that caused these errors. Many philosophers, social scientists, theologians, and others are already trying to correct these three errors through careful analysis and good old-fashioned moral reasoning.

The first three review-essays to appear in this book, namely Chapters 2, 4, and 6, will deal with books by Sissela Bok, Max Stackhouse, Susan Meeker-Lowry, and Onora O'Neill that specifically attempt to "uncloud" the thinking about social responsibility and human agency. Each of these writers attempts — very successfully, I believe — to insert the individual, morally, into the contemporary social situation, no matter how complex that situation may be. Their four books are themselves nascent correctives on the design errors of the human moral system.

CHAPTER 2

The Trickle-up of Trust

✳ ✳ ✳

A large sign that hangs in the public parklands of a city where I used to live says: "Homelessness: together we can solve this problem." On first seeing it I was struck by the reasonableness of the message — that social problems can be solved with intelligence and will. Sissela Bok, author of *A Strategy for Peace*, believes that our over-preparedness for war is a social problem whose solution lies in fairly ordinary measures. She has worked out a strategy that depends largely on citizen participation and that involves social trust. Her book is an elaboration of a statement she made in the journal *Ethics:* "Since distrust grows through reciprocal and repeated actions, it stands to reason that it can also be cut back thus" (1985, p. 721).

Bok is the world's self-made leading authority on the subject of trust. In her two earlier remarkable books, *Lying* and *Secrets* (published in 1978 and 1982, respectively), she recounted the human predilection for deception and secrecy, analyzed the implications of these behaviors for society, and laid bare the ethical issues involved. It is natural that a person with an eye for the crucial relationship between moral principles and a society's functioning would suggest that a climate of distrust, such as we experience contemporarily, is itself a very dangerous thing. Where integrity has stopped being a consideration, where "partisan" morality is ascendant, and where governments seem to act on an "anything goes" attitude, people cannot act to carry out even something as vital to their survival as disposing of nuclear weapons. They cannot act because they are paralyzed by the loss of an element necessary to group living, namely, trust, or good faith.

Deception and secrecy have become pervasive in government behavior even in democracies — one thinks of the testimony in

Review of Sissela Bok, *A Strategy for Peace: Human Values and the Threat of War* (New York: Pantheon, 1989).

the trial of Oliver North or of the allegations about the British intelligence system made in Peter Wright's book, *Spycatcher* (1987). Bok shows that secrecy "represents the greatest possible threat to democracies, since it renders ordinary citizens powerless to the extent that it keeps from them information they need to influence policy" (p. 105). Moreover, she notes, "when public officials disregard fundamental values in the conduct of foreign policy, they are led to do so domestically as well, if for no other reason than to conceal these activities and to silence critics" (p. xv). A further result is that many people in private life lower their standards accordingly, and many young people, Bok observes, refuse to vote or take any part in public life. This book emphasizes two components equally: that dishonesty at high levels *corrupts society in general* and that it is up to *individuals,* working in many different ways, to *reassert fundamental moral values.* Taking a stand, even a very personal stand, counts.

Bok divides her short book into two parts. In the first part she cleverly uses Immanuel Kant and Carl von Clausewitz — strange bedfellows, to say the least — as her spokesmen. First, she has Kant demonstrate that four moral principles — or constraints — are essential to social life. Restraint on *violence* is number one, and restraint on *deception* is number two; all civilizations and religions incorporate laws about these into their commandments. Moral principle number three is restraint on *betrayal of one's word,* or to put it positively, it is the admonition to keep promises and contracts, to practice fidelity. These three principles can easily be seen as essential to society. Moreover, Kant, writing in the nineteenth century, broke new ground by recommending a fourth restraint — on *excessive state secrecy.* This is needed, he observed, because without it, massive breaches of the other three can take place clandestinely. Governments — whose power must always be monitored — can easily escape accountability to the moral rules of society by invoking the need for secrecy.

Mercifully, the chapter on Kant leaves out, or criticizes, some of his more objectionable ideas, such as the all-or-nothingness of moral rules. Bok is able to pick out from Kant's notoriously difficult writings (her references are nearly all primary sources, particularly Kant's *Perpetual Peace*) those gems of insight that suit her polemic. She also notes how the Indian leader Mahatma Gandhi shared Kant's belief that the moral principles of nonviolence, truth, and fidelity are bound together. Gandhi, too, is one of her examples of how the private moral life influences the public one. "Through making and holding [publicly announced] vows, he trained himself to become someone who could trust himself and who could be trusted by others" (p. 47). Bok also finds ways in which Kant was ahead of his time in his cosmopolitan sensibilities. She writes that as a result of the reach of today's communications media, Kant's words about the world community are increasingly apt: "It has developed to the point where a violation of rights in *one* part of the world is felt *everywhere*" (p. 104). She also emphasizes the important Kantian idea that to use one's free will to obey laws is a mark of human dignity.

The next chapter in Bok's book concerns Clausewitz, whose great work *On War* was published posthumously in 1832. He himself had entered war in Prussia, against Napoleon, at the age of thirteen: he had been present at the Battle of Borodino in which seventy thousand men were slaughtered in one day. While his work covers strategy *in* war, his most important advice is to keep sight of the goals *of* war. Bok paraphrases him: "Neither vested interests, nor hatred for the adversary, nor war's allure for the gullible should be allowed to deflect the conduct of war from [its political] purpose" (p. 60). The twist in Bok's tale is that she considers war itself to be the great enemy — especially in our century when total annihilation is possible. She uses Clausewitz's methods (in a way she thinks he would have approved) to design a "strategy for peace."

"No one starts a war — or should — without first being clear in his mind what he intends to achieve," declared Clausewitz (quoted in Bok, p. 63), but Bok notes that "leaders will never again be able to start a major war with anything like the clarity of purpose that Clausewitz had prescribed, or even with certainty about their nation's survival. Consequently, nuclear wars have no place today in sound strategy . . . nor do world wars fought with conventional weapons [which could] create a catastrophe beyond anything humanity has experienced" (p. 65). Regarding the war between Iran and Iraq that lasted for most of the 1980s, she says "Neither nation could have aimed for the millions of lives wasted, or the impoverishment and brutalization of so many of those who survive" (p. 65).

Bok cites many examples of persons who orchestrate a complex long-range strategy for peaceful goals, such as Martin Luther King or President Oscar Arias Sanchez of Costa Rica, who won the 1987 Nobel Peace Prize for his efforts to end the cycle of violence and hatred in Central America. This, she says, takes the same coordination of efforts as the most intricate military campaign. Using Clausewitzian language, she says we can "unite in rendering [war] less powerful, immobilize some of its allies, cut back on its resources, and find openings in its flanks" (p. 66). Bok's writing is invigorating — this book is among the few I know of that puts reasonable citizens back into the driver's seat. She notes, for example, the practical steps that are taken every day by members of such organizations as Amnesty International or the American Friends Service Committee — or just private persons who devote themselves to overcoming hatred between groups, such as between Sikhs and Hindus. In short, hers is a refreshing antidote to fatalism, especially the fatalism most of us seem to feel toward war.

The second part of the book is devoted to offering practical advice and answering potential critics. Among the practical items, Bok discusses line-drawing. When all parties agree to the rightness of Kant's four moral constraints (on violence, deception, betrayal, and excessive secrecy), it is possible to begin the debate on the acceptability of specific policies. Lines can be drawn, even in difficult cases. Some practices such as terrorism and disinformation, Bok states, fall wholly on one side of the line — the side to be ruled out. Terrorism is unjustifiable because it hurts citizens randomly. "All who place bombs on buses or planes, say, or strafe health clinics or schools, must be seen as terrorists, however dedicated they may be to the cause of freedom" (p. 93). In a balanced move, the author cites both the sinking of the *Rainbow Warrior* by the French government (in which Greenpeace was the target) and the Shepherds of the Sea case (in which environmentalists sank two of Iceland's four whaling ships) as instances of unjustifiable violence. Predictably, she sees the harm done to the reputation of governments and private organizations, in these cases, as the biggest long-term costs. Such acts damage the atmosphere in which nations must work. "Once set, such examples of disrespect for law and morality linger long after particular incidents have ceased to dominate newspaper headlines. Such policies invite retaliation and imitation on the part of adversaries . . ." (p. 93).

Finally, she meets her academic critics — the realists such as Hans Morgenthau and George Kennan — boldly but with a disarmingly light touch. To Kennan she says, "The fact that not all cultures have identical moral standards should not lead us to conclude that they can agree on none" (p. 115). To Morgenthau she says, "Moralistic language can indeed be counterproductive. But this conclusion hardly proves that moral principles should be set aside in practical contexts" (p. 117). Overall, "it was an illusion . . . one increasingly anachronistic in the nuclear era, to believe that if every nation tried to steer clear of moral language, common survival would somehow be better ensured through the workings of some unseen hand or of a balance of power" (p. 118). Of the archetypal realist, Max Weber, Bok says, "He offers no support for his bitter assumption that all who engage in politics must open themselves to diabolic forces. . . . He overlooks the dangerous seductiveness of seeing oneself as a tragic hero, forced to do the unspeakable for the sake of the community's greater good" (p. 127). In another section she demolishes the vulgar rationale of "dirty hands" in politics.

The only flaw obvious to me in Bok's thesis is her agreement with Kant that the restraints on violence, deception, and betrayal constitute the three fundamental principles of social life. I should have thought that a restraint on *theft* figured at least as high as a restraint on deception. But to bring this matter into such a book could open the way for a philosophical debate about the right to property, territory, or resources — things that are sometimes the causes of war. This would unnecessarily detract from what is an extremely valuable articulation of the problem of distrust in our society.

I hope I have not given the impression that this is a utopian treatise, full of idealistic beliefs about the transformation of mankind. Rather, it leans strictly on basic moral principles that are already part of people's normal behavior and expectations. "This book," says Bok, "rejects the many calls for a 'new ethics' (p. xiii). It is multilevel in its appeal: "I see all who strive to reduce distrust as working for peace, even if they produce no immediate and direct effect on the nuclear balance of terror" (p. 152).

Shortly after *A Strategy for Peace* was published, the nuclear peril — at least the one involving the two superpowers — diminished dramatically for reasons mostly unrelated to the problem of trust. That pleasant historical circumstance may render a small portion of Bok's work obsolete, but it does nothing to diminish the value of her philosophical approach. She insists on "telling it like it is" in the face of both government whitewash and academic cynicism. She lucidly states the moral values involved and calmly calculates the consequences of their interaction.

One can only wish that if nuclear peace continues to break out, Bok may turn her attention to homelessness.

CHAPTER 3

Ten Commandments of Interethnic Relations

✳ ✳ ✳

> Moslems of Russia, Tartars of the Volga and the Crimea, Kirzig and Sarts of Siberia and Turkestan, Turks and Tartars of Transcaucasia, Checkens and mountain Cossacks! . . . Hence forward your beliefs and customs, your national and cultural institutions are declared free and inviolable! Build your national life freely and without hindrance. It is your right.
>
> — V. I. Lenin, 1917

> In the beginning, God gave to every people a cup, a cup of clay, and from this cup they drank their life. They all dipped in the water, but their cups were different. Our cup is broken now. It has passed away.
>
> — as told to Ruth Benedict by a Digger Indian

In a recent radio broadcast, five out of the six news headlines, by my count, had to do with interethnic conflicts. By *interethnic* I mean to include domestic conflicts (in any country) involving minorities, and international conflicts in which the issue is between peoples rather than strictly between governments. If this activity occupies so much of the daily news, one might expect that political scientists have long since carefully categorized the issues involved. One might think also that if people are laying down their lives in interethnic conflicts, the values they are fighting for must be crystal clear. Yet, as far as I can glean, this area is mired in confusion. It has "more heat than light."

In this chapter I undertake three assignments. The first is simply to present the argument that confusion, or vagueness, surrounds the subject of interethnic conflicts. The second is to specify that moral issues are involved, at least insofar as important values are at stake. A third thing is to demonstrate ways in which ethical principles could be sorted out, especially so they could be applied by outside observers. This last exercise will result in my proffering a ten commandments of interethnic relations.

Questions That Lack Consensus

Consider the following eight questions:

1. Does every ethnic group or people have a right to self-determination (including the right to secede from a long-established state)?
2. Do nation-states have the right to maintain their territorial integrity in spite of tribal divisions?
3. Should outside powers intervene to help a suffering minority group, say, in cases of genocide?
4. Should a nation be ostracized by the world community for blatantly practicing racism?
5. Is terrorism acceptable where a group has no other means of prosecuting its claims?
6. Do ancient groups, for example, some South Pacific islanders or African nomads, have a right to maintain their cultures in the face of the technological rationalization of the globe?
7. Do the more advanced civilizations have an obligation of self-restraint over their urge for cultural imperialism? (Or conversely, do they owe it to their "little brothers" to drag them into modernity?)
8. Is it civilized for Great Powers to take sides in communal strife or local "wars of liberation" by sending in sophisticated weapons?

If the reader assumes that his opinion is shared by most of the public, by scholars, and by Western governments, he may be in for a surprise. There is, in fact, a lack of consensus. For one thing, many people, I assume, would readily answer "yes" to both questions 1 and 2 — groups have a right to secede from states (on the principle of self-determination), but nation-states have a right to maintain their integrity. Yet these two things are incompatible. If you say yes to one, you should say no to the other.

In regard to question 3, on whether outside powers should intervene to help a suffering group, especially in cases of genocide, I assume most Western citizens would say yes. I suspect they would not realize that their governments would most likely say no. Many genocides have occurred since the Genocide Convention was approved by the United Nations in 1947, but very few interventions or rescue missions have followed. (The United States refused even to sign that convention until the 1980s.) The fact is that governments tend to give highest priority to the principle of national sovereignty. Thus they would also tend to answer no to question 4, concerning ostracizing a state because of racism, claiming that racism is an internal issue. (The unusual solidarity shown against apartheid was late in blooming and required domestic pressure in various countries.) As to question 8, concerning taking sides in wars of liberation, governments would often be compelled to answer yes, on the grounds of geopolitical reality and the need to maintain the balance of power (see Keal, 1983).

In short, although the "right" answers to these questions may seem obvious at first glance, the matters are politically complicated and, as I shall now argue, ethically complicated.

Five Values

Partisans in a conflict can usually articulate their moral claim — at least to their own satisfaction. (To onlookers, they often overstate it.) They rarely acknowledge the reasonable claims of the other side and seem to revel in denying the possibility of such. The well-known intransigence of parties to ethnic disputes may discourage outsiders from trying to help and may even persuade people that no point of leverage can be found. I believe, however, that a simple guide to the values involved would be helpful. I suggest in this section that five values be isolated for consideration.

The first is simply the *value of cultures themselves.* Each culture is unique; it arose over time in such a way as to make life coherent for a people living in a certain ecological and historical setting. A culture has its own rules, myths, technology, arts, and traditional practices. Thus it is sometimes said that a culture has intrinsic value in the way that each unique plant or animal species has value: it is a product of life that will not be repeated and therefore has a sort of right to exist. A diversity of cultures may also have practical value, in that it provides each culture with a source for borrowing from others.

A somewhat separate matter is that when one defends the value of a culture, one often means to defend the lives of those who depend on it now. Thus to argue that a culture be saved (say in the case of a "primitive" people) is tantamount to arguing that the individuals living in it today be given their human right to survive.

A second value worth picking out, in relation to interethnic conflicts, is that of a *functioning unit* of society, by which I mean an economically and/or politically functioning unit. The five billion people of this planet do not exist "on their own." They are all organized into functioning units (or sometimes they are left as "marginal people" because they do *not* belong to a functioning unit). Such units are not always coterminous with cultures. Quite often people are willing to join economic or political units that do not share their culture because joining gives them a way to make a living, or military protection from enemies, or the chance for education, or some other benefit. The value of separate, economically viable functioning units thus appears to be something worth upholding without reference to ethnicity.

A third value is the value of *modernization*. This value seems to me to have two component parts. One is the improvement in standard of living that may accompany modernization, notably in health, hygiene, agricultural productivity, creature comforts in housing, and consumer goods. These things are generally considered desirable — they are sought after, whether or not their consequences later prove ill. The other value that modernization promotes and sustains is that of rationality (in the sense of efficiency and logic). Once an ethos of rationality develops there seems to be a drive to rationalize everything — from physical things such as technology, to human things such as the labor market, to abstract things such as principles of law. As with the standard of living, the consequences of rationality may prove ill, but for the most part this does not dissuade people from valuing modernization. Certainly modernization is considered a goal in most of the "underdeveloped" world.

A fourth value is that of *nationalism* or *national pride*. I could alternatively call this ethnocentrism, implying that groups throughout human history have had some important sense of self-identity (and feeling of superiority to other groups), but I mean *nationalism* to suggest the recent form, dating back only a couple of centuries. I refer particularly to the passion with which a nation — usually a nation-state, but sometimes a linguistic, racial, or religious group — claims its right to exist and to be free from rule by outsiders. Nationalism is generally thought of in positive terms, like patriotism. One refers to a leader as "nationalist" with approbation. This value could at times coincide with either of the first two values listed above — the values of culture and of functioning units — but here it refers more specifically to ethnicity. It is the value usually invoked in relation to the right of peoples to self-determination.

The fifth value to be mentioned here, last but not least, is the *value of the human being*, the individual. Although the rights of the individual are in the forefront in many other political discussions, the individual suddenly vanishes when intergroup conflicts are the issue. It is perhaps the least talked-about value (which may offer us a clue as to what the moral worth of the group over the person is considered to be!). I bring the value of the person into the discussion here to enable it to be measured explicitly against other values. When two ethnic groups fight over, say, the right to run the country (or even over some minor point of pride), it may seem that the two values that are clashing are equal — namely, the right of each group. But thousands of families who take the loss of a soldier-son must figure into the equation as well. The moral claims of persons must be reckoned in terms of their individual human plight.

Types of Clashes

With these five values identified it is easier to see some of the moral issues involved. I realize that most political scientists would say that they are not moral issues but political issues — *political* being the proper designation for struggles for power and control. I agree that they are power struggles and hence political issues, but I maintain that they also have a moral dimension. The whole area of interethnic affairs is redolent with "right" and "wrong" and "good" and "bad" — a point to which I shall return later.

Allow me to give examples of just two types of clashes that involve the above five values. One is that of a small, low-technology culture in conflict with the forces of modernity. In various parts of the world, small indigenous cultures are being made extinct, for instance, by being thrown off their land. The victims often resist and to some extent may get some outside help for their cause. The moral apathy they meet with from the public, however, has much to do with the fact that the government or business that is displacing them can nearly always say that this activity is necessary for progress. Often there is an economic benefit to another group as well. For instance, building a dam on traditional land may put an end to a small culture, but the hydroelectric power from the dam will help the overcrowded cities. My point is to emphasize that there are two *competing* values, not merely an inevitable march of progress (or some such idea that masks the moral claims). Articulating the value of the culture may at least help persons to stand their ground against a force that would otherwise be overwhelming.

Another common type of value clash occurs when a small nation wants to secede from a larger state. It may at first appear that these are just two of the same values — two nationalisms — fighting it out. But according to my scheme, there is also the value of maintaining the integrity of a functioning political-economic unit (which is often the larger state). Many separatist movements today — in Europe, Africa, and the Pacific — are made by groups of people whose ability to function as independent units is questionable. Some of these movements arouse in their members the belief that "salvation" consists in getting free from a particular rule. That is, the value of belonging to the larger federation is kept out of discussion by the rebel leaders, who must emphasize ethnic purity — and injured pride. I do not wish to say that it is automatically better for a smaller group to remain in a larger state. The opposite case — that smaller economies are more viable than larger ones — can be made persuasively. I merely wish to emphasize that various values are involved.

28

The five values — of a culture, a functioning unit, modernization, national pride, and individual human beings — can and
do take part in a much greater number of types of clashes than
I have attempted to discuss here.

Reasons Why Articulation of Values Is Needed

The clear articulation of the values involved in ethnic relations is crucial, I believe, for at least two reasons. The first is
that *this is an area in which fuzziness about values creates an
atmosphere that is easily exploited.* If one side can vividly state
its case in morally compelling terms, it has an automatic advantage. Public relations efforts may be crucial in interethnic
conflicts. Moreover, the willingness of a few people to be mar-
tyrs for an ethnic cause often elevates that cause in the minds
of onlookers. Likewise, the commission of acts of terrorism may
give a group a certain moral status (desperados must be des-
perate about something), even though such acts receive official
condemnation.

Political leaders, moreover, know how to play on the righteousness of the group's cause and to attack the domestic
opposition for disloyalty. They famously know how to turn
economic or class problems into racial or religious issues when
it is personally convenient for them to do so. In sum, I argue
that it is important for scholars and the public to try to articulate the entire range of values involved — not just a select few of
them — because without this corrective, the strong moral language surrounding one particular value tends to give it an
unfair edge.

My second reason for claiming that clear articulation of the
five values is advisable is that *all thinking about groups has an
inherent muddle factor.* The human brain is equipped to perceive directly such individual items as individual people or
individual chairs. But agglomerations of things are always
made at a higher level of cognitive abstraction. The word *society*, like the word *furniture*, is already an abstraction — even
before it acquires the inevitable emotional connotations. Once it
acquires those emotional connotations it may be taken out of
the realm of reason altogether. An additional problem is our

imprecise usages of the words *society, culture,* and *nation* in the first place; although these entities may overlap, they are not identical.

Ethnic claims often get even more fuzzy when they refer to such things as a nation's blood brotherhood or its special relationship to the soil — but of course those romantic phrases are deliberately meant to call up sentiments of group loyalty, not to give analytically accurate definitions of group membership. In my opinion, it would be a service of social scientists to the world, or at least to social science itself, if they would sharpen these labels, making some demand for accuracy. This would expose some of the blatant uses of ethnic-arousal language.

Value-Free Social Science

This book is about morality. In seventeen chapters I deal with a wide variety of moral topics and different ways of analyzing the human moral system. A recurring theme is that morality is a fundamental social thing: it is meant to govern social relations. As such, moral behavior must be of central interest to social scientists, yet (with a few notable exceptions) academic researchers shy away from the subject of morality. No doubt this results from the important methodological principle of social science that its practitioners should not impose their values on the object of their study. A social science study of homicide, for instance, should not contain comments about the author's personal disapproval of homicide. The author should merely present the facts.

In a study of interethnic conflicts, what would it mean to present just the facts? One could report how many people get killed or injured, how the leaders stirred up the population, what the alleged grievances are, and so forth. In a comparative study, one could try to find patterns of interethnic behavior. But social scientists do not feel it is their prerogative to sort out the values that are at issue, because that is not their province. And they certainly should not comment on the rightness or wrongness, or the cruelty or the hypocrisy, of either side — much less take sides.

Or *so they say*. But in fact many anthropologists in the field become partisans, and many sociologists who teach race relations on university campuses become champions of various civil rights causes. Academics frequently lend their name to petitions and declarations, giving their professional title or university affiliation or their membership in scholarly associations. It would appear that they assume that such groups do have special authority to speak out against discrimination, unfairness, and inhumanity of various sorts. What I am getting at here is that since there are massive breaches of the value-free rule of social science, it may be better for us to admit — when the subject is interethnic affairs — that the area is highly emotionally charged, and morally charged, instead of continuing to pretend that it is not.

My tentative suggestion is that social scientists be forthright about the fact that interethnic conflicts do involve a number of values. The participants already know this: the perceived rights and wrongs of the situation are what give rise to agitation among tribes and nations. And the participants' rhetoric is particularly heavy with "morals" where the issues concern, for example, a people's sacred tradition or homeland, or where they have to do with claims of exploitation, discrimination, or rule by an alien power.

I suspect that, as academics, we have got ourselves into a ridiculous mess by accepting the idea that a study of a value-ridden subject must be value free. To suggest a way out of this mess, I propose in the following section ten commandments of interethnic relations. This proposal is not meant as a social science proposition as such. Rather, it represents my personal views. Still, it could be of some use to social scientists in their attempt to weigh up the moral issues that are already there.

Ten Commandments of Interethnic Relations

Given that moral values are involved when one group confronts another, is there any way priority could be assigned to one value over the other? If an outside group — say, a benign third party — wanted to propose rules, would it be possible for it to formulate neutral rules (neutral in the sense of not playing favorites either with particular groups or particular values)? Is there a way to be ethical without being partisan? I think it is possible, in a rather abstract way, to come up with such rules. I offer the following ten commandments of interethnic relations. These, I must admit, do take for granted the prior acceptance of two principles: the value of human life and the desirability of fairness. (And one of them — commandment 2 — assumes that all cultures are valuable, which may not be a very solid assumption.) Beyond that, however, they are merely "logical" commandments.

1. *Protect minorities.* Minority groups, simply by being in the minority, are vulnerable. By virtue of being vulnerable they need protection or special care. Moses Moscowitz has stated: "Everywhere where ethnic diversity clashes with the ideal of national homogeneity, only iron restraint and relentless probing from within and without can stay the hand of oppression which always reaches out to crush those of another race, another creed, or another language" (1968, p. 125). The minorities I refer to here are those ethnic groups that live within a majority nation. Of course, in a few cases, ethnic minorities wield power over the majority. Those minorities would, perforce, not need protection.

2. *Protect cultures.* Many cultures are small and are in danger of extinction. They deserve protection for the same reason as minorities — because they will be overwhelmed; the odds are against them. The cultures I have in mind are mainly the indigenous, nonmodern ones, but it would be reasonable to protect all cultures from destruction or invasion. It *is* possible that one homogeneous world culture lies ahead, but we cannot know this and should not take it for granted; to do so would certainly make it a self-fulfilling prophecy. In the meantime, even though we are not yet very clear on the merits of various cultures, it seems wise to protect all of them, in the same way that endangered species of plants and animals are protected.

3. *Encourage compromise.* It seems to be in the nature of ethnic struggle that it sets all-or-nothing goals for a people. Often each one of two groups, with similar chances for success, is determined to have it all. It may be virtually impossible for a member of either group to shout "compromise," since in the heat of the fray this is seen as treason. Thus it usually falls to

outsiders to arbitrate and to try to point out the merits of compromise.

4. *Call a demagogue a demagogue.* This commandment could alternatively be called "cut through the bluster of nationalism." One can identify many instances in which the volatile issue of nationalism or ethnism is used to manipulate people, either for personal aggrandizement of political candidates or to focus attention on an outside enemy to cover up incompetence or illegal rule at home. An obvious way to cut through the bluster would be to articulate other criteria besides patriotism for measuring a leader's right to rule. Similarly, one could measure the actual prospects of a given ethnic movement (for instance, could a secessionist group function as an economic unit?) as a test of the movement leader's "genuineness."

5. *Eschew the double standard.* Here I refer to the fact that racism practiced by whites against persons of any other color has always been a fit subject for discussion, but to criticize racism when it is practiced among non-whites is thought to be unsporting. Hedley Bull has remarked, "The racism displayed by Vietnamese in relation to Chinese, black Africans in relation to East African Asians, Brazilians in relation to Amerindian minorities will engender opposition within the Third World, but it will not unleash the torrent of protest, to which every stream of opinion throughout Asia and Africa will make its contribution, as racism does when it takes the form of white supremacism" (1984, p. 150). Perhaps academics tend to be squeamish on this because they assume wrongly that racism is always a function of classism or colonialism. The thrust of this commandment is: be alert for racism everywhere.

6. *Rate the effects on individuals.* Ethnic clashes often result in long-enduring wars and in the creation of refugees. Wars have well-known disastrous effects on economies, on environments, and last but not least on individuals. Death and disabilities are experienced by human beings, not by statistics. Refugeeism, for its part, is an almost invisible issue, although millions of people today live in refugee camps, some for their whole lives. In such an artificial setting it is difficult or impossible to maintain one's culture, or economy, or even one's marriage. Also, since human dignity is largely related to self-sufficiency, human dignity must be said to be at a low ebb in most refugee camps. Thus, it is worth considering the effects on individuals of wars and refu-

geeism, as part of the overall picture of who is winning and who is losing in clashes between nations or between ethnic groups.

7. *Expose outside interests.* Onlookers are often aware that ethnic hatreds are being inflamed by persons who are nonparties to the clash, yet they do not often think of this factor as falsifying the clash. The outside party may be a superpower conducting a proxy war, a neighbor wanting to destabilize a rival state, or just an arms dealer looking for customers. I think that all such factors should be enunciated as clearly as possible. If we have a name for this activity, its practitioners are less likely to get away with it than if we are only able to talk about the ethnic clash itself. For lack of a better name, I suggest "external inflaming."

8. *Recognize the advanced forms of nationalism.* It is not only "tribalist barbarians" who practice vicious forms of nationalism or ethnism. Consider the fact that a few civilized nations have produced weapons that stand ready to wipe out whole countries, if not the human race itself. Moreover, as John Dunn has pointed out, persons in advanced nations who do not go around with machine guns may practice a more laid-back form of economic nationalism. "And thus the nationalism of tariff barriers . . . appears as simply a component of modern political reason [while] the nationalism of those as yet unable to erect tariff barriers, and the violence which disfigures this, seems archaic and irrational, irredeemably morally ugly" (1979, pp. 70–71).

9. *Identify racism's breeding grounds.* It is frequently hard to discern whether or not a particular racial, religious, or ethnic problem is really a class or economic issue. It would therefore be helpful to know which situations tend to bring out the racist sentiments — hatreds and fears — of populations and which of these are likely to lead to scapegoating. For example, an influx of migrants to cities that have high unemployment often provides interracial tension because it arouses economic fears and jealousies. Preventive measures against racism appear to be underutilized. For example, even where there is a legal right to free speech it is possible to outlaw incitements to hatred. Article 20 of the United Nations Convention on Civil and Political Rights states that "any advocacy of national, racial or religious hatred that constitutes incitement to discrimination, hostility

or violence shall be prohibited by law." Nations that sign the treaty are expected to incorporate such laws domestically. On the other side of the coin, the value of tolerance can be publicly played up. This could include educating the majority about the way of life of the minority in order to stave off gross misinterpretation (see Pettman, 1986).

10. *Be aware of the politicization of the United Nations.* An organization such as the United Nations may appear to be the best bet for outside monitoring of the troubles that occur among peoples, and indeed it has accomplished much. But a whole layer of politics and bureaucracy at the United Nations frustrates the causes of peoples. (See Leo Kuper's remarkable documentation of this in *Genocide*, 1981, and *The Prevention of Genocide*, 1985.) There is also a tradition in international diplomacy there that gives highest protection to the principle of national sovereignty, ahead of any such unpolitical principle as "humanity." For example, it is taboo at the United Nations for members to propose the breakup of any existing state. Leo Kuper has written, "One has to ask whether the slaughter of millions in Bangladesh, Biafra, the Sudan and now in Eritrea can possibly be justified by the interests of the Territorial State in the relatively unrestrained exercise of its internal sovereignty. . . . Or is there a need for the United Nations to abandon a dehumanized scale of values which effectively condones the sacrifice of human victims to the Territorial State?" (1981, p. 183).

In sum, here are the ten commandments of interethnic relations and the reasons why they are recommended: 1. Protect minorities (because we value lives). 2. Protect cultures (because diversity of ways of life are worth maintaining). 3. Encourage compromise (because unnecessary violence seems stupid). 4. Call a demagogue a demagogue (why let people manipulate others?). 5. Eschew the double standard (recognize that racism is a universal habit). 6. Rate the effects on individuals (why leave them out?). 7. Expose outside interests (don't assume that two peoples are simply blind enemies living in a vacuum). 8. Recognize the advanced forms of nationalism (we have quiet, sophisticated ways of hurting other nations). 9. Identify racism's breeding grounds (to put the onus on the racists rather than on the victims). 10. Be aware of the politicization of the United Nations (which is more a guardian of governments' prerogatives than a champion of humanity).

The first three of these are statements of my value preferences and sympathies that I assume are widely shared. The last seven urge skepticism in dealing with the morally loaded area of ethnic relations; they are suggestions for clearing away some of the distractions and deceptions that characterize dealings between peoples and between governments and citizenry. I do not claim an iota of originality for any of these commandments — at most I may be credited with arranging them into a mosaic pattern.

CHAPTER 4

Christianity: The Voluntary Society

✳ ✳ ✳

There was David and there was Goliath, but David had a slingshot. Now there is Max Stackhouse, and there is the whole of modern political economy, but Max Stackhouse, too, has a deadly weapon. That weapon is theology — not exclusively the study of God but the study of godliness in humans. Stackhouse uses the Christian view of what a moral person is and what the correct society is to slay the giant of the ungodly socioeconomic structure of our time. The little stones in his slingshot are words — words we have heard before, such as *piety* and *sin,* but which take on a sharp new value as they are aimed, ever so accurately, at the institutions of modernity.

In *Public Theology and Political Economy,* Stackhouse accomplishes three remarkable things. First, he persuades the reader that theology is indeed relevant to the study of political economy. For instance, he shows that the influence of Christian preaching on Western culture has been normal and routine and that the contemporary split of social decisions from ethics is the oddity. The antislavery movement, for example, started in the churches; it included intense debate about property, work, and wealth and used "the principles of Jesus" as the standard for judging social institutions. Later, in the same way, Martin Luther King "captured the moral imagination of the world on theological grounds to confront racism" (p. 3). Stackhouse also presents a short history of religious reaction to that most rapid social change, the Industrial Revolution, outlining, for example, the work of the Evangelical Social Congress of 1889.

Let us not forget, he says, that "under the impact of Christian theology and ethics, political life was being democratized and legal institutions had established equality as a governing

---

Review of Max L. Stackhouse, *Public Theology and Political Economy* (Grand Rapids, Mich.: Eerdmans, 1987).

principle" (p. 39). When the industrial "robber barons" arose as a new elite to threaten this system there was a new religious debate. "Decadent theories of Calvinism" (which saw personal wealth as a sign of special divine favor) came under increased criticism. Stackhouse recounts the work of late-nineteenth-century and early-twentieth-century theologians, such as Walter Rauschenbusch and Shailer Mathews, who discussed "persons in community" and what this concept meant for economics. "One of the remarkable things about these [theological] developments is that they entail a social view of economics rather than an economic view of society. The social nature of the human self and the necessity of applying spiritual and moral principles to the structured tissues of social relationship . . . are presupposed, *and are viewed as empirically and normatively prior to economic activity*" (p. 65).

Stackhouse insists that "public theological matters have concrete historical consequences" (p. 71). Thus, "when the pressure of the Depression of the 1930s struck America, it was the specific policies advocated by . . . church leaders that became the policies of the nation" (p. 71). Obviously, however, the involvement of churches in public issues has declined since then. "Members of congregations take their cues for social and economic policies from the secular press, from political ideologies, or from the sheer calculation of . . . interest without references to either piety or theology" (p. 71). The author attributes this trend to several factors. First, there was the Bultmannian turn in theology itself that questioned the historical accuracy of scripture. Second, there were "economic developments which grew in geometric ratios of increasing complexity" (p. 72), and third, there was the fantastic growth of the secular university. He notes that "the skyscraping towers of industry and finance began to dwarf the steeples of the churches" (p. 72). Economics thus got cut off from overtly religious and ethical issues, while most theologies remained confessional, focusing on the individual and on otherworldly matters (p. 75).

The second and more important thing that this book accomplishes is to show why theology should influence political economy. The broad answer is that *all civilizations need moral rudders*. If such guidance is not provided, coercive power, economic influence, and technology will decide everything for arbitrary, self-serving reasons. And a more specific answer, for Stackhouse (to the question of why theology should influence political economy), is that *Christian theology happens to provide a very valid anthropology.* The "Kingdom of Heaven" as portrayed in the Bible is a vision of a moral society toward which humans naturally — voluntarily — incline. The author disparages the depiction of human nature implied in various economic theories. "The individualism of conservative capitalist theory is an abstraction of the worst sort. . . . Christians understand that all humans are joiners; they are members of communities and must be responsible in communities. People do not live in isolation . . . and it is a lie to say they do . . . in economic life" (p. 47).

Stackhouse has equal contempt for vulgar Marxism and for Adam Smith's "Invisible Hand." "Perceiving the human creature as merely a rational calculator of costs and benefits does not fit with the New Testament message" — the message not just of what we should be but of what we actually are (p. 46). Similarly, understanding society in terms of automatic harmonies resulting from the efficient pursuit of private interests does not fit with a Christian interpretation of society. These perspectives fail to understand that sin deflects the rational capacities when interests are at stake.

Scripture, says Stackhouse, does not contain any blueprint for social institutions, but it offers boundaries. For example, the parable of the vine and its branches or of the mansion and its many rooms can be taken to indicate some necessary relation between the individual and the whole society. The exhortations to love one's fellow man reveal that the plan of Jesus is for a voluntary social life, that is, one based on freely chosen restraint and moral commitment. At the same time, there are clues for an ethical confrontation with power. "Liberationists know that the only God worth worshipping is biased in favor of the oppressed, and that truly pious living involves active . . . advocacy of their rights" (p. 21). Any ideology that claims to offer salvation for human life is false if it fails to challenge "the pretense of the arrogant and open horizons of hope to those who suffer" (p. 22). The Christian understanding of human nature is person-centered. To be human is to be both body *and* soul. Stackhouse quotes the turn-of-the-century theologian Shailer Mathews, "To disregard the promptings and needs of the social part of the personality is to invite an intellectual and moral death whose earliest symptoms are sin and abnormality of all sorts" (Mathews, 1897, pp. 27–28, cited in Stackhouse, 1987).

The lessons that scripture holds for political economy are thus based on these essential features of "Christian anthropology." They are also conveyed even more explicitly in the biblical concept of stewardship. Economics, according to Stackhouse, refers to "common decisions about managing the resources of common life," and stewardship indicates that we are responsible for the fate of the community. As stated in the gospel, property is a loan for which a stewardly account has to be given. Industry, for example, *should not be based on the desire for individual profit but should be conducted for the service of the community.* Moreover, the tremendous power of modern political economies is not an end coinciding with the national good but a means to be employed in stewardly responsibility for humankind.

The subtitle of Stackhouse's book is "Christian Stewardship in Modern Society." If that phrase raises the question of why Stackhouse ignores non-Christians, atheists, and agnostics, one need only recognize Stackhouse's very broad view of Christianity as the anthropology on which Western values are based. It is not an exclusive club, and its mission is fluid. At one point, he defines "the community" as "all those among humankind who are willing to discuss the most important things." Yet it must be admitted that Stackhouse *is* a partisan for the Christian faith. In his earlier book, *Creeds, Society, and Human Rights* (1984), he entered into a comparison of various cultures and concluded that Christian-based Western culture is "objectively" best. His style is to identify a society's values and then to see what institutions are capable of arising from them.

Thus, the third and most creative accomplishment of his book has to do with using the scriptural model of the Kingdom of Heaven as grounds for judging some of the political and economic realities of modern life. This approach gives Stackhouse an amazing ability to criticize both capitalism and communism; he finds that the dominant forms of modern political economy are "morally and spiritually corrupt." He is particularly nimble at measuring what the effects will be on society if either politics or economics is given too much control. I first thought it curious that a man of the cloth should have such facility for measuring the effects of one social institution on another, but on later reflection decided it is not so curious.

In a surprise move, Stackhouse identifies the corporation as an entity that can control (or at least historically *did* control) other forms of power — such as the power of government or of traditionally wealthy families. The notions of "trustee" and "limited liability" were once liberating. Yet, he notes, when modern Western corporations are exported to Third World countries that have no similar background in breaking the power of governments and families, the corporations end up reinforcing those powers (for example, in Latin America). Stackhouse appears to be resigned to the fact that for the foreseeable future, decision-making about production and distribution will be centered in the corporation (p. 113). Thus, in a not-so-far-fetched chapter entitled "Spirituality and the Corporation," he looks for ways in which corporations can be stimulated to act more morally.

A theme present throughout Stackhouse's book is that of the relationship between politics and religion. Have no fear — he has no truck with theocracy, noting wryly that "efforts to weave piety and power into a single fabric never work for long" (p. 98). Yet he shows that some degree of piety in leaders is always demanded by the public — as legitimacy for their authority. Stackhouse uses Max Weber's thesis that religion sets the basic attitudes within which certain types of politics are possible. Piety, Stackhouse says,

> is the least tangible aspect of power, but it is perhaps the most potent. The failure to recognize this fact is one of the great failures of much contemporary theology that tries to be politically relevant. . . . Many [theorists] have thought that in dealing with power, they are being realistic only if they become more Machiavellian. But this concentration on "realistc" analysis, on the hard calculations of who holds sway over the guns, dollars, brains, and law, has contributed to the creation of a vacuum at the moral and spiritual level on the question of legal authority (p. 102).

The author notes that "into that vacuum are flooding the new fanaticisms of both the left and right . . . struggling for control over the piety of the people" (p. 102). Stackhouse observes that "both fundamentalists and liberationists know, better than most . . . , that this is a decisive arena for the shape of power" (p. 102). He believes "the shape of the dominant piety will shape the future of power as much as any other single factor" (p. 102).

Quiet bombshells such as this appear throughout *Public Theology and Political Economy*. A particularly unexpected one is the author's attack on liberation theology. He jibes at his clerical colleagues in Latin America in a manner that may strike the reader as unsporting. However, Stackhouse seems genuinely sad at what he considers to be their errors: they make the too-easy link between righteous wrath, blaming the system, and adherence to Marxism. "The liberationists have seldom made the case for their position much better than the fundamentalists have made the case for their stance" (p. 22). Indeed, I suspect that the misguided faith of the liberation theologians caused Stackhouse to write this book. Above all, however, he wants to give pastors and theologians confidence in their role as social critics. He tries, extremely successfully, to articulate a language and map out a tradition for a public theology.

Stackhouse is by no means backward-looking in his references to the Bible, recognizing that any attempts to meet contemporary circumstances call for all sorts of flexibility and creativity. And he admits that "the use of Scripture as a boundary line in public theology . . . is both a way of testing our contemporary claims about what is adequate as a word for today, and a way of testing the adequacy of Scripture and its interpretation to provide civilization with the spiritual and moral principles of meaning able to guide life" (p. 7).

This book is at once crisp and profound. It can be recommended both as a fascinating tour of church history and as a treatise that may forever unfix the reader's categorizations of politics, economics, and religion.

CHAPTER 5

Natural Law, Social Contract, and Sociobiological Theory

❊ ❊ ❊

Men are not gentle creatures. . . . Their neighbour is . . . someone who tempts them to satisfy their aggressiveness on him, to exploit his capacity for work without compensation, to use him sexually without his consent, to seize his possessions, to humiliate him, to cause him pain, to torture and kill him. . . . Who in the face of all his life experience and knowledge of history will have the courage to dispute this assertion?

— Sigmund Freud

The moral precepts are species-specific. They are the essence of humanity.

— E. O. Wilson

A major theme of this book is that morality is a social affair. A study of the origins of morality in human evolution shows that morality first arose as a facilitator of cooperation among individuals. Hence, morality primarily concerns social relationships. This chapter will be concerned with both philosophical and biological approaches to the problem of human morality.

Among the great questions philosophers have asked about humans are these: What is the underlying basis of the social order? What motivates people to cooperate? Is human nature basically disposed to be sociable, compassionate, and self-sacrificing? Or is the more primary instinct a drive for individual satisfaction and self-aggrandizement? Must human competitiveness lead to great destruction? How can we solve the problem of the ruthlessness of a few at the expense of the many?

Similar questions have been asked by zoologists concerning social life in the animal kingdom. In several species, such as ants and chimpanzees, members live in stable societies. Zoologists for a long time wondered how they did this. They asked: What is the mechanism by which individual animals act (at least sometimes) in concert? What prevents them from going their selfish way instead? How did animal societies get started in the first place? The key to solving this problem has now been found. The sociobiological theory of altruism explains how cooperative behaviors among individuals led to the formation of society in animals.

I believe that sociobiology is very useful in resolving the paradox of the coexistence of individual selfishness and social cooperation in humans, too. Later in this chapter I shall lay out the sociobiological hypothesis concerning the evolution of morality, which I consider to be essential for understanding the role of morality even in contemporary society. Before doing that, however, I shall sketch the two most important traditional philosophies that explain why humans act morally: natural law and social contract.

Natural Law

Natural law originated as an idea of the ancient Greeks and has continued to flourish over the centuries. It made its way into Christian theology and Roman law and hence is a fundamental element of Western thought. Natural law theory holds that people act morally in society according to rules of right and wrong, which in some cases are codified in public law but which are in any case knowable by reason. Natural law means a law of nature in the way that gravity, for example, is a law of nature. God — or some kind of World Soul or Logos — runs the universe both in its physical aspects and in its spiritual aspects, through reason.

The Greek philosophers, particularly the Stoics, believed that this was obvious — the world of nature runs smoothly. It was also obvious to them that individual humans have some kind of direct access to this divine reason. That is, humans participate in the World Soul, intellectually. The correct thing for each person to do is to follow natural law and not to resist or destroy the system. (This participation in reason, incidentally, made all men equal — an idea that later figured in Christian teaching and in the theory of human rights.) The Roman Stoic Seneca expressed this perfectly when he wrote *"Non pareo deo, sed adsentior"* (I do not obey God, I agree with him) (*Epistula* 96.2, in Arnold, 1911, p. 284).

The natural law idea has received many refinements over the centuries, but its core idea about morality has remained essentially intact. It holds that people know right from wrong. Laws are not arbitrarily invented; they are discovered by reason. The world runs in a certain way that requires people to behave in an orderly and cooperative manner. Theft and murder, for example, are *obviously* breaches of the social law of nature. Control, in this view, is self-imposed. And what is the (supposed) motivation for this self-imposed control? It is simply that people want to participate harmoniously in the proper running of the world. The Greeks produced an elaborate metaphysics in connection with natural law, which I shall not attempt to describe here. Suffice it to say that the dominant theme of natural law, as far as explaining social cooperation is concerned, is human reason and conscience. People "naturally" obey natural law.

Social Contract

How else could social cooperation be explained? It could be explained not as a natural urge but as a somewhat grudging agreement by individuals to forfeit some of their selfishness in exchange for greater benefits. Such benefits may include personal security, in the form of freedom from constant violence, and the general advantages afforded by group activity, such as creation of complex products. Either self-restraint could be left up to an individual's calculation of how much restraint to apply in a particular exchange, or the group could agree to a set of rules and then leave punishment in the hands of law enforcers.

The theory of a social contract was first put forth by the ancient Greeks but is best known from the seventeenth-century writings of Thomas Hobbes. He elaborated the two ideas mentioned above — that people would prefer security over a life that was "nasty, brutish, and short" and that they would prefer civilization over a life that had no art, no industry, no letters (1909, p. 97). In other words, enlightened self-interest is the force that brings about the establishment of law and morals. For Hobbes, enlightened self-interest also brings about specific political forms, including authoritarian rule. People, he thought, are sufficiently willing to come together in society that they will accept even harsh rule. The justification for this government is the contract that the people have made.

This theory of social contract requires a two-stage history of humankind. In the first stage there *was* no social contract, and people lived as in a "jungle" according to their selfish instincts. Later, in the second stage, they deliberately gave up or suppressed these instincts. Presumably, there could be a third, future stage in which the social contract is nullified, and people opt to return to the jungle once again. After all, in the social contract stage human nature has not changed — for Hobbes it is only contractual agreements that keep people's behavior in line.

Human Evolution (Sociobiological Theory)

The foregoing two ideas — natural law and social contract — are both plausible as the explanations of human social and moral life. Each of these theories has many adherents, and indeed most people seem to accept both (not noticing, perhaps, their incompatibility!). I shall now present a third explanation for human social and moral life — that of human evolution — that I believe is more enlightening in regard to the origin of morality. Later I shall return to compare this one to natural law and social contract. At once it can be said, however, that human evolution theory disagrees with the Hobbesian suggestion that there was a past stage in which humans were loners. Humans were never loners; not even caveman or the earliest ape-man were loners. Humans and their hominid predecessors, according to this theory, evolved from other primate species that were already social.

Outlining the sociobiological theory of human evolution in a short chapter requires that I limit myself to only a few of the main ideas. First I shall briefly discuss the dates and names of species involved in human evolution. Then I shall present E. O. Wilson's model of the four pinnacles of social evolution. This will be followed by a discussion of William D. Hamilton's theory of inclusive fitness and Robert Trivers's theory of reciprocal altruism and of the moral emotions.

Dates and Species Names in Hominid Evolution

The earliest mammals evolved about 225 million years ago. It is believed that by 70 million years ago the type of mammals known as primates had come into existence; these were small, agile, tree-dwelling creatures. By 30 million years ago the great apes had evolved from these. The fossil record of early apes is not very good, but from what is available it appears that a creature living about 16 million years ago was the common ancestor of at least three modern species: gorilla, chimpanzee, and human. The gorilla line branched off from that common ancestor, leaving behind a branch that may have existed unbroken until 5 or 6 million years ago. Biochemical comparison of modern creatures (rather than fossil evidence) leads researchers to think that a species existing 5 or 6 million years ago gave rise to both the modern chimpanzee line and the hominid line (Cherfas and Gribbin, 1982).

Thus, hominids are, at the most, 5 million years old. The narrative of human evolution from that point to the present is based mainly on a collection of fossils. The first ape-man, dating to 3 million years ago, was found by Raymond Dart in South Africa in 1924. He named the genus *Australopithecus* — "southern ape" — and it was later found to have two species: *Australopithecus afarensis* and *A. africanus*. Clearly *Australopithecus* walked upright and had a humanlike skeleton, but its facial structure was more like an ape's, and its brain size was similar to that of the modern chimpanzee, namely 700 cubic centimeters. Almost certainly this primate had stopped living in trees and had ventured out onto the ground, with all the new risks and opportunities that entailed.

The next hominid genus, *Homo*, dates from about 2 million years B.P. (before the present) and has at least two species, *Homo erectus* and *H. sapiens*. The two million years of *Homo* fossils are marked by more or less steady increase in brain size, steady reduction of jaw protrusion, and, most importantly, an increase in the number of artifacts — mainly stone tools — found in association with the bones. There is some evidence of communal living and use of fire by *Homo erectus*. Its social life is by no means recorded, although this does not dissuade anthropologists or sociobiologists from estimating that it had social life. The use of tools, for example, implies a method of teaching, and the apparent transportation of minerals from one location to another suggests trade. The very fact of ground-dwelling, in an area of many predators, may persuade us that there was a need for group defense.

Homo sapiens's date of emergence is highly disputed: it could have been 500,000 years B.P. By 100,000 B.P. there is plenty of evidence of *Homo sapiens Neanderthalis* in Europe, lasting until 60,000 B.P. The Neanderthals clearly had social organization: they herded reindeer, built houses, sewed fur clothing, and so forth. Modern man, sometimes called *Homo sapiens sapiens*, is thought to have evolved completely by 40,000 B.P. The main specimen of that date is Cro-Magnon man, whose skeleton and brain are indistinguishable from those of modern humans. Among *Homo sapiens*'s early artifacts are works of art, such as the cave paintings of bison found in France and Spain (see Richards, 1987; Reader, 1981).

Although I have used words such as *emerged* or *arose* to indicate the beginning of a new species, it must be remembered that each new set of traits (anatomical or behavioral) was forged under the pressure of natural selection. Random mutation of genes provides the raw material for change, but the environmental situation of the animal determines which of those mutations will be adaptive and hence which will survive. This was true of the primates' evolution into the two hominid genera, *Australopithecus* and *Homo*, and of the genus *Homo*'s speciation into *Homo erectus* and *Homo sapiens*. It should also be noted that once *Homo* existed, some of the further "selection" may have been by competition among groups. For example, it may be that Neanderthals did not evolve into Cro-Magnons but rather that some other group came into Europe and displaced the Neanderthals, and from their descendants came Cro-Magnon man.

The point of this chapter is to suggest that humans evolved biologically as social creatures (instead of consciously inventing society). Thus, we might conclude so far that *some direct progenitors of modern man were undoubtedly social.* If the progenitors were the Neanderthals, we know from the fossil record that they were social. If the progenitors were another species clever or strong enough to displace the Neanderthals, we can virtually be certain that they were social: it is difficult to imagine an unorganized group conquering an organized one.

E. O. Wilson's "Four Pinnacles of Social Evolution"

Now let me backtrack from the story of human evolution to another interesting phenomenon: the evolution of *social life.* Throughout the animal kingdom there are certain species (some small fraction of all species) that exhibit a kind of social organization, ranging from simple to complex. The social behavior of these animals — like any other behavior — is guided largely by their genes. Interest in this has given rise to sociobiology, which is "the systematic study of the biological basis of social behavior" (Wilson, 1980, p. 4).

E. O. Wilson has noted that of all the species that have evolved a society, four types can be nominated as the pinnacles of social evolution (1980, pp. 179–180). The first is the unicellular marine type of creature, such as corals and sponges. The large coral or sponge that we are able to observe is in fact an agglomeration of thousands of one-celled members of the society. The members work in concert to perform the functions needed for, say, the nutrition of the coral or sponge. The biological explanation for the "willingness" of the members to agglomerate rather than go their separate ways is simply that *they are genetically identical.* Reproduction is accomplished by asexual budding; the members are clones of one another and so, in a sense, do not have conflicting interests.

The second pinnacle of social evolution is that of those insects that live in colonies: ants, bees, and certain wasps. (These are called Hymenopteran insects.) Their mode of reproduction is known as haplodiploid. It results in offspring that are not identical but that are more similar to their siblings (and thus have a higher convergence of "genetic interest") than the offspring of fish, birds, mammals, or, for that matter, the non-social species of insects. As with the corals and sponges above, but to a lesser extent, the genetic similarity of the colonial insects makes society possible. The members of these societies are thus biologically able to render service to one another even to the point of forming castes for the division of labor. For instance, there are ants in a given colony that are exclusively devoted to defending the nest or to getting food for the larvae.

Wilson's third pinnacle is occupied by a few highly social mammalian species — this includes not only primates but also social carnivores such as the African wild dog. They have evolved a fairly complex social organization. Here the mode of reproduction is the normal sexual type, with each offspring taking half of its genes from each parent and therefore never having more than a 50 percent genetic identity with any other individual. For this reason, mammalian individuals remain predominantly selfish: this generally makes cooperation difficult. Nevertheless, certain ecological circumstances, such as a need for group defense against predators and a need to obtain food by group effort, may make it worthwhile for the species to evolve traits of cooperativeness. In baboons, the need for group defense seems to account for social life; in the African wild dog it is the need to obtain food by group effort.

The fourth pinnacle of social evolution is the fully evolved human species. Our species seems to defy the laws of biology, in that its members, being mammals, are *selfish* yet perform *cooperative* acts as intricate as those of the social insects. They also have a far more complex division of labor and system of communication than ants. Wilson has referred to this phenomenon of high sociality in humans as the "culminating mystery of all biology." As noted earlier, that mystery has inspired philosophers to come up with the theories of natural law and social contract as ways of explaining human sociality.

Hamilton's Theory of Inclusive Fitness

Not only is human sociality a great mystery, but the phenomenon of social behavior in any animal species was a mystery until 1964. In that year, William D. Hamilton discovered how the social cooperativeness of insects could be an inherited trait. Until then it was believed, in line with standard Darwinian theory, that only those traits could be passed to offspring that gave the individual an advantage in survival or reproduction. But the slavish devotion of an ant toward its colony hardly appears to give that ant an advantage. A biologist would expect this behavior to die out in the population and be replaced by the behavior of ruthless selfishness. In the theory of natural selection, nice guys finish last. Hamilton's discovery consisted of the recognition that the success one has in leaving descendants can be measured not just in *direct descendants* but in *collateral descendants*. If an individual produces no offspring, but helps a sibling to produce offspring, its genes will still end up in future generations.

By "its genes" I mean genes just like the ones it possesses. After all, siblings have many genes in common. In mammals, individuals have 50 percent of their genes in common with their nearest kin, that is, with their siblings, their parents, and their offspring. In social insect species (the Hymenopterans), individuals have 75 percent of their genes in common with siblings, due to the haplodiploid mode of reproduction referred to above. And here, in this mathematics, lies the solution to the evolution of society. Hamilton found, simply enough, that the 75 percent sharing of genes within the Hymenopteran insects meant that an individual had a greater interest in helping a sibling than in producing offspring. He wrote: "Consider a species where the female consecutively provisions and oviposits in cell after cell so that she is still at work when the first of her female offspring . . . leaves the nest and mates. Our principle tells us that even if this new adult had a nest ready constructed and vacant for her use, she would prefer . . . returning to the mother's and provisioning a cell for the rearing of an extra sister to provisioning a cell for a daughter of her own" (1964, p. 28). Thus, if the individual bee would rather help others than "go her own merry way," we have the beginnings of a society — though in this case the society also happens to be the family.

In short, the concept of inclusive fitness solves the *mechanical* problem of how altruistic traits can be heritable: helping those who have the same genes you have is a way of increasing your own fitness, measured in future terms. But this in itself does not explain the evolution of a particular social structure. For that, one must see the larger environmental picture. *Why* would it be adaptive for the bees to take up the practice of cooperative behavior? The incentives for such evolution, as mentioned earlier, may be the presence of large predators that are best deterred by group defense or of hard-to-get food resources that are best obtained by a joint labor force.

Trivers's Theory of Reciprocal Altruism and of the Moral Emotions

"Kin altruism" — as just described in bees — can go far toward producing a complex society; indeed, it may completely explain insect society. But in human society the giving of favors is not always directed at kin: humans are often altruistic toward strangers. Thus, there cannot be a hidden genetic benefit in terms of one's collateral descendants. Yet there may be a benefit for the individual if the altruistic act evokes a *reciprocal* act. The theory of reciprocal altruism is considered one of the major building blocks of sociobiology, along with the theory of inclusive fitness. George C. Williams first put forth this idea in 1966, and in 1971 Robert Trivers published the key article, "The Evolution of Reciprocal Altruism." Trivers's theory holds that the tendency to be altruistic — even to nonrelatives — can evolve genetically, so long as it benefits the altruist. If, by giving aid to a fellow creature today, the animal can extract aid from that individual later, the aid-giving behavior may be adaptive.

In nonhuman animals, reciprocal altruism seems to be much rarer than kin altruism. It can come about only when certain conditions are met. First, the animals must be of sufficient intelligence to recognize each other individually and to remember favors performed. Second, they must live in proximity to one another for a sufficiently long time to reap repayment of the favor. Third, pairs of animals must be "able to render roughly equivalent benefits to each other at roughly equivalent costs" (Trivers, 1971, p. 37). To date, reciprocal altruism has been reported in several species. For instance, male baboons help one another in fighting off a rival (Packer, 1977). Dolphins and whales may help a sick individual by swimming along under it, pushing it up to the surface for air (Connor and Norris, 1982). In a species of bat known as the vampire bat, individuals regurgitate blood to a starving fellow bat (Wilkinson, 1984).

In two of these cases, the baboon and the bat, the donor of altruism has been observed to seek help from the recipient later, on a tit-for-tat basis. In the case of dolphins and whales it is assumed that the donors may be able to get help from the recipient later, although no actual instance of this has been recorded. In early hominids there may have been such a one-to-one exchange of favors, but among fully evolved humans the system of reciprocity is much more generalized. People perform helpful deeds for strangers and expect *other* strangers to do the same for them. In other words, the exchange of favors is not limited to tit for tat. The motivation to do the favor becomes channeled into obedience to society's rules.

This raises the question, At what point in time did hominids change from a purely instinctive system of reciprocal altruism, based on one-to-one exchanges, to a rule-based system? Trivers believes that the change to a rule-based system need not have occurred as a rationally worked out social event; it could be a biological, evolved phenomenon. This could have come about if the physiological basis for following rules was developed gradually, under the pressure of natural selection. Such selection pressure, according to Trivers, did exist in the earliest social milieu, because the very phenomenon of altruism *elicits the evolution of cheating.* A subtle cheater can take advantage of altruistic exchanges by giving a repayment of less than he received.

Cheating obviously puts the cheater at an adaptive advantage, so this behavioral trait can be expected to spread. Individuals then have to evolve mechanisms to keep their altruistic acts from becoming detrimental to them: they have to find ways to guard against cheaters. Certain emotions could be useful in this regard. For instance, the emotion of anger toward one who cheats could help deter the potential cheater (Trivers, 1985). A whole set of such "moral emotions" may have evolved in hominids to make the monitoring of reciprocity sharper. The emotion by which one senses that his acts are socially wrong can be called *guilt.* (Note that the "purpose" of guilt in this scheme is that it helps Ego to be good so that *he* will not suffer the penalty of ostracization. Natural selection does not try to protect the victim of the cheater.) Although we do not know the exact process by which the transition was made from the feeling of guilt experienced during a one-to-one exchange to the more generalized socially manipulable phenomenon of guilt, it seems reasonable to postulate that this took place very long ago.

What I have sketched here, from Trivers's theory of the evolution of the moral emotions, could form the basis for a more general theory of the evolution of morality, as will be discussed further in Chapter 9. This biological moral system (or protomoral system), consisting of emotional, physiological responses in personal interactions, had to wait for later hominid developments of language and culture before it could become a recognizable system of morality. It is my guess that soon after language became available, humans began to articulate rules of behavior and to make distinctions between "right" and "wrong." From that point on, concern with morality would have become a large part of the cultural environment.

Comparison of Natural Law, Social Contract, and Human Evolution

To the question, Why do humans cooperate in society?, three answers have been briefly outlined in this chapter. The theory of natural law holds that the universe works a certain way with people fitting into the divine plan and using their reason to cooperate. It holds that people are naturally conscience-bound and that social life has obvious requirements for restraint of individual impulse.

Social contract theory holds, on the contrary, that the natural scene is one of individuals running wild, as their selfish instincts would prompt. The fact that we see people instead living in harmony is due to a social contract. People realize that it is better to act in a restrained manner, not for God's sake or their neighbor's sake, but for their own sake. Enlightened self-interest persuades them to join the group and submit to its rules.

Sociobiological theory holds that humans cooperate because, despite the fact that they are basically selfish mammals, they have an evolved ability to engage in complex exchanges. This ability depends on the existence of some sort of moral emotions, which grew out of simple reciprocal altruism.

Does the theory of human evolution support or refute either the natural law or social-contract ideas? I believe it clearly refutes the metaphysical natural-law idea that there is a law of nature governed by reason. Evolution itself is driven by chance and by environmental pressures, not by reason. But in a general way sociobiology *supports* a major tenet of natural law: that people are conscience-bound. I do not mean that people are conscience-bound to do such-and-such a specific deed. Rather, they inherit the physiological apparatus that makes them experience pangs of conscience — after they have been taught what is right and wrong by their culture. And no doubt fully socialized persons could figure out the necessary rules of society, even in a new situation, by consulting reason.

As for social contract theory, I have already stated that human evolution theory denies the occurrence of a period of human life that was presocial. By the time humans came into existence they were already social. Yet there is an aspect of social contract theory that accords perfectly with Trivers's idea of reciprocal altruism. It says that we are willing to do apparently generous or self-restrained things because we will reap a return. So, both Trivers and Hobbes acknowledge that self-interest can promote social cooperation. For Hobbes, though, it must be enlightened self-interest, whereas for Trivers the evolved behavior — say, in bats — need not have been a product of conscious awareness. It may have started on a trial-and- error basis of some sort, in which the individuals with a genetic mutation for this behavior proved more fit than the others.

In this chapter, I have wanted to call attention to the fact that the coexistence of individual selfishness and social cooperation has long been considered a mystery but that the mystery is now basically solved. I should admit, though, that the sociobiological theory in regard to humans is far from proven. Trivers's "moral emotions" cannot be seen under a microscope. But, in the absence of refutation, I find his hypothesis compelling. (Further corroboration of the evolutionary role of altruism in humans will be found in Chapter 14.)

The argument that morality, or at least protomorality, evolved by natural selection helps to demonstrate that moral behavior is normal, is pervasive, and is well provided for psychologically. The fact that the original object of moral feelings was the monitoring of social transactions further helps explain why we have so much concern about fairness.

This chapter is thus the main introduction in this book to the idea that such moral capacity as humans may possess today derives from their biological constitution. It justifies my claim, stated in other chapters, that morality is a routine intellectual and emotional guide to the solving of social problems.

CHAPTER 6

Green Ideas and the Ethics of Hunger

✳ ✳ ✳

"*Economics as If the Earth Really Mattered* is a remarkably complete guide to investing one's money and time in social change," says the back cover of this book. The front cover shows ticker tape from the New York Stock Exchange, out of which is emerging a heart, in the shape of a green summer leaf — a very clever cover that depicts the three elements in this book: the passions of the heart, the beauties of the earth, and money, money, money.

Reading Susan Meeker-Lowry's book made me feel like Rip van Winkle — as though I had slept for many years and then woken up in a changed land. In this new United States, small businesses have the laugh on large corporations, people trust their neighbors and care about each other's welfare, and citizens act responsibly toward the earth. Meeker-Lowry's effective tactic is to emphasize the things that *are* being done and to downplay the odds against social change. As the founding editor of *Catalyst: Investing in Social Change,* a quarterly report on business that she writes "from the woods of Vermont," she is in a position both to know of many enterprising activities and to take inspiration from the trees, the lakes, the birds and even the insect life around her.

The book's practical-guide section offers a discussion of "socially responsible investing." As we shall see, Meeker-Lowry considers this pretty tame stuff compared to "investing for social change," but at least it is somewhere to begin. She notes that one way concerned individuals can invest responsibly is to buy stock through a mutual fund that screens out companies with bad records. *Bad* is defined differently by different groups;

Review of Susan Meeker-Lowry, *Economics as If the Earth Really Mattered* (Philadelphia: New Society Publishers, 1988) and Onora O'Neill, *Faces of Hunger* (London: Allen and Unwin, 1986).

for example, the Pax World Fund, founded by Methodists in 1971, avoids all investments in weaponry. Others screen "for" certain things, such as for good labor conditions. The book is replete with names and addresses of groups you can write to and companies you can invest in and provides evidence that money invested in screened funds generally yields a higher return than money invested in nonscreened ones. The bi-monthly newsletter *Good Money* (P.O. Box 363, Worcester VT 05682; $75 per year as of 1988) contains information on the ethical and social practices of publicly traded corporations and offers investor services. Socially conscious investing is no longer a "fringe" activity. Meeker-Lowry mentions, for example, The Social Investment Forum, a national professional associa-tion of bankers, analysts, and brokers in Boston (who will "furnish you with a list of advisors on socially responsible investing in your area" [p. 56]).

A slightly more active way of making one's money, or one's voice, count in the corporate world is by filing a shareholder resolution. Any individual (or pool of individuals) who owns at least $1,000 worth of stock in a company and has held it for eighteen months may file such a resolution. A corporation can exclude a resolution that involves "legitimate shareholder con-cern" only if it sends notice of its reason for exclusion both to the filer and to the Securities and Exchange Commission. To present such a resolution one need not be present at the annual meeting — one may mail it in. The author notes that shareholder resolutions "are most often filed to raise aware-ness, rather than with the expectation that the resolution will pass. Media attention can make such resolutions far more effective" (p. 29). Churches and other large investors such as pension funds have actually had some success with resolu-tions. The Interfaith Center on Corporate Responsibility (475 Riverside Drive, New York NY 10115) coordinates such activi-ties, along with letter-writing campaigns, and provides informa-tion to others on the practices of major corporations. (They are also the publishers of the exposé-style magazine, *Multinational Monitor*.)

More to Meeker-Lowry's taste is the type of financial invest-ment in which the individual can feel more directly involved. She favors "investing in social change" for at least two reasons. First, her bias is toward small, local economies that give the people in their area more control over decisions that affect them. This accords with her ecological bias toward webs of small communities. Second, she sees the activities of people who engage in these businesses as *empowering*. People who have actually started an alternative business, say, or who have organized a land trust for community control over housing emerge from their experience with a sense that they *can*, with the aid of like-minded people, make life better. They can get rid of certain absurdities in the economy and ameliorate social injustices and ecological tragedies merely by putting their minds (and money and time) to it. She writes, "As I have met more and more skillful, incredibly committed people working both here and in the Third World to heal some of the damage done by corporations, I have become more and more convinced that to save this Earth and its communities, we must transform our corporate economy" (p. 96).

The difference between socially responsible investment and investing for social change may be pictured as follows:

> Cleaning up toxic discharges is an improvement, but social change involves developing technologies that do not leave us with toxic discharges in the first place. . . . Social change is not just saving the rain forest: it is developing a culture that provides for the needs of the people *and* the rain forest. Social change means recognizing the importance of history and of other cultures and the absolute necessity of diversity. Social change takes into account (and celebrates) the small differences between and the nuances of each of us within our communities; it does not expect to franchise (or clone) itself around the world (pp. 97–98).

To see some of the projects Meeker-Lowry has in mind, let us take a quick tour of the acronyms WON, CLT, LETS, and GRI. In the Appalachian area of Ohio, where unemployment is 20 percent, some folks have founded the Worker Owned Network (WON) to provide assistance to low-income people who want to create their own jobs. Initially, volunteers helped a group of welfare mothers start a homemaking and home health aide service. After obtaining some funding from the state of Ohio, WON was able to add three new businesses: a Mexican-American restaurant, a cleaning service, and a wholesale bakery for natural foods. "As each business gets underway, it helps the next one take its first steps" (p. 115). WON sees itself as a model of community-based economic development (it was inspired by the Mondragon Cooperatives in Spain) and is willing to help others. A packet of its materials can be obtained for $3 (better make it $5) by writing to 50 S. Court St, Athens OH 45701. Marty Zinn, an organizer at WON, says, "We believe it does not work simply to create new businesses with cooperative workplaces only to set them adrift, isolated in our economy with the deck stacked against them" (p. 115).

CLT stands for Community Land Trust. *Economics as If the Earth Really Mattered* gives two case studies of CLTs. One is the South Atlanta Land Trust, which shows how a run-down, condemned neighborhood can be reclaimed from absentee landlords by the local community. Civic groups buy the land (with the houses on it) and set it up as a public trust — no one may own pieces of it. Then, houses are rehabilitated and sold at a fairly low cost. Public ownership of the land helps to take the real estate out of the speculative market and makes it possible for the neighborhood's long-term residents to stay there. The other example, Community Land Trust in the southern Berkshires, involves a middle-class community in Massachusetts. This mountain area is considered a resort, and persons from out of town have been buying up land there for second homes, putting land prices out of reach of locals. Moreover, the local wilderness area is fast coming under development. The CLT buys up land, participates in having it zoned for housing, recreation, and wilderness — permanently — and arranges financing to lease homes to Berkshire County people. One of the few truly radical remarks in Meeker-Lowry's book, a quote from Ralph Borsodi, who was one of the developers of the CLT model in the 1960s, may provide food for thought: "The only way to make possible a truly good life for mankind is to utterly abolish the principle of absolute ownership of land and other natural resources, and completely replace it with agreements of tenure in trust. No amount of legalization can provide an honest title to any portion of the earth" (p. 105).

GRI, Grassroots International, is a social-change organization that funds community-based relief and development programs in Africa, the Middle East, and the Philippines. For example: "Black South Africans have rejected the township councils chosen for them . . . and have begun to organize new civic associations, parents' crisis committees, women's organizations, youth groups and the like. Since many community leaders have been arrested, street committees have been elected to protect against disruption when a leader is in detention . . . GRI is committed to supporting these organizations . . ." (p. 100). It also supports trade unions, paramedic training to give first aid to victims of police and army repression, and so forth. GRI's newsletter can be obtained for a donation of $25 or more from P.O. Box 312, Cambridge MA 02139.

The ultimate example of economic restructuring, perhaps, is the Canadian LETS — it is hardly meant as an example for all to follow but is interesting enough to mention. LETS stands for Local Employment Trading System, but LETS is as much a word as an acronym. Let's do it. Let's work for each other in a system where no money actually changes hands. In this arrangement, people barter their labor and talent. Imagine that Joe cuts firewood, and Peter is a welder who wants wood. But Joe doesn't need welding service from Peter. However, if they both belong to LETS, they can do the following:

> When Joe delivers the wood, Peter picks up the phone, dials the LETS office, and says into the machine there, "This is Peter, No. 48; please acknowledge Joe, No. 83, $75 for firewood." Joe's account balance increases by $75 (since he provided the service), and Peter's decreases by $75 (since he used the service). In turn, Joe employs a carpenter, the carpenter gets a haircut from a barber, and buys food from a farmer. The farmer now has a way to pay for a welder, so Peter gets to work again (p. 161).

Sophisticated city dwellers need not feel left out. There is still a way to invest in social change and feel some personal involvement. A guest writer, Michael Kilcullen, provides a section entitled "For a Good, Safe Investment, Think About Your Local Minority-Owned Bank." Depositing your savings there is low-risk, convenient, and pays market rates, yet also promotes housing and business development in low-income neighborhoods. One study showed that for every dollar deposited in a bank in Bronx, New York, only two cents were re-lent to local residents! The federal Community Reinvestment Act (CRA) of 1977, however, encourages banks to first meet the needs of the community where they are based. You can stroll into any bank and ask to examine their CRA files before deciding to open an account there.

Meeker-Lowry's devotion to local business is explained frequently in this book by way of analogy with "the leaky bucket." A bucket riddled with holes cannot hold water. Likewise, a community whose money and talent are leaking out cannot be economically healthy and cannot control the decisions that affect its well-being. Many — most — of our communities are leaky buckets. The value of participating in social investment, she admits, is partly just psychological. "Some of the most exciting changes I see involve shifts of perception. When we begin to make choices based on values — for example, refusing to invest in companies that produce nuclear weapons — we become more open" (p. 9).

Much of the book, though I cannot cover it here, is devoted to the search for a Gaean Economy, and there is a considerable section on the economics of waste, a specialty of Meeker-Lowry. (She is not without humor. There is a description of how the environmentally protective Ben and Jerry's Ice Cream company attempted to get rid of its dairy waste in the soundest possible way. The owners found that pigs could successfully consume it. The pigs accepted almost all flavors, but drew the line at Mint Oreo Cookie.) The book infuriatingly lacks an index but does contain an astonishing reference section entitled "Resources." Among the items mentioned there are such books as *Robin Hood Was Right* (by the Vanguard Foundation), *Green Politics: The Global Promise* (by Charlene Spretnak and Fritjof Capra), and *The 100 Best Companies to Work for in America* (by Norman Myers).

I bring this review of *Economics as If the Earth Really Mattered* into my book for at least three reasons. First, Meeker-Lowry is extraordinarily articulate in the often very vague realm of how various values relate to one another. In her introduction, she says, "The key to affecting our economy is to consciously choose to apply our values to economic interactions. If we do not choose our own values, then we subscribe by default to the values of the present system" (p. 1). Second, I believe that the issue that seems to concern her most, the health of the earth, is a moral matter par excellence. In later chapters, I consider various definitions of morality, but it goes without saying that morality has something to do with restraint, with discipline, with sharing. It seems inconceivable that our relationship with this planet and its resources and with the other people (including future generations) who need to use it could be somehow divorced from moral considerations.

Third, I have taken the opportunity of paraphrasing Meeker-Lowry's report on already existing activities (WON, GRI, CTL, and so on) because it is such a good example of how to overcome moral inertia. Namely, one can overcome it by recounting some victories. As far as I know, the adventures in her tale really did take place. But even if they were only fanciful, the exercise of "reporting" them would still be worthwhile. It makes me think: what if during the early 1980s, some Romanian underground groups had circulated a mock newspaper describing how their popular revolt had succeeded, how Nicolae Ceausescu had fled the presidential palace, how the various opposition parties had subsequently run for election — how might such an encouraging scenario have speeded up the actual events?

In the introduction to her 1934 book, *Patterns of Culture*, the anthropologist Ruth Benedict remarked that in every culture a child soon absorbs whatever is "in the atmosphere" around him — all the attitudes of his culture. "By the time he is grown . . . its beliefs are his beliefs, its impossibilities, his impossibilities" (p. 2). Perhaps our common belief that it is impossible to do anything about our present economy — and the ecological havoc it wreaks — is an example of such innocent acceptance of impossibilities.

This brings me to the next book under review, *Faces of Hunger*, by Onora O'Neill. It is virtually the opposite of Meeker-Lowry's book in that it does not — cannot — rely on examples of "how things are being done" in regard to hunger and poverty in the world. Rather, it concentrates on the problem of how we *think* about hunger and the morality of sharing. O'Neill's book is, in fact, purely a work of philosophy, albeit applied philosophy. In it, she makes a very persuasive case that the discourse on hunger is faulty and troubled and that, until this is dealt with, it is unlikely that there will be any change in ethical attitudes about hunger. To the cynic who may say, "Any idiot can see that the present distribution of food is wrong, and that the problem is one of motivation to share, not one of philosophical discourse," I can only say, wait, give this book a chance.

Where would a thinking person begin to tackle the subject of the ethics of hunger? Probably by seeking facts about the causes of and solutions to the food problem. Yet facts here are difficult to acquire. A likely source of information would be the development theorists, but they are divided among themselves on this issue. As O'Neill points out, there are "expert" opinions to support many different views. Some defend immediate importation of food, whereas others argue that helping a country to establish self-sufficiency in food production is more important. Some believe efforts at population control should come first; others show that health and security precede voluntary birth control. Some favor development of the industrial sector, others of the rural sector, and so forth.

These and other views are themselves not ethically neutral: they embody ethical or ideological presumptions. O'Neill comments: "Economic discussions that take centralized (or decentralized) decision-making for granted, or that assume some (but not other) property relationships, and social investigations that use (or shun) explanations in terms of class or ethnicity . . . embody substantive ethical assumptions. Development studies are filled with *ethical* as well as other disagreements over what the problems of development are and whose problems they are" (1986, p. 5).

In short, the first difficulty for anyone who wants to "do something" about world hunger is to know what to do. The second difficulty, the one to which most of O'Neill's book is devoted, is that there is no widely accepted principle of ethics concerning persons in need. There are local and religious ethics of this type — liberation theology, for example, is proving appealing to activists in Catholic countries — but what we need are principles that are accessible to everyone. "Philosophical writing in ethics," she notes, "has traditionally aspired to show how ethical reasoning could be prised away from local context" (p. 31). The classical, eighteenth-century solution to the problem of addressing a mixed audience was to rely on modes of discourse which were thought to be accessible to "rational beings as such" (p. 32). Paradoxically, what that level of abstraction entails is that universal ethical reasoning can address only individuals. This, O'Neill says, is a high price to pay because it makes ethics a private matter, relevant to thinking about personal dilemmas and relationships but not accessible to powerful institutions. Such ethical reasoning "could not guide the action of states, international bodies and transnational corporations. . . . None of these are ideal rational choosers. All are bound to the particular categories and concepts embodied in their constitution or tradition" (p. 33). As the author observes, "No individual can devalue a currency or irrigate a desert. . . . Individuals can only take part in such activities in appropriate social contexts" (p. 38).

One might think that the notion of human rights — to which most peoples today ostensibly aspire — takes care of this problem by setting up structures in which such collectivities as governments must act. Let us look more carefully, however, at the idea of rights to see how or whether it can result in action. When we speak of rights, "we assume a framework in which performance of obligations can be claimed" (p. 100). Yet holders of rights can press their claims *only when the obligations to meet these claims have been allocated to specified others.* It is true that certain "negative" rights, such as the right not to be injured, are incumbent on all persons — that is, everyone is obliged to refrain from injuring others. But "positive" rights, such as rights to receive benefits, are special rights for which there must be a special agreement, such as an employer's agreement to pay wages. O'Neill says, "A list of universal rights might provide a grid of categories which make certain problems salient and show who ought to act to remedy them. If, for example, we could establish that there is a universal right to food, each hungry person would have legitimate claims against specifiable others. However, unless the obligation to provide food to each claimant is actually allocated to specified agents and agencies, this right will provide meagre pickings" (p. 101).

Using P. Alston and K. Tomasevski's (1984) observation, O'Neill remarks, "Unless obligations to feed the hungry are a matter of allocated justice rather than indeterminate beneficence, a so-called 'right to food,' and the other 'rights' of the poor, will be only 'manifesto' rights" (p. 101). Interestingly, she points out that it is perhaps because rights talk has become so important, that beneficence, or generosity, has been downgraded. No one feels that charity is mandatory, and the factor of need is often left out of discussion. "If we lavish our attention and help on those who already have enough, or on our own families, that will count as beneficence. In discussions of rights, mere need carries no independent weight" (p. 102).

O'Neill's solution to these anomalies is that we shift our ethical deliberation so that *obligations*, rather than rights, are seen as fundamental. As noted by A. Sen (1984) and Henry Shue (1984), if obligation were the starting point, then institutional structures to secure the right to food could be sought on this basis. Rights language, according to O'Neill, speaks most forcefully to suffering claimants, but the message may be inaccessible or half-heard by those with power to bring about change (p. 120). Those with power need to have their obligations spelled out for them.

Hence we come to her main contribution, presented in the final chapter of *Faces of Hunger*, which she calls a "maverick Kantian theory of obligation." It is action-centered and, she believes, potentially accessible to agents and agencies who are in a position to do something about hunger and destitution. Although abstract, it does not confine itself to "rational individuals" but takes in contexts, institutions, and collectivities. Here are its main points: it is concerned with both justice *and* beneficence, and it makes human autonomy and human needs central; it relies on the Kantian notion that we must respect other persons and not coerce or deceive them. Most importantly, it calls for "far-reaching political activity which transforms the basic principles of economic, and social structures" (pp. 142–145).

I must pause to note that although O'Neill is about to launch into a polemic, she does appear to have got there on strictly philosophical grounds. Her argument relies on Immanuel Kant's proposition that respect for other persons, which is a universal obligation, derives from the fact that all persons could wish this to be a universal rule. The way in which respect is carried out is by *not* coercing or deceiving others and also by giving help when it is needed; this may include helping the development of people's talents or capacities. The test for the universality of this obligation is that no one could will (or want) "to find themselves part of a world in which respect, help, and the development of skills and capacities are universally neglected" (p. 146).

The originality of O'Neill's work consists of her allocating to specific agents the obligations to alleviate hunger, based on the universal obligation not to coerce or deceive. She always takes into consideration the wider context of people's actions and is critical of institutions, structures, and historical circumstance. She states, "Circumstances of justice are lacking so long as material and social needs are so great that coercion and deception are not merely easy but virtually unavoidable" (p. 146). Here is an example of her "action-centered reasoning": "A company might initially represent its dealing with representatives of a poverty-stricken country as guided by standard and acceptable negotiating practice. . . . The management might insist that there was nothing either coercive or deceptive, and so nothing unjust, in the negotiating. However, others might think that the desperation of those with whom the deal was made meant that it amounted to a coercive 'offer they could not refuse' " (p. 147). The author compares this approach with that of most philosophers by saying, "Seen in a wider context, adherence to standard forms of commercial bargaining, which might not coerce either the ideally rational or the materially self-sufficient, may be fundamentally coercive" (p. 147).

A major contribution of this book is the author's observation that we suppress the factors of coercion and deception in most of our discussions of democratic political forms and market economies. That is, we leave out a large part of the real picture.

Commentary

O'Neill's *Faces of Hunger* and Meeker-Lowry's *Economics as If the Earth Really Mattered* are vastly different but both invigorating books. The intellectual integrity of each is reassuring, and the novelty of their arguments is refreshing. Meeker-Lowry's style is easy (which is not to say it was easy to write), and O'Neill's is difficult (which is not to say it was easy to write!). *Faces of Hunger* was no doubt aimed at colleagues in academia, but I believe it is sufficiently self-contained that an amateur philosopher could enjoy working through it. It is unusually free of jargon. (In fact, my only complaint about

O'Neill's English is that she appends "ly" to inappropriate adjectives to make them adverbs: the word *standardly* appears dozens of times, and there's even a *Kantianly* somewhere in the text.)

Both women, it seems to me, face an economy that strikes them as ethically absurd, and both want to go to the heart of the matter to find what is wrong with our system. Let me now try to place these two works within the larger context of this book that is concerned with moral inertia. It could be noted that O'Neill's complaint about the underdeveloped ethics of hunger is a pinpointing of one aspect of moral inertia. Bodies at rest (in this case, intellectual bodies!) tend to remain at rest. It is difficult for them to break out of the closed circle of philosophical discussion and drag in the realities of world hunger. By contrast, Meeker-Lowry's activist approach recalls the other definition of moral inertia. Once moral action is put in motion, it tends to stay in motion. As she says, the mere effort of doing something, such as trying a new approach, is empowering and leads to more action.

The success of Meeker-Lowry's book is largely related to her direct confrontation of the issue of power. Later, in Chapter 15, I shall inquire in depth into the relationship between morality and power, but we must at least mention this important topic now. Morality often takes the form of a *confrontation with power*. In the introduction, I stated that morality can be defined roughly as "what people agree on." In some circumstances, all the members of a society might agree. If their interests are roughly similar, and they stand to lose or gain equally in their compromises, they can be expected to arrive easily at moral rules that others would also accept as just. Where some have an initial advantage, however, they may be able to set up a morality that masquerades as justice but that consists mainly of protection of their privileges. When this happens, moral action may eventually take the form of confronting the status quo on behalf of the powerless.

Meeker-Lowry's approach is both moral and political. She advocates certain values, such as the value of a healthy planet and the value of a community's maintaining control over its fate. She suggests specific ways to assault the powers that hinder these values, especially the large, uncaring corporations. Her book, *Economics as If the Earth Really Mattered*, is a veritable how-to guide for changing the power system. Essentially, she appeals to citizens to use their numbers to bring about social change. A little effort placed here, a little money spent there, she says, adds up to social and economic power that can bring the desired values into effect.

By contrast, O'Neill is not able to urge the hungry to vote with their feet. In fact she cannot appeal to them directly. By the nature of the case they are very powerless people. Her tactic instead is to go to philosophers and tell them to be more forceful and precise in their moral reasoning and moral language. She advocates what I would call ethics-smithing. Her particular contribution to such smithing consists of finding logical flaws and helping to correct them. For instance, she allocates obligations to relevant agents and brings the factors of deception and coercion into the picture of economic bargaining.

Clearly, O'Neill cannot appeal to our interest in working for a more equitable distribution of food. Morals aside, it is in our interest to keep the distribution as it is, as we thereby enjoy longer and more comfortable lives. The most she hopes to do is get us to follow through more honestly on our stated beliefs about people's rights. I would characterize her book, *Faces of Hunger*, as an appeal to our integrity. Oddly, it is not an appeal to our sympathy. I believe O'Neill has missed an important opportunity to incorporate into the ethics of hunger the factor of sympathy as a motivator of moral behavior. It is not enough to develop an ethics of hunger by saying that people have a *right* to food. (Indeed, on at least one view it is incorrect to say they have a right, insofar as rights are something won, not merely requested.) What needs to be shown is that there exists a moral relationship between a rich man and a poor man based not on the poor man's "rights" but on the poor man's suffering and the rich man's sympathy with that suffering.

The greatest oddity of O'Neill's book is that despite its title, *Faces of Hunger*, it provides no actual portraits of hunger. This is a crucial omission, since portraits would have the effect of drawing sympathy. Let me give a portrait of hunger expressed in factual, clinical terms. In adults, hunger involves weight loss, energy loss, apathy, depression, and susceptibility to infection, most often manifest in diarrhea. In pregnant and lactating women, the condition of hunger additionally encompasses likelihood of miscarriage, small or premature babies with attendant problems, high neonatal death rate due to infection, and lack of breast milk and therefore slow growth of the baby, including head size. In children, hunger is expressed as listlessness, stunted mental and physical development (often permanent), and very high rates of infection, including fatal diseases.

I have not, in that portrait, gone into any emotional description, such as the grief of loss of a loved one or the parent's frustration over a stunted child, nor have I described the pain, discomfort, and disability involved in most of the hunger-related diseases. Yet all these things are surely part of the moral picture here. To be fair, O'Neill should not be saddled with the task of inventing a complete and perfect ethics of hunger — it is enough that she has opened the discussion. My point is only that she has neglected to utilize a key aspect of the human tendency to be moral — namely, sympathy — in her effort to clarify the relationship between the haves and have-nots. It would be my guess that a flourishing of sympathy for the hungry billion individuals in our world will be the only method by which redistribution of wealth will come about — or, at least, the only method by which voluntary redistribution will come about.

CHAPTER 7

Moral Inertia: Contributing Factors

✳ ✳ ✳

For evil to triumph all that is needed is for good men to do nothing.

— Edmund Burke

When visible, palpable, banal evil shows itself, few will speak out.

— Hannah Arendt

This must stop!

— Nicholas to Mr. Squeers
in Charles Dickens's *Nicholas Nickleby*

The subject of this chapter is moral inertia in the "mark one" sense of moral inaction or moral malaise. As lamented in the introductory chapter, we witness horrific things happening in the world, yet often do little to stop them. Examples of things that would widely be regarded as "evils" are the practice of torture by governments, the irreversible pollution of habitats by industry, extreme economic injustice, and the buildup of grotesque weaponry. Undoubtedly, some people are moved to act against these evils, as the plethora of voluntary organizations shows. Yet the majority of us stand idly by. We do not throw our moral weight against these evils.

Why is this so? In Chapter 1, I identified seven "design errors" in the human moral system: the option of deviance, tribalism, demographic limitations, the arbitrariness of values, the diffusion of responsibility, the moral immunity of group persons and officeholders, and the coexistence of voluntarism and structuralism. It was not my mission there to inquire specifically into the causes of moral inertia but more generally to isolate flaws in our moral system (though these undoubtedly account to some extent for moral inaction in the face of evil).

In this chapter I limit myself to three categories of items that help account for the phenomenon of moral inertia: certain cognitive traits, problems of moral language, and ideological factors. In the category of *cognitive traits,* I shall list several characteristics of the human mind that limit people's ability to perceive certain social or moral facts. The category of *moral language* will have more to do with linguistic mental processes or with particular cultural habits concerning the use of words. The third category, *ideological factors,* is related specifically to two major modern ideologies: liberalism and Marxism. I shall show how these have a way of assisting moral apathy and the tolerance of evil.

Cognitive Traits

The first in my list of broad cognitive impediments to moral action is simply *perceptual selectivity.* A principal reason why people do not respond readily to eradicate evils could be that they have difficulty perceiving those evils. As psychologists Bernard Berelson and Gary Steiner (1964) have demonstrated, a person tends to see only the facts that fit his prejudices, theories, and expectations. Conflicting facts are suppressed, ignored, or somehow rationalized (Berelson and Steiner, 1964, pp. 578–580). If a person is not trained to recognize evil, to receive it into his awareness, the evil may remain more or less invisible to him. In the discussion of cruelty in Chapter 8, it will be noted that cruelty flourishes best in isolation — when the cruel acts are genuinely out of people's sight. Cruel acts can also be out of sight if people agree to pretend they are not there: for instance, neighbors may not "see" wife-beating.

A second cognitive trait — actually a combined cognitive and emotional trait — is the general human *proclivity to be optimistic.* Most people much of the time see the world as rosier than it is. Even when they agree that the world is not too rosy their presumption is that things will improve. Perhaps one chance in a hundred that things will improve is enough to make people feel that there is a reasonable chance. In the behavior of gambling, such as playing roulette or lotteries, individuals routinely overestimate the favorable odds. Sociologist Lionel Tiger has suggested that such a habit was an adaptive trait in the days of early human evolution when individuals faced great difficulties (1979, pp. 20–21). In any case, we now routinely upgrade positive indications of hope into general reassurance.

A third cognitive trait pertinent to our search for the causes of moral inertia could be called *the Emperor's New Clothes syndrome*. If it has become a culture's habit to soft-pedal the existence of certain social problems, it will be difficult for an individual to insist on their importance or urgency. Self-censorship operates here: one simply is too embarrassed or intimidated to deviate from the norm. Hence, this behavioral trait may be primarily emotional; nevertheless, it is cognitive in that it actually prevents the full perception or recognition of social evils. One begins to doubt one's own senses if they are not in accord with the majority's. Occasionally, however, someone breaks out and announces that the emperor is not wearing any clothes; then others can change their perception and join in. This happened, for example, during the 1970s and 1980s when some U.S. journalists began to claim that it was wrong for their nation to engage in "covert actions" abroad.

A fourth cognitive trait that contributes to moral inertia is *dichotomization*. Humans like to think in either-or terms, and it is possible that subconscious human decision-making is done in the mode of a binary computer (Pugh, 1978, pp. 98–99). Some examples of dichotomization in relation to the evils mentioned earlier are "The opposite choice to an arms race is the extinction of my nation," or "The opposite of polluting the environment is the removal of all technological comforts." Expanding the imagined alternative into an evil as great as the one under consideration makes the options equal and the decision easy. Such all-or-nothing thinking is characteristic of everyday moral thought, but it also colors much ethical philosophy. As Isaiah Berlin (1980) and Marshall Cohen (1984) have noted, few philosophical writers bother much about moral complexities and conflicts.

A fifth cognitive trait limiting human action on social evils is one that could be called *solutionism*. This is the belief that there must be a perfect solution, somewhere, to every problem. And since there is a perfect solution to evil — such as a new type of political arrangement — then we should wait for it rather than carry out piecemeal reform. This mode of thinking is the stock-

73

in-trade of academic theorists, but it is a layperson's trait as well. Susan Meeker-Lowry, author of the book on economy and ecology reviewed in Chapter 6, writes: "It is tempting to sit around analyzing theories and waiting for the one idea that will save us. . . . But as long as we wait for the definitive solution, nothing will change, or rather, we will have no say in the changes . . . [Moreover,] if we wait for experts to come up with brilliant one-time solutions, we will simply watch — and help — our planet, ourselves, die" (1988, p. 10, p. 20). I believe that solutionism is not a well-recognized phenomenon and that it gets much of its power from this lack of recognition.

Finally, I list as the sixth cognitive problem the *numbing effect of statistics* on the human mind. It seems almost as though the larger an evil is in numerical terms — such as "200,000 prisoners tortured this year" — the less is the emotional impact on the individual. If there were only six prisoners tortured, we could learn the names and background of each and feel more involved in their plight. In the case of Soviet dissidents during the cold war, the *names* of a few, harped on by the Western press, made the situation more real to the public. Likewise, some charitable organizations operating among starving populations use the tactic of asking people to support an individual or family, whose photograph they furnish to the donor. This allows the effect of one's charitable effort to be felt in a personal sense. In general, not only do large statistics convey a less vivid picture, they tend to suggest that the matter is hopeless. Thus, individuals feel that they might as well not try to influence the outcome.

In sum, at least six cognitive traits contribute to moral inertia: perceptual selectivity, the proclivity to be optimistic, the Emperor's New Clothes syndrome, dichotomization, solutionism, and the numbing effect of statistics. These cognitive traits evolved as part of our multifaceted mental apparatus; they did not especially evolve in connection with moral life. Their effect on moral thinking and action is incidental to their usual function. Nevertheless, anyone concerned with moral inertia as a problem needs to know of their existence.

Moral Language

In this section I shall discuss various ways in which aspects of language lead to, or support, moral inertia. These are ways in which words or linguistic mechanisms dull our moral sensibility or help to prevent the expected human response to evil. The first three of these result from emotions that probably evolved in connection with other areas of life, namely religion, authority, and nationalism. The remaining five show how one linguistic feature or another — such as the flexibility of words, or the lack of vocabulary for certain concepts — has an influential effect on moral thought and hence on moral action.

The first aspect of moral language to be noted is the *realm of the sacred.* Some words, phrases, or ideas have a certain aura around them. Whether in primitive or modern religion, there is a sphere of moral belief that is not available for criticism or debate; to question holy truths is to blaspheme. It may seem odd that I list this as a factor contributing to moral inertia: often the strength of religious belief is an *aid* to moral action. However, the point being made is that some forms of language put *restriction on thought.* Leaders wishing to control thought can, moreover, use or misuse religious words or inappropriately conjure up the realm of the sacred in order to curtail people's rational response to evil.

The second item to be listed here is a related one, namely *the force of authority.* In each generation the subject of right and wrong is not open for reworking by all people (in the way that scientific theories are said to be). The existing set of moral rules — whether secular or religious — seems paramount and unchallengeable. Our natural tendency is to accept the authority of tradition; this inhibits critical moral thought. Moreover, respect for authority is entangled with deference to political power. Our acquiescence in the present distribution of power in our society may lead us to accept some of the evils mentioned earlier — torture, pollution, poverty, the arms race. At the moment, I am not arguing that power is coercive, that it prevents us from acting — an important but separate point. Rather, I am pointing out that the very analysis of evil is hindered by a general belief in the rightness of what "authority" says and a belief in the rightness (or perhaps the inevitability) of "the way things are."

75

A third aspect of moral language that contributes to moral inertia has to do with *the logic of nationalism* or more generally with the phenomenon of in-group/out-group behavior. As social psychologists have shown, people quickly form loyalties to the group to which they are assigned (even if the assignment be arbitrary) (Sherif, 1956, pp. 54–58). One's in-group becomes the object of praise and devotion, whereas the out-group is fair game for derision and attack. The obstacle that this poses to moral reasoning or discussion is the obvious one — that rightness or goodness is automatically associated with the behavior of one's own group and wrongness is uncritically attributed to the foreign way of life. Moreover, if the out-group is a threat to the survival of the in-group for any reason — such as competition over a vital resource — then its badness takes on an even more indisputable quality. I have investigated this "dual code of morality" in my book, *Morality among Nations* (1990).

The aforementioned three factors — the realm of the sacred, the force of authority, and the logic of nationalism — are not strictly characteristics of language itself. The language relevant to those behaviors no doubt came about as a consequence of them. Nevertheless, I think it is worth including these factors in the list of moral language problems since they limit the human ability to approach the problem of evil. In each case, key words set up emotions that curtail further moral exploration.

The fourth language item that I propose as a contributor to moral inertia can be called *sloganeering*. By this I mean the linguistic trait of oversimplification in speech to reduce an issue to its salient elements, leaving out all modifications and exceptions. Many heated debates in our society, such as those concerning abortion or racism, become reduced to slogans. This use of words probably reflects the mental habit of drawing conclusions from a few clues: cognitive psychologists have demonstrated that we do not usually reason logically to a conclusion but use shortcuts, clues, and stereotypes. The relationship between thought and speech is apparently two-way: the very existence of slogans can cut short the process of thinking as well.

The fifth item I shall call *Orwellian euphemism*. Here a party, such as a government, that wishes to get away with reprehensible acts simply calls them by another name. Unpleasant objects or facts can likewise be rendered innocuous by linguistic fiat, as when devastation by bombing is referred to as "taking out" a city. Orwellian euphemism has been developed to a fine art in the twentieth century. So also the sixth item, which can be labeled *Nukespeak*. Here a government or other organization obfuscates its policies by the use of technical or mathematical-sounding terminology. The effect is to put the subject out of public reach, since most individuals will feel daunted by their apparent lack of expertise. The impression meant to be created is that somewhere there is a group of experts in whose capable hands these matters are best left.

The seventh moral-language problem has to do with the *open-endedness of language itself*. Human language is not tied to a static universe of ideas, nor are words something that reflect objective reality in a one-to-one manner. Rather, language is fluid and open-ended. Hence, many and varied social or moral values can be proclaimed simultaneously by a particular group or even by a particular individual. It does not matter that these may be incompatible; that is, the expression of one set of values does not automatically demand the suppression of another. Erich Fromm has pointed out, for example, that Westerners live with two sets of values simultaneously. The official, conscious values are those of the religious and humanist tradition — such as love, compassion, and hope. But the unconscious values of the social system — property, consumption, social position, fun — are more influential (1968, pp. 94–96). If these two sets of values were explicitly pitted against each other, many people might opt for the former over the latter, but there is never a requirement that one make such a choice. Individuals can get around the problem of carrying two sets of values at once by choosing their words carefully.

The eighth and final language factor contributing to moral inertia concerns the *unavailability of words* needed to express certain concepts. For example, there may be no word or phrase available to portray the relationship of responsibility and blame in particular situations. Jonathan Kozol, in his study of American education (1980), found that schoolchildren are not given the linguistic means with which to connect individual action to social problems. Events such as war and starvation, he says, are discussed in the third person, passive voice, as though they were uncaused misfortunes or technological and biological mistakes. Linguistically we do not place ourselves into the center of historical action, by saying "I choose this" or "I am responsible for that." Thus, Kozol notes, because schoolchildren cannot see the possibility of their own moral potency, they will hardly come to exercise it.

In sum, we can identify eight language problems related to moral inertia: the realm of the sacred, the force of authority, the logic of nationalism, sloganeering, Orwellian euphemism, Nukespeak, the open-endedness of language, and the unavailability of needed words. Each of these helps to channel our mental processes in ways that deter moral action.

Ideological Factors

The question we are investigating in this chapter is, Where the majority of people agree that something is evil, why do they not act morally against it? Four evils to which I alluded were torture by governments, pollution of habitats, extreme economic injustice, and buildup of weaponry. Here I cannot attempt to unravel the historical causes of these evils, much less account for all the forces that sustain these particular things at present. Yet I think it is possible to isolate some of the factors that undergird widespread moral inertia in the face of these evils. In the preceding sections I listed very general background factors — cognitive traits and problems of moral language — that cause humans to be less morally responsive than might be expected. Now let me switch the focus to more specific factors, namely, ideological factors that operate in two of the dominant nations in the late twentieth century — the United States and the Soviet Union. For the remainder of this chapter, I shall briefly look at the ideologies of Western liberalism and of Marxism, with an eye to the way each one has hampered moral initiative. (Of course, a large part of the problem is that these two ideologies have existed in a mode of fierce competition with each other; this also will be discussed.)

Western Liberalism

Ideologies come about in specific places at specific times, that is, with reference to the circumstances of a particular culture, a particular economic situation, a particular form of government. Yet it seems to be in the nature of ideologies that the values they set up are construed as being values for all time, for all people. This may relate to some tie-in with religious thinking: when a way of life is described as the good way, it seems logical that it should be universally appreciated.

The ideology of Western liberalism contains values that were important in nineteenth-century America, such as emphasis on individual initiative, the right of citizens to be free from governmental coercion, and the value of economic development. These values no doubt contributed greatly to the success of U.S. society, and they continue to be honored in the lore without any particular concern for their contemporary relevance. Acceptance of these values is seen by most Americans as a basic part of their self-image. Emphasis on the positive nature of these values may, however, tend to mask their deficiencies and in any case deflects attention from the worthiness of other values.

The question before us is how ideological factors specifically contribute to moral inertia. In the case of the liberal ideology several ways can be noted. Michael Walzer observed in the late 1970s that one feature of the cultural ethos of liberalism in America is that moral discussion becomes unfashionable (1978, p. 11). To some extent this intellectual embarrassment or reluctance to talk about moral issues is part of the overall American dislike for authority and is also related to the "each-man-for-himself" philosophy. Walzer calls attention to two typical liberal approaches to morality that have been personalized by major figures in American cinema: the hard, seasoned, lonely frontiersman and the tough, sophisticated urban wise guy.

> The first American liberal approach to moral life is a special kind of relativism. Values, it is said, are deeply personal and private. . . . In public, we can only hold a man to his own standards: honor, sincerity, grace under pressure. These can be talked about, but not virtue or goodness. Moral judgement focused on questions of virtue or goodness is moralizing, the sure sign of self-righteousness, priggishness and hypocrisy (1978, p. 12).

The second kind, also a stereotype of the American, involves a utilitarian approach to morality, a sort of cost-benefit analysis:

> When decisions are unavoidable, they must be hard-headed, tough-minded, unsentimental, worked out in terms of the actual or supposed preferences of discrete individuals. The standard must be clear — utiles of pleasure, dollars, lives — qualities that can be turned into quantities, so that the ultimate decision is as undisputable as addition and subtraction and so that there is, once again, no room for moralizing (1978, p. 12).

In short, the Western liberal ideology can act to inhibit the normal human disposition for moral judgment and grappling with evil.

A second commentator on liberalism's obstacles to moral reasoning is Alexandr Solzhenitsyn. In his famous Harvard Commencement speech in 1978, he noted that the Western sense of what is right or wrong is colored by an interest in what is legal. Such emphasis on legality cuts out whole areas from moral consideration. For example, Solzhenitsyn found it shocking that in the United States oil companies are allowed to buy up the inventions of alternative energy production for the sole purpose of preventing their use. "If one is right from a legal point of view," he said, "nothing more is required, nobody may mention that one could still not be entirely right, and urge self-restraint. . . . Whenever the tissue of life is woven of legalistic relations, there is an atmosphere of moral mediocrity, paralysing man's noblest impulses" (1978).

There are other critiques of liberalism as well, such as Michael Sandel's (1982) view that concern with the rights of the individual hinders perception of the community's needs and rights. This is somewhat related to the classical critique of democracy. As political philosopher Paul Corcoran notes, democratic governments, being formed from the interests of private groups, characteristically lack a moral vision for society as a whole or even a sense of public purpose (1983b).

In short, although ideological systems often appear to have much moral content — being concerned with defining the good way of life — they can act subtly to deter further moral investigation. I contend that the three above-mentioned features of the cultural ethos of Western liberalism — sophisticated distaste for authority, concern with legality, and exclusive emphasis on the rights of individuals — are all inhibitors of moral thought and action. Morality *necessarily* involves interpersonal relations and the competing goods of individual and society; morality also requires some regard for authority, even if it be just the authority of socially agreed-upon principles. Hence, liberal notions, and the world view they create, do act, at least sometimes, as contributors to inaction in the face of evil.

Marxism

The "opposite" ideology to liberalism, Marxism, also appears at first glance to have a large, even overwhelming, moral content, yet it too can restrict moral thought. Eugene Kamenka refers to the familiar picture of Karl Marx as "an Old Testament prophet hurling anathemas at bourgeois civilization and exposing its inhumanity, exploitation, hypocrisy and greed" (1986, p. 20). Marx himself had written in 1844 that the "essential sentiment of criticism is *indignation:* its essential activity is *denunciation*" (Kamenka, 1986, p. 20). But later he changed his approach from that of denouncing the immorality of capitalism to that of proclaiming that it would come to an end through its own internal difficulties. Karl Popper wrote in 1944, "Marx's hatred of hypocrisy . . . together with his amazing optimism led him to veil his moral beliefs behind historicist formulations" (1944, pp. 206–207). Whereas for Hegel "might is right," for Marx "the coming might is right." This scientific certainty about the future, Popper notes, leads to a scorn for human reason and an appeal to violence.

Just as the United States prides itself on its championship of human rights, Marxist societies can deservedly rest their reputations on their general crusade for social justice. Yet the Marxist ideology has led to an even greater rigidity and exclusiveness of moral thinking than the liberal ideology. Steven Lukes noted in 1985 that in the USSR and Eastern Europe, "both marxist and moral vocabulary have become wholly devalued, the worthless currency of an empty rhetoric" (1985, quoted in Kamenka, 1986, p. 20). This probably has much to do with the inherent dogmatism of Marxist-Leninist theory, with its demand for party discipline, and with the inconsistency between the dream and the reality of a socialist state. However, two further aspects of this ideology can be singled out as specific contributors to moral inertia. The first of these is Marxism's *lack of a theory of the state*, and the second is its *lack of a theory of ethics.*

Allow me to elaborate. John Hoffman (1984) — echoing Antonio Gramsci — points out that a great paradox of Marxism is that it lacks a theory of the state. Marxism restricts politics to mere superstructure (or epiphenomena) of the ownership of the means of production. In doing so, it denies any autonomous realm for political activity. Thus, for example, the concept of a power-hungry leader is not available for analysis in this tradition; it has to be ignored. Similarly, Marxism was never able to absorb Robert Michels's pertinent observation of 1903 (Michels, 1958) that an "iron law of oligarchy" is likely to operate in socialist parties. Moreover, the failure of Marxism to deal in any way with the issue of consent by the governed is notorious. As Colletti declared, any political theory that neglects the question of consent will facilitate leaderships that, as in much of the Communist world, exercise power "without any control by the masses over whom they rule" (1977, p. 315). In short, repression by the state is simply a non-issue where there is no theory of the state.

The second problem is that Marxism does not have a philosophy of ethics that defines a person's duties to his fellows. Rather, as George G. Brenkert points out, Marxism contains a strong ethics of virtue. Like many of the ancient Greek philosophies, Marxism questions which ways of life are worthy of humankind (1983, pp. 12–13). Thus, Marx wrote, "The moral law . . . has to be expressed in the form 'be this,' not in the form 'do this' " (Brenkert, 1983, p. 17). Most likely Marx would not have felt that this lack of a practical ethics was a failing in his work. On the contrary, he held adamantly that ethics cannot be rationally imposed on people where the structure of society goes against it. It is the essence of Marx's critical theory that persons operate in a social context of which they are not consciously aware. Again, however, by concentrating only on the ideal future system, Marx denied his followers the means by which to criticize, piecemeal, the social relations of their present. Indeed, he caused them to have to abandon the wisdom of traditional morality. A remarkable example is that it has taken half a century for some Marxists to find the words in which to charge Stalin with moral blame for his murder of millions of Russians.

Since Stalin was acting for the revolution — for the future — it was as though his deeds could not be wrong.

In short, during its years of prominence as an ideology, Marxism managed to deflect a huge amount of moral debate by leaving political behavior as such out of its basic analysis and by concentrating so intently on the future ethical ideal as to render present social relations unfit for critical discussion.

Nationalist Competition

So far I have suggested that various intrinsic features of both the Western liberal ideology and the Marxist ideology contribute to moral inertia. But, I should add, the fact that two powerful nations held these ideologies and pointed to each other's ideology as a foremost evil made their respective systems become even *more* intellectually rigid. Over time, each developed a caricature of its own position. Moreover, when nations are in a state of constant military preparedness vis-à-vis each other, criticism of one's ideology from *within* can be considered treasonable. (As I finish writing this book, this situation is happily changing in regard to the United States and the Soviet Union.)

At the very least there is self-censorship on both sides. If something is part of the enemy's intellectual kit — for example, the "liberal enemy's" concern with civil rights — it must automatically be given no consideration by the other side. Just as many Americans go into an irrational frame of mind when they encounter "communism," for Marxists the thought of "capitalism" is enough to shut down some of the cerebral processes. This habit may be related to the cognitive trait of dichotomization mentioned earlier, whereby all thinking must be either-or. It is also reminiscent of nationalist thinking in which one's own group is unquestionably considered to be morally superior and the other group thought villainous — with or without evidence.

Thus I claim that the very competition between two historical ideologies has stunted the development of the moral tradition of either side. (Where might America's moral-intellectual energy have been directed over the last several decades if it had not been burdened with the preoccupation of "fighting communism"?) An equally serious problem is the way in which the existence of an evil enemy has exempted both nations' international behavior from domestic moral scrutiny. The logic of nationalism here is that any action taken to counter the evil enemy is itself "good" — even if by any other standard of moral judgment it would be bad. For example, the United States frequently finds itself helping Third World governments to put down popular organizations such as trade unions in the interest of preserving freedom (Herman, 1982, pp. 207–208). The logic of superpower confrontation has at times gone so far as to support the idea that to risk the extinction of the human species is a lesser evil than to let down our guard with the enemy. Only in recent years have ethical thinkers started to cut through this absurdity, for instance, by reviving the traditional Christian moral philosophy that states that the ends cannot justify all means (Beitz, 1988, pp. 219–236).

In sum, ideological factors have an influence, perhaps an overwhelming influence, on moral inertia. Ideologies are sacrosanct both because they define the good life and because they give self-identity to a nation. Yet, as we have seen, they are always deficient models; by playing up one factor they leave another out of consideration, perhaps even out of perception. The liberals overemphasize the individual, forgetting the community, and overemphasize legality, sometimes forsaking moral principle. The Marxists overemphasize economic determinism, neglecting the significance of political power, and overemphasize the virtue of the future system rather than articulating an ethics for existing social relations.

Instead of each ideology seeing itself as a lopsided picture — needing the balance of the other — it customarily proclaims the other ideology to be simply wrong and sinister. The United States and the Soviet Union stayed in more or less hostile confrontation for decades, for reasons purportedly having to do with their ideological differences. That state of enmity stiffened each ideology in a way that helped to perpetuate social evils — namely, by preventing the citizens' normal moral sensibilities from running their course. Thus, both the nature of ideologies and their entanglement with the force of nationalism have helped to constrain moral reasoning and inhibit moral action.

In the wake of the demise of the cold war and the "fall of the wall" in late 1989, we should expect to see a great flourishing of ideas that are eclectic and integrative of these two ideologies.

Other Explanations

The search in this chapter for the causes of moral inertia was conducted against a background assumption that moral action is normal and moral inertia is peculiar. The explanations for moral inertia listed in this chapter concerned rather neutral or accidental items — cognitive, linguistic, and ideological factors. I ignored the category of human "badness" as an explanation for the lack of moral action. The reader will realize, however, that it is more customary to cite human badness as the main explanation for moral inertia. "Why don't people fight evil?" "Because they are selfish, lazy, greedy, cowardly, and so forth."

Certainly I would not be able to refute the argument that human badness is an important contributor to moral inertia. "Negative" human traits must account in large part for the persistence of the four evils named above. For example, the basic selfishness of humans could account for the fact that extreme economic injustice is allowed to continue and could also account for environmental pollution. The basic fearfulness of humans could explain why weaponry tends to develop out of control and why vehement protest against torture is lacking.

I acknowledge, also, that I have deliberately omitted here, as an explanation for moral inertia, the bigness and the anonymity of modern society. Social life today is perhaps structured in such a way as to cut the individual out of much decision-making. Indeed, decisions often seem to be made by "internal logics" of organizations rather than by human beings at all. Nevertheless, persons genuinely interested in the phenomenon of moral inertia should not be content solely with these all-encompassing explanations. There *are* other factors, and it would be my guess that some of the ones named above — the cognitive, linguistic, and ideological factors — have a great effect on the limiting of moral action.

Now let us turn, in the following chapter, to a specific evil — *cruelty* — and attempt to account for its apparent acceptance by society.

CHAPTER 8

Is Cruelty Okay?

❋ ❋ ❋

Robert Hughes, in *The Fatal Shore*, tells us that the Reverend Thomas Rogers, a chaplain in 1875 at Australia's most terrifying convict-hold, Norfolk Island, noted that the quantity of lashings doled out there on some mornings ensured that "the ground on which the men stood at the triangles was saturated with human gore as if a bucket of blood had been spilled on it" (1988, p. 535). One of the jailers later recalled that the clothing of a particularly energetic flogger "usually presented an appearance of a mincemeat chopper, being covered in flesh from the victim's body" (p. 115). Such descriptions of corporal punishment of prisoners do not necessarily tell us that *cruelty* was taking place. The use of the lash was prescribed by British law, and in at least some cases the convict deserved or even "asked for" what he got. But is there any person who could deserve such punishments as those described by Hughes as having taken place under the direction of the infamous John Price at Norfolk Island?

> Some men, after flogging, would be laced into a straight-jacket and tied down to an iron bedstead for a week or two, so that their backs mortified and stank . . . (p. 547).

> For striking [the overseer], a convict named Lemon was bludgeoned unconscious by the constables, tube gagged, and chained up with his arms, one broken, behind him around a lamp post. . . . Men were sentenced to work "on the reef," cutting coral in water up to their waists, in 36-pound leg irons; they were condemned to fourteen days' solitary for "having some ravelling from an old pair of trousers [to protect their ulcerated ankles]" (pp. 547–548).

Review of Robert Hughes, *The Fatal Shore* (New York: Pan, 1988); M. Scott Peck, *People of the Lie* (New York: Simon and Schuster, 1983); and Edward Peters, *Torture* (Oxford: Blackwell, 1985).

Surely this is cruelty for cruelty's sake, pain inflicted for some motive other than merely to punish or deter crime.

In this chapter I attempt to sort out some of the causes of cruelty and to inquire about the moral status of cruel behavior. What is cruelty anyway? *The American Heritage Dictionary* records that the word is derived from the Latin *crudelis*, meaning "morally unfeeling." That dictionary performs a useful service of sorting out cruelty's different features by providing the following discussion of synonyms at cruel: "inhuman," "sadistic," "vicious," "pitiless," and "ruthless."

> These adjectives mean predisposed to inflict violence, pain, or hardship; or to find satisfaction in the suffering of others. *Cruel* implies both disposition to harm and satisfaction in or indifference to suffering. . . . *Inhuman* means markedly deficient in such qualities as tolerance and sympathy. . . . *Sadistic* implies the experiencing of satisfaction, specially sexual gratification, from cruelty inflicted on others. *Vicious* suggests native disposition to malicious and destructive behavior. . . . *Pitiless* refers specifically to absence of mercy. *Ruthless* also stresses lack of compassion and often implies relentless pursuit of personal ends regardless of hardships to others (1976, p. 318).

Is it human nature, then, that brings about such cruel acts as described above? The foregoing dictionary list seems to imply that indeed cruelty is a phenomenon explicable in terms of the nature of the perpetrator of cruelty. If that is so, then perhaps there is not much that can be done about cruelty. It is just a fact of life: some people *are* that way, and some others, by bad luck, will fall into their hands.

There is another way to look at cruelty, however, that seems to carry with it greater implications for society's role in the commission of cruelty, and hence society's power to curtail it. That way of looking at cruelty is with the use of historical analysis. In this chapter I shall review three unusual books — unusual in that they try to show how certain famously cruel activities came about historically. Robert Hughes, in *The Fatal Shore*, covers the history of the convicts who settled the early colony of Australia — that "hell-hole of chain gangs ruled by the cat-o'-nine tails" (from a review by *Listener*). M. Scott Peck, in *People of the Lie*, examines how "ordinary American boys" ended up massacring over five hundred helpless villagers at MyLai in Vietnam. Edward Peters shows, in *Torture,* how weapons of torture used by governments today have a respectable history in European judicial systems. I believe that these studies can be used in an attempt to separate out the "inevitable" causes of social evils (especially human nature) from other causes that are more susceptible to change.

The title of Hughes's book, *The Fatal Shore,* refers, of course, to the shore of the Australian colony of New South Wales to which prisoners were transported from the British Isles as an alternative to execution for crimes. Their crimes were mostly crimes against property — only 3 percent of the prisoners had committed assault against persons. This fact and the general plight of the poor in England at the time are themes of Hughes's book but must be omitted here. My interest begins with the arrival of the convicts on the fatal shore in 1788. There the circumstances for both the convicts and their guards (the New South Wales Corps) were dire. For the first five years everyone lived on the brink of starvation. Australia had only one supply ship, which could be sent to China or South Africa for vital stores, but it sank in 1790. After that, Governor Arthur Phillips had to cut rations even further and eliminated any difference in allotment between convicts and guards — to the great resentment of the latter.

The New South Wales Corps — later called the Rum Corps — was a unit of the British marines but did not contain regular enlistees, as those would certainly not have wanted to take the dreadful journey. In Hughes's words, "Most of them were scum, and they found service in New South Wales the best alternative to beggary or crime" (p. 105). Moreover, he notes, few of the officers were better than the soldiers (p. 105). Nevertheless, the Corps was able to get ahead not only of the prisoners but of the free settlers. Hughes notes that the impact of the Corps "was to be all out of proportion to its quality. . . . Between 1791 and 1808 the Corps was defacto . . . the most powerful single internal influency on the colony" (p. 106). When Governor Phillips decided to return to England in 1792, the colony was taken over by Corps officers Francis Grose and William Paterson, who "set the pattern of private management and slave labor that created the wealth of Australia's first elite" (p. 109). Hughes writes:

Grose did not forget his own rank and file. He cancelled Phillip's policy of equal rations for all and gave the troops more food than the convicts. He also let it be known that any member of the New South Wales Corps could have twenty-five acres of free land [and he gave] 100 acres land grants to corps officers — along with ten convicts, free of charge and maintained at government expense, to work each one. . . . Under Grose, officers had the economic edge on civilians; they could raise capital by borrowing against their regimental pay, and as a junta they seized a monopoly on most consumer goods arriving in Sydney Harbor (pp. 109–110).

A crucial event in the Corps's rise to power was the arrival in 1793 of a U.S. trading vessel, the *Hope*. It carried 7,500 gallons of rum and such badly needed stores as flour and cloth. The captain refused to sell the latter until all the rum was bought. The New South Wales Corps formed a ring to buy all of the *Hope*'s cargo and sold it to the colonists and the government at hugely inflated prices. The Rum Corps (having thus gained that name for itself) was soon able to predominate. By 1799 its members controlled much of the acreage of land, as well as 59 percent of the colony's horses and 75 percent of the sheep (pp. 110–111).

With the aid of Hughes's study, *The Fatal Shore*, it becomes possible for us to isolate some of the specific factors that contributed to the cruelty shown by guards to prisoners. The first was simply money. Keeping the prisoners in abject condition made them a better supply of workers. If there was abuse of prisoners, few members of the Rum Corps would be inclined to protest it since the "system" was now in their personal financial favor. Money enters the story at other places, also. For instance, there was a reward system for informing within the prison, and a nice compensation paid to settlers who caught escaping convicts. One thinks here of Alexandr Solzhenitsyn's remark in *The Gulag Archipelago* that no Soviet political prisoner in Siberia could count on the mercy of neighboring families if he escaped. The police paid a ransom of a herring for catching escapees — a luxury those people would otherwise never obtain. So great was the association of herring with Gulag escapees that the locals simply called them herrings. "Mama! There's a herring coming" (1975, p. 318).

Money and power are inextricably linked in the unique Australian situation of the Rum Corps. However, I believe power — or, more precisely, status reinforcement — can be isolated as a distinct motivating force in the issue of cruelty. The Rum Corps was surely anxious to establish its superiority to the convicts. Recall that Hughes tells us that in the early years there were few signs of status available — even the uniforms were threadbare — but "if clothes and rations could not symbolize rank, then actions would, and one may be sure that every kick and blow the marines rained on the exhausted 'crawlers' was meant as a reinforcement of superiority, not just an incitement to work" (p. 103). The convict artist, Thomas Watling, transported for forgery, wrote that "instances of oppression, and mean-souled despotism, are so glaring and frequent, as to banish every hope of generosity and urbanity from such as I am: — for unless we can flatter and cajole the vices and follies of our superiors, with the most abominable servility, nothing is to be expected" (quoted in Hughes, p. 104). In short, the ill treatment of prisoners gave a rise in status to the "scum" of the British marines.

Another power struggle should be mentioned here, since it was equally ominous for the convicts. I refer to the competition between the Rum Corps and the rest of colonial officialdom. As the Corps rose in power, it felt the need to render impotent any political force that could challenge it, such as that of civil magistrates. Hughes notes, "Grasping, haughty, jealous of their privileges and prerogatives, MacArthur and his friends in the Corps were on top and meant to stay there; and the official governors . . . had the utmost difficulty controlling them" (p. 111).

A third power factor that can be identified separately, among the causes of cruelty in Australia, was that of the *rivalry* between the Corps and the prisoners. Each became a tribe, as it were, seeing the other as the enemy and thus lowering its sense of respect for members of the other tribe as humans. Not all prisoners were broken. Some showed their contempt openly, none more so perhaps than the convict who had his friends tattoo on his back a message to the lasher: "Flog well and do your duty." That the men could act as a team was shown in their reaction to internal traitors. "Anyone who betrayed a fellow prisoner to Authority was denounced as . . . a dog and his punishment was swift: The men would kill him, or at least mutilate him by biting his nose and ears off, an operation known as 'taking the dog's muzzle' " (p. 539).

Thus, my claim so far is that rather ordinary human behaviors — the seeking after money, the need for status, the banding into rival groups — can enable cruelty to occur. Undoubtedly, though, there is pure unadulterated sadism, too. In a random sample of any human population there will be individuals who delight in inflicting pain. Prison guards, military officers, hangmen, and lashers are not a random sample. They are to some extent self-selected for the job and also selected by others who are glad to leave the dirty work to them. Two sadists of renown in the Australian colony were Major Joseph Foveaux and John Price. Beginning in 1800 and 1846, respectively, they ran the last outpost of the penal system, Norfolk Island, which was deliberately intended as a hellhole to terrorize other convicts on the mainland. Those sent to Norfolk Island had no hope of eventual emancipation.

Hughes explains that under Foveaux, the men had to break stones for new buildings. "When the picks and hammers broke, for they were of poor quality, their users were severely flogged" (p. 114). There was a black isolation cell, where a man would be made to stand waist-deep in water, unable to sleep for fear of drowning, for forty-eight hours at a spell (p. 115). As recorded by the head jailer, a certain prisoner named Joseph Mansbury had received two thousand lashes in three years. As a result, his back was "quite bare of flesh and his collar bones were exposed looking very much like two Ivory Polished horns. It was with some difficulty that we could find another place to flog him. Tony [the overseer] suggested doing it on the soles of his feet next time" (p. 115). As Hughes puts it, "Under Foveaux the military contempt for convicts would approach the level of mania" (p. 113).

John Price, one of fourteen children of a minor aristocrat, was said by his biographer to have had a psychopathological love-hate relationship with the prisoners. He was obsessed with the men and spoke their slang fluently (an indication that he himself may once have "done time"). According to Hughes, "He ruled by terror, informers, and the lash, to which he added the public force of his own indomitable character; he was known to walk into the lumber yard unescorted and, before five hundred hostile men, face down a convict who showed signs of rebellion. He once stared down a convict who snatched the pistol from his belt, taunting the man as a coward and a dog, until the prisoner handed back the weapon and fell beaten to his knees" (p. 545).

Price's second-in-command was Alfred Baldock. He was ruthless with the men but totally servile to the commandant. Indeed Price saw to it that all free persons on the island were in league with him. The sole medical officer, says Hughes, was "so much in cahoots with Price that he claimed a desperately sick prisoner had to be kept in an airless cell because ventilation would be 'prejudicial' to him" (p. 549). In general, Price purged Norfolk Island of civil officers. "Everyone who showed signs of opposing his autocratic rule was suspended or recalled to Hobart, until no one stood between Price and the prisoners" (p. 547).

This brings me to the last in my list of explanations of cruelty in early Australia, namely, the *isolation* of the prisoners from *protection by society*. The whole colony was thousands of miles from "civilization" (and Norfolk Island itself a thousand miles from Sydney). Prisoners did not have their families to plead their cause for them, and until at least 1810 "England had not equipped its colony with a normal judicial framework" (p. 118). The excesses of men like Foveaux were hidden from view. During Price's regime in Norfolk Island, a chaplain there, Thomas Rogers, made proper complaints, but these were ignored at first. In the end it was Robert Willson, the first Catholic bishop of Tasmania, who, in response to rumors, visited the island, and did get Price removed.

The fact that on-site inspection does make a difference in the treatment of prisoners can be seen in the statistics of deaths on the transport ships themselves. Hughes tabulates that of the first six convict ships from 1792 to 1794, all had supervisory agents, and the death rate was one man in fifty-five. By 1795, however, the Napoleonic wars deflected naval surgeons to other areas, so that only two of the next six convict ships carried naval agents or surgeons: the death rate on these ships was one man in nineteen. The last group of six had no naval supervision of any kind, and one man in six died.

It is worth noting here how essential privacy is to the practice of most cruelty. Physical abuse often thrives in prisons, in military barracks, and in the privacy of home. Violence seems to be infectious, and once it is begun there is little to stop it — the perpetrators are unlikely to hold back, and the victims, almost by definition, are powerless to stop it. The main thing that does control such outbreaks is discipline imposed by the larger society. Thus, publicity of the cruelty is important. (One wonders how long Nazi concentration camps would have lasted if their conditions had been broadcast on television.) Publicity alone is not enough, however. Action by third parties is required.

Let us turn now to another analysis of cruelty, M. Scott Peck's book, *People of the Lie*. Peck is a psychiatrist who identifies a certain type of person as "evil." That type practices cruelty, usually of a psychological rather than a physical type and usually on his or her own children or spouse. Peck very rarely encounters these evil people as patients: as we shall see below, it is an essential part of their syndrome that they not admit to any mental illness or even to the slightest imperfection. Rather, he sees their victims, their children, in his office, suffering from the destructive effects of the evil person. (I should say here that I disagree with Peck's choice of the word *evil*, as it tends to debase the currency of language: we should save the term *evil* to mean something stronger. Perhaps *wicked* or *malevolent* would suffice to describe these people. However, it is useful that he has categorized them at all.)

Psychiatrists have had a diagnosis for some time of a personality disorder in which the major feature is *the inability of the person to accept responsibility for his or her own actions.* Among standard symptoms in this disorder are extreme intolerance of criticism and, perhaps relatedly, a pronounced concern with keeping up an image of respectability. Peck explains that such persons engage in any amount of intellectual deviousness when confronted with evidence of their bad side (p. 129) — hence the name of the book, *People of the Lie*. Peck notes that a foremost strategy of the sick evil person is *scapegoating* or displacing his sins onto others. This word refers to an event in the Bible: "And Aaron shall lay both his hands upon the head of the live goat, and confess over him all the inequities of the children of Israel, and all their . . . sins, putting them upon the head of the goat, and shall send it . . . into the wilderness" (Lev. 16:10). In psychiatry the technique of scapegoating is also known as projection — one projects one's imperfections onto others.

Some persons, early in their life, cannot come to terms with their faults — psychoanalysts would say they cannot get past their narcissistic stage. This word recalls the mythological character Narcissus, who was in love with his own image, reflected in a pool. It is a normal part of development for a person to begin to admit his imperfections, but certain people — for unknown reasons — fail to make this adjustment. One result, Peck says, is that "they project their own evil onto the world. They never think of themselves as evil — on the other hand, they consequently see much evil in others" (p. 74). If such persons become parents, they are likely to be very cruel to their children, in subtle ways, as a way of punishing evil. "Strangely enough, evil people are often destructive because they are attempting to destroy evil. The problem is that they misplace the locus of the evil. Instead of destroying others, they should be destroying the sickness within themselves" (p. 74). Peck explains how their problems give rise to cruelty:

> We all of us tend to be more or less . . . self-centered in our dealings with others. . . . Nonetheless, particularly if we care for the other person, we usually can and eventually do think about his or her viewpoint. . . . Not so those who are evil. Theirs is a brand of Narcissism so total that they seem to lack, in whole or in part, this capacity for empathy. . . . Their narcissism makes [them] dangerous not only because it motivates them to scapegoat others but also because it *deprives them of the restraint that results from empathy and respect for others* (emphasis added) (p. 136).

Although much of Peck's book focuses on cruelty by parents, that is not my main interest here. Child abuse is perhaps statistically the greatest type of cruelty in existence, and a reasonable amount of analysis has been devoted to it. Major causes of assaults on babies and children are alcohol and drugs as well as the so-called culture of violence in which a parent who was himself beaten as a child thinks it is natural to do likewise. Peck's work adds an important psychological dimension to this. However, I wish to concentrate in this review on his penultimate chapter, entitled "MyLai: An Examination of Group Evil." In 1972 Peck was chairman of a committee appointed by the U.S. Army Surgeon General to make recommendations for research that might shed light on the psychological causes of the events in MyLai, South Vietnam. The question before him was, How could ordinary Americans commit such atrocities and what could be done to prevent this in the future?

The MyLai incident occurred on March 16, 1968. Members of C Company — known as Charlie Company — of Task Force Barker of the U.S. Army were sent to conduct a search-and-destroy mission at a group of hamlets known as MyLai in South Vietnam. For a month these troops had not captured any enemy, yet they had suffered some casualties themselves from mines and booby traps. They looked forward to the chance to succeed at last, but when they entered MyLai they did not find any combatants or any armed person. They found only women, children, and old men.

Charlie Company proceeded to kill between five and six hundred of those villagers with guns and grenades. Some soldiers stood at the door of huts and sprayed machine-gun fire inside. Others, under the command of Lt. William L. Calley, herded villagers into groups of twenty to forty and shot them. They also shot children who were running away. About fifty Americans pulled triggers, and about two hundred directly witnessed the killings. Six of these later were brought to trial and one was convicted (pp. 212–214). Peck writes: "The killing took a long time. It went on throughout the morning. Only one person to try to stop it. He was a helicopter pilot. . . . Even from the air he could see what was happening. He landed on the ground and attempted to talk to the troops, to no avail. Back in the air again, he radioed to headquarters and superior officers, who seemed unconcerned" (p. 214). Presumably the incident would never have received public attention, except that an ex-soldier — who heard about it from friends — wrote to several congressmen a year later.

Who is to blame for this act of ultimate cruelty? Is anyone to blame? Is the helicopter pilot the only one who is innocent? Or is he perhaps the most to blame since he thought the massacre was wrong yet did not appeal to higher authorities to stop it? Should soldiers refuse to follow orders in the battlefield? Were there many other unreported MyLais? Isn't this just an ordinary instance of the lowered human sensitivity during war? What's all the fuss about? Peck's analysis goes "up the ladder of collective responsibility" — from the individual soldier, to Charlie Company, to the military in general, to American society, in order to find who is to blame. I shall outline his main insights here.

The individual soldiers were under constant stress. They were in a hot climate, molested by insects, unable to sleep well, and on a diet of unpalatable food. Besides being away from all the normalcy of home, they were in continuous danger of stepping on mines or being shot at. As well, morale was low because the United States was not winning the war. Peck notes that in situations of prolonged discomfort, people naturally regress. Psychological growth reverses itself while childish traits come to the fore. Thus, stress would have affected the soldier's maturity. They may also have undergone "psychic numbing" — a phenomenon described by Robert Jay Lifton in his study of the survivors of Hiroshima. Peck describes this defense mechanism as follows: "In a situation in which emotional feelings are overwhelmingly painful or unpleasant, we have the capacity to anesthetize ourselves. . . . The sight of a single, bloody, mangled body horrifies us. But if we see such bodies all around us . . . day after day, the horrible becomes the normal and we lose our sense of horror. . . . [Furthermore], when it no longer bothers us to see mangled bodies, it will no longer bother us to mangle them ourselves" (p. 221).

The soldiers' behavior can also be explained by two well-known phenomena of group dynamics. The first is simply that of *dependency on the leader*. Peck says that "most people would rather be followers . . . it is probably a matter of laziness. . . . It is simply easier to be a follower than a leader. There is no need to agonize over complex decisions, plan ahead, exercise initiative, risk unpopularity, or exert much courage" (p. 223). The person who hands over to the leader his power becomes a bit like a child in relation to a parent — dependent.

The second phenomenon concerns the fact that groups have a characteristic narcissism. "There are profound forces at work within a group to keep its individual members together. . . . Probably the most powerful of these is narcissism. In its simplest and most benign form, this is manifested in group pride . . . the group feels proud of itself" (p. 225). As Peck points out, the military goes out of its way to foster group pride, by issuing unit standard flags, shoulder patches, and other insignia and by broadcasting the body counts of different units. A less benign "but practically universal form of group narcissism is that one that might be called enemy creation, or hatred of the out-group. . . . Those who do not belong to the group are despised as being inferior or evil or both" (p. 225). In short, the individual soldier's ability to do the right thing was impaired by various pressures on him and by the very nature of groups.

Peck then looks at Charlie Company as a whole and notes that it was certainly the members of that company who pulled the triggers. But they had been assigned, more or less, to do this. Task Force Barker had been put together as a specialized group solely for the purpose of conducting search-and-destroy missions. It is worth mentioning that these particular men were not there against their will: until late 1968 the American forces in Vietnam were volunteers. Peck notes that "for many career personnel a tour of duty in Vietnam was highly desirable and sought after. It meant medals, excitement, extra money, and an invariable promotion" (p. 228). At the very least, each volunteer for Vietnam got an immediate furlough and a bonus.

A consideration of the background of Charlie Company's personnel reveals clearly that they were not a cross section of American youth. For one thing, boys strongly opposed to particopating in the war could find many ways out of combat duty — from escaping to Canada to enlisting in the Navy. For another thing, in 1968 they were mostly career Army men. As such, they were self-selected: persons with certain traits are probably more likely than others to join the military. Peck claims, too, that they were selected by society: in some instances, he says, they were dumped into the Army by their communities because they were misfits. Even within the Army, selection was further made to choose boys for Task Force Barker according to their willingness (or even eagerness) to kill. Once selected, these boys were specially trained and equipped for search-and-destroy work. Thus, the author asks, "Is it realistic to encourage and manipulate human beings into specialized groups and simultaneously expect them . . . to maintain a breadth of vision much beyond their specialty?" (p. 230).

Peck's bugaboo is specialization itself. "I am thoroughly convinced that much of the evil of our times is related to specialization and that we desperately need to develop an attitude of suspicious caution toward it" (p. 217). Specialization brings fragmentation of conscience. Thus, for instance, the men who drop napalm say, "We don't make the weapons, we just use them." The manufacturers of napalm say, "We don't make the policy as to which type of weapons to be used," and so forth. "It is not only possible," Peck says, "but easy and even natural for a large group to commit evil without emotional involvement simply by turning loose its specialists. It happened in Vietnam. It happened in Nazi Germany. I am afraid it will happen again" (pp. 231–232).

Next up the ladder of responsibility, Peck looks at the military itself and observes that it is a group that is by definition in favor of action in battle. As humans we all want to feel useful, and once people find themselves in the military, they will naturally come to feel especially useful in time of war. Peck says "we must fully expect, without rancor or recrimination, the military man to always vote and stand on the side of war" (p. 234). Another thing to consider is that the U.S. Army in the 1960s was particularly high on technology. The interest in finding ways to win wars by smart machinery, Peck points out, helped to take some of the ugliness out of war. "We went technologically 'hog-wild' in Vietnam, employing our bulldozers and weapons systems and precision bombing and chemical defoliants with a Strangelovian fervor" (p. 235). All of this fervor in some way clouded the moral issue of killing people, at the time of MyLai.

The ease with which Peck seems to explain away the blame of various parties for the massacre may cause the reader to think that he will be most forgiving of the largest responsible group, namely, American society. Not so. The buck stops here. Although it was the members of Charlie Company who pulled the triggers, and although the military put them in the mood for killing, it was American society that decided to undertake that war in the first place. It did so primarily in the belief that communism was a monolithic evil force hostile to human freedom in general and to American freedom in particular (p. 238). But this, Peck says, shows intellectual laziness. By 1968

> there was a wealth of evidence to indicate that communism was not (if, in fact, it had ever been) a force that was either monolithic or necessarily evil. Yugoslavia was clearly independent of the USSR . . . China and the USSR were no longer

allies but potential enemies. As for Vietnam, any slightly discerning examination of its history revealed it to be a traditional enemy of China. The impelling force [there] was not the expansion of communism but nationalism and resistance to colonial domination. Moreover, it had also become clear that . . . people in communist societies were [in many ways] faring better than they had under their pre-communist forms of government [and that the people in many of our allied countries] were suffering violations of human rights that matched those of the USSR and China (p. 239).

Along with such intellectual laziness was simply our narcissism: we kept assuming we were better than everyone else without trying to reflect critically on ourselves. Peck believes that "the task of preventing group evil — including war itself — is clearly the task of eradicating or, at least, significantly diminishing laziness and narcissism" (p. 252).

Lastly, Peck implies that we cannot, as a society, say that the massacre of innocent people carried out at MyLai was due to the low moral character of those individuals, whereas that of the rest of us was higher. We chose those boys to do our dirty work for us. We seduced them into Vietnam with bonuses, and then trained them to be mindless in combat. "We Americans as a society deliberately chose and employed them to do our killing for us. In this sense [all the members of Charlie Company] were our scapegoats" (p. 231).

The laying of blame on a large entity such as "American society" does not mean that individuals are exempted from responsibility. Individuals, Peck says, must resist the temptation to do certain things; for instance, they should resist the temptation to create specialized groups that may get out of hand. He recommends that we "come to know that the natural tendency of the individual in a group is to forfeit his or her ethical judgment to the leader, and that this tendency should be resisted" (p. 253).

In concluding this review of Peck's book, I should acknowledge that he has omitted the more general reason for the killings at MyLai, which was that the soldiers almost certainly thought of their victims as the enemy — they were, after all, "gooks." He also has not dwelt on the corporate military rage routinely manifest in the battlefield — a soldier wants to kill anything that moves. Almost certainly there were many MyLais, though we happen to know about this one because it was reported. (Peck mentions that his committee recommended that further inquiries be made about such events but was turned down: the government did not want further embarrassment.) In any case, as with Hughes's book on Australia, Peck's book performs the service of demonstrating that inhumanity cannot be solely chalked up to "human nature." At least it cannot be chalked up to the inevitable cruelty of people. Cruelty, we see, results from a combination of circumstances and involves a congeries of human traits.

Finally, let us look at Edward Peters's book, *Torture*, which is a history of the legal use of torture. Surely the use of torture is the last word in human cruelty. What could be the explanation for this brutal behavior? *Brutal* is defined by *The American Heritage Dictionary* as "characteristic of a brute; cruel," and *brute* is defined as "any animal other than man; a beast." It is perhaps widely considered — when it is considered at all — that torture as practiced by humans is a throwback to our bestial past, that the urge to hurt is some sort of primitive instinct. Peters shows clearly that this idea is incorrect, and in doing so he shows how important is historical knowledge of a subject.

Peters's study of torture is specifically limited to "torment inflicted by a public authority for ostensibly public purposes" (p. 3). Torture is first mentioned in ancient Greece. The word Aristotle uses for it is *basanos*, which Peters says "is philologically related to the idea of putting something metallic to a touchstone in order to verify its content" (p. 14). Slaves, but not free citizens, could officially be tortured in regard to legal disputes to see if their testimony (as witnesses) was truthful. Since a more powerful echelon of society was thus committing the cruelty on a less powerful echelon, a cynic might conclude that it was just another instance of status reinforcement — like the Rum Corps's lashing of the Australian convicts. However, I believe Peters's alternative explanation is persuasive. The torture of slaves came about because of a particular act of *rationality* or abstraction, having to do with law.

The Greeks invented the idea of an abstract law. It emerged from earlier unarticulated custom. Prior to the sixth century B.C., the law had consisted of the conflict between two litigants exercising self-help in a contest, known as an *agon*. Voluntary arbitrators made decisions in favor of one or the other party.

Their statements were called *dikai* — these "accumulated over time into a recognized body of opinion, until the popular perception of their abstract moral quality made the term *dike* come to mean justice itself" (p. 12). Gradually, the *agon* shifted to a trial, and evidence became important. A primary type of evidence was the testimony of a citizen. His personal honor was considered an important indication of the truth of his evidence. Hence, no slave could give equivalent evidence merely by speaking. Slaves "had to be coerced into a special status in which their testimony became acceptable. Their testimony became equal to that of citizens by means of physical coercion" (p. 13).

Under the Romans, who incorporated many of the principles of Greek law, the number of people on whom torture could be practiced widened, and the types of cases in which it could be used increased. Slaves could now be tortured in cases of pecuniary crimes as well as capital crimes. Treason, too, became a common reason for torture. Peters quotes the Roman Arcadius Charisius: "When the charge is treason, which concerns the lives of Emperors, all without exception are to be tortured, if they are called to give evidence, and when the case requires it" (in Ulpian's *Digest* 48.18.10.1, quoted in Peters, p. 28). By A.D. 75 Christians had lost their status as Jews, that is, as members of a protected religion, and fell into the category of followers of an illegal religion. "Torture and aggravated death sentences under Nero, beginning in A.D. 64 constituted a precedent for regarding Christians as both impious and subversive and therefore subject to investigation by torture" (p. 25). In the fourth century Constantine made soothsayers, magicians, sorcerers, and diviners liable to interrogatory torture, and by the fifth and sixth centuries simply a designation of "low condition" or *infamia* (bad reputation) exposed more and more freemen to torture (pp. 31–33).

Already we see that what started out as a very limited idea — verifying the testimony of slaves during litigation — seems to have caught on. Peters notes that "the appearance of a class of bureaucratic magistrates, no longer the learned jurists of the second and third centuries, probably made the application of torture more routine and less considered" (p. 33). The methods of torture themselves became more developed also. The standard means was the rack, meant to pull a person's joints and muscles, as well as torture with red-hot metal and the *ungulae*, hooks that lacerated the flesh (p. 35). Peters emphasizes the paradox that there is a vast legal literature, even from early times, in which the usefulness of torture is questioned. The truth did *not* necessarily come out, as the torture victim was just as likely to lie to save himself from further torture. Yet instead of questioning the method, the Romans "surrounded it with a jurisprudence that was designed to give greater assurance to its reliability, a jurisprudence that is admirable in its scepticism and unsettling in its logic" (p. 35).

The next period we should look at is the twelfth century, when legal procedures were introduced that lasted until the eighteenth century. A major change involved the use of the *inquisitorial* rather than *accusatorial* method. That is, public officers were in charge of discovering crime, rather than waiting for the injured party to report it. In this period, law and administration became much more homogenized as popes and kings centralized their authority, and the influence of literacy, Peters notes, was enormous. Romano-canonical legal procedure reflected a new specialized profession. In the new system it was required that "proofs be sought, produced, and examined, that witnesses be classified and interrogated under oath, and that the accused have some rational means of defense against the charges" (p. 44).

The important point for our narrative is that, in the change to the inquisitorial method, confession became all important. Confession was named "the queen of proofs," and it was, in the absence of two eyewitnesses, the *only* means by which a guilty verdict could be found in serious cases. In short, the courts needed confessions "and to obtain confession, torture was once again invoked, but on very different grounds from those of ancient Roman law" (p. 47). R. C. Van Caenegem states, "In the last analysis it was the need of criminal practice and new principles for the pursuit of criminals that were responsible for the reappearance of torture in Europe" (quoted in Peters, p. 50).

This counteracts the popular belief that medieval torture was an invention of the Church. However, it has to be said that the Church quickly adopted, and adapted, secular methods, especially in the case of "intellectual crime" — dissent. "The steps taken against heretics by central ecclesiastical authorities after the middle of the twelfth century were based largely on the increasingly sophisticated scholarship dealing with universal canon [church] law" (p. 52) — which was itself drawing closer and closer to Roman law. Pope Innocent III in 1199 announced in a decree that heretics were traitors to God, exactly comparable to traitors to Caesar in Roman law — which of course, says Peters, opened up another avenue for legal torture of heretics (p. 53). Innocent IV added that heretics were thieves and murderers of souls: "They should confess to their own errors and accuse other heretics whom they know . . . just as rogues and thieves of wordly goods are made to accuse their accomplices" (p. 65).

With God now involved as the backer of torture, it was easy for inquisitors to slip away even from the standard regulations. Peters notes the following corruptions: the personnel doing the torturing started to include clerics themselves (even though this was forbidden); they also withheld names and testimony of witnesses and restricted the aid of counsel for the defendant. Worse, they admitted the testimony of legally incompetent witnesses, such as interested parties and those convicted of perjury, and they deliberately deceived the accused by introducing spies into their cells. In short, the ecclesiastical inquisitors altered the rules of the game, and "in turn, the secular courts found themselves influenced by the ecclesiastical procedure in the fourteenth and fifteenth century" (p. 69).

Overall we have seen that torture was first used as a touchstone, to validate the testimony of slaves, and was later used to extract confessions, these being necessary for justice to be done — that is, for genuine criminals to be convicted. Concomitant with these developments were certain world views about the honorableness of free citizens, about the value of law itself, about God's majesty, and the evil of sin. Peters points out that in every age there is a human anthropology, a sense of what human beings are like, what they are for, what universe they occupy, and so forth. In the ancient and medieval periods, the respective anthropologies allowed torture to exist as a reasonable or logical procedure.

The human anthropology of the Enlightenment period, however, did not have a place for torture. Thus, the story of the Romano-canonical encouragement of torture ends in the late eighteenth century. With the Enlightenment and its reforms, and particularly with the French Revolution, such relics of the *ancien regime* as torture became despised and were publicly abolished. Peters writes, "Seventeenth and eighteenth century theories of natural law focussed often on torture as violating their most essential tenets, that of the natural dignity of humans" (p. 82). Nation after nation, including Russia, banned torture, so that by the nineteenth century it could be considered a thing of the past.

The final task of Peters's historical study, therefore, is to explain the tremendous revival of torture in the twentieth century. He does this first by admitting that torture is no longer a legal procedure; it is a manifestation of the power of the state over the individual. It serves not so much to verify testimony or to elicit confession as to intimidate, to terrorize, to degrade, to punish. The only connection we might see between torture today and the torture of old (besides the methods, but even these differ greatly) is in the one category under which, even in early Roman law, it was permissible to torture a free citizen — namely, treason. In those days treason was associated with the ruler's person and his household, but by the end of the eighteenth century there emerged "a concept of treason against the abstract state and people" (p. 104).

The right of the state, indeed the obligation of the state, to protect its citizens from internal enemies became extremely diffuse. By 1942 in Germany, Heinrich Himmler was able to say, apparently without courting total ridicule, "The third degree [i.e., torture] to elicit information may be used only against communists, Marxists, Jehovah's Witnesses, saboteurs, terrorists, members of resistance movements, antisocial elements, refractory elements, or Polish or Soviet vagabonds. In all other cases, preliminary authorization is necessary" (quoted in Peters, p. 125). This obviously reflected a new human anthropology, the extreme expression of which was given by Benito Mussolini, writing in the *New Italian Encyclopedia* of 1932: "Man is nothing. . . . Beyond the state, nothing that is human or spiritual has any value whatsoever" (quoted in Peters, p. 122).

So it is the change in the nature of the state, therefore, that best accounts for modern torture. Peters emphasizes that European states throughout the nineteenth century became far more powerful than ever before. "Their strength derived from their ability to mobilize vast resources and from a broader-based concept of governmental legitimacy" (p. 104). At first it had seemed, in the post-Enlightenment period, that increased state power would actually enhance the security of citizens —

that the state would be the watchdog of now publicly recognized human rights. "But by the early twentieth century a number of states were strong enough virtually to abolish conventional courts . . ." (p. 104). And in some places there emerged "a doctrine which proposed new classifications of political crime, the subordination of the law to the sense of rightness held by the people, and effected by transforming statute law and traditional procedure into administrative law and *ad hoc* procedure" (p. 109).

As to the actual avenues by which torture was reintroduced, Peters looks to the suggestions made in 1949 by Alec Mellor in his book *La Torture*, one of the earliest analytical works on the subject. Mellor believed that the concern for "military intelligence" aided the return of torture. Although the state's strength was growing, so too was its vulnerability, thanks to the destructiveness of modern weapons. Peters notes, "the kind of information that might now be provided by prisoners [of war] or captured spies could prove crucial and was needed quickly. The interrogation [was] carried out in the heat of battle, guided only by the least enforceable rules against an enemy . . ." (p. 115). Peters notes Mellor's suggestion that "Asianism" was responsible for new tortures. Mellor imagined that a peculiarly non-European treatment of people was imported into Europe by means of the Russo-Japanese war of 1905. This theory has been discredited, however, by the finding that such brutality exists in many parts of the world.

Peters also discusses Mellor's third explanation for torture: the emergence of totalitarianism. The police state was given its greatest thrust by — of all things — philosophy. The doctrine of communism was full of loathing for the existing "kingdom of evil" and passionately concerned with the arrival of its replacement. The Russian Revolution of 1917 proclaimed the right of a revolutionary government to take measures to protect itself and the revolution in general, similar to the measures once taken to protect a nation, state, or *volk* (p. 127). Thus it is not surprising that revolutionary states became the first states to use torture in a more visible and routine way (p. 121). It was said by the Cheka (the Soviet secret police, the predecessor of the KGB) that "we stand for organized terror — this should be frankly stated — terror being absolutely indispensable in current revolutionary conditions" (p. 128). Suspects were arrested late at night, were verbally and physically abused, rushed to a prison, and even led to a place of threatened execution several times. Different Chekas developed innovative tortures. One went in for scalping; another thrust its victims naked into an internally nail-studded barrel. Rats were encouraged to eat the prisoner's flesh (pp. 128–129).

As the decades have gone by, torture has become used by more and more nations of both the Right and the Left (Amnesty International estimates one in three). The technology of torture has become more intricate and, starting with experiments by the Nazis, has become a medical specialty. Peters comments at some length on the way in which pain can be intensified both physiologically and pharmacologically by those with know-how. A modern torture victim is often subjected to combinations of physical and psychological torment designed to upset the natural means by which the human body copes with pain and anxiety. It is as though the ability to perform these tortures is a new incentive to carry them out. As Peters observes, this reflects a new human anthropology — one enamored of technique.

Two more of Peters's observations should be mentioned here. The first concerns the weakness of the public reaction to revelations of torture. In the mid-1950s it became known that the French army was using torture in Algeria, thus making people realize for the first time that even a democratic country could engage in such practices. French citizens were forced to ask how their own country, so tied to the doctrine of human dignity and civil protection, could engage in torture. Jean-Paul Sartre wrote: "In 1943, in the Rue Lauriston [the Gestapo headquarters in Paris], Frenchmen were screaming in agony and pain; all France could hear them. In those days the outcome of the war was uncertain. . . . Only one thing seemed impossible in any circumstances: that one day men should be made to scream by those acting in our name" (quoted in Peters, p. 133).

The question does seem to be, Who hears them? In regard to the soldiers in Algeria, Peters says "rough handling of those in their power was hard to stop, particularly when the judiciary was unaware it was happening and the public and legislators hard to convince" (p. 138). In 1963 Pierre Vidal-Nagut published *Torture: Cancer of Democracy*, in which he said, "The cancer was not the torture itself, but the public indifference to it that eroded and rendered meaningless even the most explicit protections afforded by civil rights and public law" (quoted in Peters, p. 140).

The second observation of Peters is that the future of torture depends on the availability of torturers. The question of who the torturers are has been investigated in our generation in the case of Greece during the 1970s. After the rule of the colonels ended, the torturers were brought to trial amid considerable publicity. Peters says that the conclusion of observers was that "although many sadists are indeed drawn into the role of torturer when such a role is available, it is also arguable that the institution of torture creates as many sadists as it attracts" (p. 179). As the father of a young Greek torturer, Alexander Lavranos, said, "We are a poor but decent family . . . and now I see him in the dock as a torturer. I want to ask the court to examine how a boy whom everyone said was a diamond become a torturer. Who morally destroyed my home and my family?" (p. 179). Even many of the sexual perversions of the torturers struck the observers as the consequence, not the cause, of the practice of torture (p. 180).

The record of the Greek trials shows that the government recruited potential torturers from conscript soldiers whose families were sympathetic to the regime. They received intensive political indoctrination that emphasized danger to the country caused by "terrorists," "communists," and "imperialists." Moreover, they were invited to join an elite corps that gave special privileges such as higher rank, access to cars, and favors for their families. They then were subjected to beatings and humiliation themselves to make them obey unquestioningly and were taught a specialized jargon to describe their work (pp. 182–183). These recruitment and training tactics sound at least vaguely like those of Charlie Company mentioned above.

Commentary

Now let me comment, as a whole, on these three books and on the title of this chapter, "Is Cruelty Okay?". I intended that title to have some smack of irony or absurdity, yet at the same time to suggest that most people much of the time do seem to think that cruelty is okay. At the very least, cruelty is taken for granted as a fact of life, rather than as a problem to be solved. I find it anomalous that even though the word *cruel* so distinctly conjures up "bad" things — pain, injustice, evil — *cruelty* does not regularly figure into discussions of morality. Other concerns of morality — such as teaching individuals how to build character, punishing criminals, getting people to do their fair share for society — have a well-established place in moral discussion, but not so cruelty. And as Judith Shklar points out, very few writers on morality — Montaigne and Montesquieu are her exceptions — have ever "put cruelty first" (Shklar, 1984, p. 8).

I would guess that the reasons for cruelty's low profile include the following. First, cruelty is so unpleasant that no one wants to think about it. Period. Second, we probably carry the vague impression around that justice will be done, even if we make no personal effort to that end. (In like manner, the suffering of oppressed masses can be thought of as the working out of history, so there is no real need to help them.) Third, we may most often think of cruelty as the consequence of aberrant personalities, bullies, rather than anything structured into society. Fourth, we may conversely think that cruelty is such a matter of structure that individuals' wills don't enter into it. Fifth, we may believe that cruelty is necessary, that individual deviants are so ferocious that they need to be dealt with in kind or that groups who oppose society's current establishment are so dangerous that punishment for them need know no bounds.

Work such as that of Hughes, Peck, and Peters puts paid to many of those illusions. These authors show that various practices of cruelty have rather distinct social histories and identifiable "causes." From Hughes's book, *The Fatal Shore*, I extracted the following causes of cruelty in the Australian convict colony: desire for money, reinforcement of status, rivalry of groups, sadism, and isolation (of the convicts) from the protection of society. Peck's *People of the Lie* identified the psychiatric phenomenon of arrested narcissism and consequent scapegoating as a leading cause of cruelty in families. With regard to the MyLai massacre, Peck put the blame for cruelty on such things as stress in battle, dependency on the leader, group narcissism, the specialization of the military and of killers, and the intellectual laziness and narcissism of the American people. Peters, in *Torture*, showed how rationality (in Greek law), logic (in Roman law), and professionalization of magistrates fostered the growth of torture from ancient through medieval times. In the modern period, nationalism, the needs of the military, the all-out devotion to a philosophy, and what he called a technological anthropology brought out the beast in man.

Here we seem to have an embarrassment of riches. Instead of cruelty appearing to have no particular cause — and therefore being impossible to stop — cruelty now appears to have many causes — and stopping it may therefore, again, be hopeless! I think, however, that some of the causes named by our three authors could be combined and that it is possible to isolate two as the most important. The first is one that I would label *the herring factor.* The reference is to Solzhenitsyn's observation that some people would do anything for a herring (such as report escaping prisoners to the police). Throughout Hughes's Australian epic there are mentions of such venality, both in the outside world, in the prison, and among prisoners themselves. The perquisite is not always money — it could be a promotion, as for the soldiers in Vietnam or the torturers in Greece — or any kind of favor. The point is simply that a person justifies his own participation in a horrible system by paying attention to the small good that he acquires — the herring — and ignoring the enormous bad that results from his action.

The second factor I nominate as an important cause of cruelty is *intellectual laziness.* This could encompass a very large area; indeed, it takes in about half of the causes of cruelty listed above. For instance, it takes in Peck's complaint that groups practice an uncritical narcissism and his observation that we too readily forfeit ethical judgment to leaders. It could perhaps cover also his ideas about specialization and our unwillingness to think out the consequences thereof. Intellectual laziness is also involved in some of the historical causes of torture identified in Peters's historical survey, notably the way in which the dynamics of rationality and logic were unthinkingly allowed to spur the development of torture in ancient times. As Peters pointed out, for instance, doubts about the honesty of slaves' testimony under torture did not lead to a questioning of the whole system but rather to more torture. And as to Romano-canonical law's need for confession as the "queen of proofs," we have to ask why at least some of the thousands of

learned jurists and clerics couldn't have said, "Wait a minute —
this is ridiculous. . . ."

Without stretching the point too far, I believe that intellectual laziness as a cause of, or at least staunch maintainer of,
cruelty could also be said to cover the factor described in the
Australian colony as "isolation from society's protection" and
the related phenomenon of indifference by the public that was
called the "cancer of torture." The essence of this laziness
consists of the public's failure to recognize that the way to stop
cruelty is to *impose discipline from outside.* Cruelty doesn't cure
itself!

Intellectual laziness could also be said to encompass those
occasions in which a person acts in a group in a way that he
would not act alone. Thus, for instance, a soldier kills innocent
Vietnamese villagers because his buddies are doing it. The
same category involves all the participation by citizens who
support a nationalistic or philosophically revolutionary government in the practice of torture. Must one really mutilate the
bodies of dissidents to protect oneself and one's people? This
does not seem reasonable. A final intellectual laziness I might
mention is the laziness of intellectuals themselves, in their
failure to establish a human anthropology that could keep
torture at bay.

Before ending this chapter I should entertain for a moment
the idea that the answer to the question "Is cruelty okay?" could
be yes. It must be obvious from the way I have argued in this
chapter that cruelty is something *I* would like to see eliminated.
The "willful infliction of pain or suffering on others" strikes me
as a straightforwardly bad and undesirable thing. That is only
a viewpoint — no doubt one I share with many or most civilized
people but still just a viewpoint. Let us consider for a moment
the validity of another viewpoint — that cruelty is okay. I quote
Marvin Harris, concerning the Yanomamo tribe of Brazil, first
studied by the anthropologist Napoleon Chagnon:

> No Yanomamo woman escapes the brutal tutelage of the typi-
> cal hot-tempered, drug-taking Yanomamo warrior-husband.
> All Yanomamo men physically abuse their wives. Kind hus-
> bands merely bruise and mutilate them; the fierce ones
> wound and kill. While Chagnon was in the field, a man who
> suspected his wife of committing adultery . . . chopped off

both her ears. In a nearby village, another husband chopped a hunk of flesh out of his wife's arm with a machete. Men expect their wives to serve them and their guests and to respond to all requests promptly and without protest. If a woman does not comply quickly enough, her husband may beat her with a piece of firewood, take a swing at her with his machete, or put a glowing stick of wood against her arm (Harris, 1968, pp. 88–89).

There is plenty of completely unprovoked violence against women as well, which Chagnon attributes in part to the men's need to prove to each other that they are capable of deadly assault. "It helps a man's 'image' if he publicly beats his wife with a club" (Harris, 1968, p. 89).

So at least half the tribe — the males — thinks that this type of cruelty is okay. As for the victims, the Yanomamo women, "Chagnon states that [they] expect to be manhandled by their husbands and that they measure their status as wives by the frequency of minor beatings their husbands give them. Once he overheard two women discussing their scalp scars. One of them was saying how much the other's husband must really care for her since he had beaten her over the head so often" (Harris, 1968, p. 91). The same men, I should note, go at one another with even greater violence.

I believe that if one wants to take a stand against something, especially something widely practiced — and cruelty is surely widely practiced in our society as well as in others — then one must be able to justify one's position. For this reason, it is helpful to recognize that we do at times think cruelty is okay. Presumably the Rum Corps, Company C, the Catholic Church, the Communist party, and other of the various torturers mentioned above thought it was okay. Hence, to challenge their stance, one must have an even more compelling stance — about kindness, decency, or the inviolability of the human body, or whatever. The stance could be taken on merely aesthetic grounds — that we moderns prefer noncruelty as a matter of taste in the same way that the Yanomamo enjoy it. Or the anticruelty position could be argued on the principle of enlightened self-interest: we would like our society to do away with cruelty, since we would not personally care to be the victims.

In this chapter I have chosen to review books about physical cruelty of the violent assault kind. Thus, I have neglected an immense area of cruelty, namely economic cruelty. The exploitation of poor and unorganized people by more "advanced" humans — which is sometimes known as structural violence — is probably the type most widely considered to be okay. It may result in hunger and hunger-related diseases of millions of people but by and large it's okay. (As with the Yanomamo's wife-beating, it is just a normal feature of the landscape . . .). Both the herring factor, as I have defined it above, and intellectual laziness help to maintain such economic cruelty. So do a number of factors I listed in Chapter 7 as contributors to moral inertia, such as perceptual selectivity, the numbing effects of statistics, the unavailability of words for expressing blame, and ideological blinders concerning capitalism and communism. Thus, to tackle the massive problem of economic cruelty and structural violence I believe we would need to have a particularly strong conviction that cruelty is *not* okay. (Also, as presented in O'Neill's argument in Chapter 6, we need an unambiguous ethic of obligation to the needy.)

In this chapter I have admittedly downplayed cruelty as an instinct or as a personal pathology. I omitted, for example, Peters's remark concerning first-century Rome that "while Caligula was lunching or revelling, capital examinations by torture were often made in his presence" (Peters, 1985, p. 23) — as this did not portray the emperor as being particularly reluctant to carry out his official duty. I have up-played the degree to which the practice of torture and cruelty comes about cooly, logically, and by default of human feeling, rather than by bloodlust. I do not deny the existence of bloodlust, but it is my guess that if we could somehow weigh up the human-nature factor of bloodlust or sadism on one side and the herring factor plus intellectual laziness on the other, as *causes* of modern human cruelty, the latter would win — by tons. In sum, I suggest that *bystanders* have much to answer for in regard to the continuing practice of cruelty.

CHAPTER 9

Three Major Components of Morality

✳ ✳ ✳

The quality of mercy is not strain'd,
It droppeth as the gentle rain from heaven
Upon the place beneath.
— William Shakespeare, *The Merchant of Venice*

My object all sublime
I shall achieve in time-
To let the punishment fit the crime-
The punishment fit the crime.
— William Gilbert, *The Mikado*

Hut, two, three, four! Hut, two, three, four!
— Anonymous drill sergeant, U.S. Army

It is my contention that morality plays a huge role in human life and that most of our social dealings are built on a framework of morality. I expect that some readers will find that theme utterly radical (or just plain wrong) while others may consider it perfectly commonplace. Those who find it radical may do so because morality has in contemporary times seemed to be considered a private affair in the life of an individual. This notion that morality is private rather than social has been conveyed by many modern philosophers who have analyzed the ethical dilemmas of persons as though those persons were completely isolated from their social setting.

Even literary writers in the late twentieth century have reduced the scope of their work, moving away from the great social issues. The novelist E. L. Doctorow blames this partly on the fact that the social sciences have moved into the area that was once covered by novelists. Anthropology, psychology, and sociology, he says, force writers to become more private and interior. "We have given up the realm of public discourse and the political and social novel to an extent that we may not have

realized. We tend to be miniaturists more than we used to be"
(quoted in Moyers, 1989, p. 83).

In this chapter I attempt to specify what morality consists of
and what it encompasses and to show how it reflects our social
human nature. I first acknowledge that morality is difficult to
pin down in a concise definition. The etymology of the word is
itself indicative of the problem: *moral* derives from the Latin
mos, which simply means "custom" or "habit." The moral things
that we do, therefore, are simply the "done" things, the things
expected of us by society. Of course many items of convention
or etiquette, also, are expected of us by society, and these are
not especially moral. Conversely, certain moral things, particularly those associated with lofty character, are not really *expected* of us by society.

The word *moral* can bring at least three separate areas of
human behavior to mind. The first, which I shall call *law and
order*, has to do with following the rules of society. Thus, a
person with high standards of, say, honesty is acknowledged to
be moral. A person who adheres to strict rules of sexual conduct is likewise said to be moral. Conversely, the person violating the rules is said to be immoral, and such behavior is itself
called "immoral." The behavior of a whole society, too, can be
rated as to its morality: in times of decadence it may be said
that the group's morality is in decline.

A second large area of human behavior that connotes the
presence of morality or morally admirable human character is
that which (for lack of a better word) I call *welfare-provision*. I
am referring to behaviors in which people help the weak, the
poor, the young, or persons who are in some other way in need.
The word *charity* might suffice here, except that it has today
garnered the meaning of condescension on the part of the giver.
The word *mercy* is also somewhat appropriate, although it
connotes an additional factor of forgiveness or clemency. The
sentiment involved in the behavior to which I am referring is
compassion. By calling the behavior *welfare* I am referring more
to the effect of the compassionate deed: it leads to the welfare or
well-being of those who, on their own, might suffer. I think it is
safe to say that this kind of behavior is considered moral:
persons win a type of moral approbation for acts of kindness and
philanthropy that they do not win for acts of, say, cleverness or

endurance. Again, I might note that the morality of a whole group may be rated according to its degrees of welfare-provision; civilized societies congratulate themselves and each other on their moral achievements in this regard.

A third large realm of moral behavior consists of moral *judgment.* People seem to take great interest in discussions of right and wrong. Gossip about who is to blame for things has been popular throughout the ages, and courtroom dramas on television give satisfaction today: the audience waits with bated breath to see if the jury will find the accused guilty or innocent. Among intellectuals, fine points of ethical principle are the subject of endless debate. As with the other two components of morality, law and order and welfare-provision, this one, too, can appear as a quality possessed by a whole culture or people. Some nations pride themselves on their high moral judgment and their advanced sense of right and wrong, as seen, for instance, in their development of the notion of human rights.

The Evolutionary Background of the Major Components of Morality

In endeavoring to show that morality is fundamental to society and is deep-seated in human nature, I find it useful again (as in Chapter 5) to stress the origin of morality. I am personally persuaded by the sociobiological hypothesis of the evolution of morality (Maxwell, 1984, 1990). And, for me, that origin of morality sheds light on the potential constructive role of moral thought in contemporary society. In the following sections I shall consider whether each of the major components of morality has a biological basis. I shall look at judgment first, then law and order, and then welfare-provision.

Judgment — Did It Evolve?

Could moral judgment be a trait that evolved through natural selection? If one thinks, in the traditional manner, that morality is an objective fact in the world, that right and wrong were preordained by God, then it is hard to see how the human brain could have *evolved* a tendency for moral judgment. Evolution, after all, is built on a series of random changes. The stomach, the hand, the whatever, did not evolve in order to meet a predesigned endpoint: evolution is not teleological. Thus, if the traditional idea is correct, that morality is a quality that exists independent of human judgment, I would find the old-fashioned idea of *tabula rasa* to be more credible than that of an evolved tendency for judgment. In that view, the brain is a blank slate — the child comes into the world and learns whatever society teaches him. Moral ideas could thus be given to him in catechism class or at his parent's knee, or he could be deprived of all moral ideas and grow to adulthood as a non-moral being.

In the cosmology that attends sociobiology, however, moral qualities are *not* objective. Right and wrong do not exist independently in the world: these are evaluations of things imposed by humans. Hence, before hominids evolved, or, say, before any mammals evolved and the world was "peopled" with reptiles, there were no right and wrong. There were dark and light, warm and cold, and other qualities in the world, but not moral qualities. There were "interpersonal" behaviors in the world, such as snakes stealing eggs from birds' nests, or large fish swallowing small fish, but these couldn't be said to be bad or good. Bad and good are ideas that come about because the human brain is formed a certain way.

And why is the human brain formed that way? I have already discussed the theory of Robert Trivers concerning "the evolution of morality." (He does not actually go so far as to call it that.) It contains, or depends on, several premises. The first is that reciprocal altruism evolved among primates — evidence of this can be seen today in the tit-for-tat exchange of favors by baboons and chimpanzees. Second, the prevalence of altruism in a population of very social primates, such as hominids, offered a niche for cheaters. So cheating (that is, accepting a favor and not repaying it) became prevalent also. That situation elicited the evolution of a mechanism for better monitoring of repayment of favors. According to Trivers, "Natural selection will rapidly favor a *complex psychological system* in which individuals regulate both *their own* altruistic and cheating tendencies, and their *responses* to these tendencies *in others*" (emphasis added) (1985, p. 387).

Third, that complex psychological system would include strong emotional responses to both altruism and cheating. We could call these the moral emotions: feelings of guilt when the self cheats, a sense of righteousness when the self does not cheat, and a sense of indignation toward others who cheat. I think it is very easy to imagine those emotions leading to more generalized concepts about right and wrong. This could have occurred *before* language evolved, but as soon as language did evolve, and people could pin a label on such things ("that is right," "this is wrong"), the sense of *objectification* of morality would rapidly come about. And from that point on, religious leaders or other thinkers could create explanations as to why certain practices have been forbidden by the ancestors, how God will punish sin in the afterlife, and so forth.

Over time, cultures more or less inevitably institutionalize behaviors that are laid down in human nature. People seem to want predictable customs and regular traditions in which to express their behavior. Thus, the mechanism for accusing, judging, and punishing wrongdoers, for example, would soon have become fixed in a given society. The institutionalization of moral debate itself must have been a landmark in the "evolution" of morality. Of course, by that stage we were past the point of *biological* evolution; natural selection was no longer designing the product. Natural selection designed the moral judgment–oriented brain, but individual human beings, with their cultures, created the actual moral rules and beliefs. These can differ widely among societies, yet have much in common.

I think that the tendency to moralize — to attribute a good or bad quality to the actions of oneself or others — *is* the core of the human moral system. Evaluation is the main activity. Appropriately enough, the first definition of *moral*, in *The American Heritage Dictionary*, is "of or concerned with the judgment of the goodness or badness of human action and character." If the new sociobiological view of morality is accurate, it seems to me to place more responsibility on individuals in modern society. It shows ordinary people that their moral sensibility is the source of judgment for social decision-making.

Law and Order — Did It Evolve?

The second component of morality to be investigated here is the one related to law or more generally to the keeping of social order. As to the question of whether the tendency for obeying laws and keeping order could have evolved biologically, I think the answer is yes. The background explanation here, though, is different from the one given above for the evolution of judgment: this one does not depend on the evolution of reciprocal altruism. Instead, the evolutionary theory to be referred to here concerns the evolution of the social behavior of dominance and submission.

Many animal species have *dominance hierarchies;* these come about as a result of competition over scarce resources. Dominance hierarchies occur both in some species that have some social cooperation and some that do not. Wherever they are found there is patterned behavior: the animals at the top exert some control over the animals at the bottom. Not only do those at the bottom lose out in actual benefits — for example, they predictably do not get the best choice of food or nesting sites — they also carry out activities of which the function is merely to record their status. For example, submissive animals may bow to the more dominant ones or may spend time grooming them.

Falling in with one's established place in the hierarchy is, predictably, a common feature of behavior in the animal kingdom. (In some species, the status achieved early in life may last permanently; in others there are frequent shake-ups based on new attempts by individuals to show their strength.) After all, the practicing of subordinate gestures and prudently staying out of the way of the more dominant individuals have adaptive value: they at least help one to stay alive. The tendency to obey the orders of hierarchical rulers may be an inherited trait of the human species. (I shall consider human hierarchies at greater length in Chapter 11.) Hierarchies are widespread among mammals and quite prevalent among primates, so it is a reasonable guess that hominids had this trait.

Finally, I may mention one other behavior related to the keeping of order that may have an evolutionary explanation: I am referring to conformity. Humans, like animals of certain other species, generally prefer to conform to the established way of doing things. Conformity is more emotionally comfortable than deviation. The adaptiveness of this trait may have to do with the fact that it is safer to stick to the beaten path than to be a path breaker. Such a psychological trait can help promote obedience to law. Of course, it may extend to other things that have nothing to do with morality, such as conforming to fashion and tradition. (Indeed, conformity may promote *im*morality, if that is the fashion.)

Welfare-Provision — Did It Evolve?

The final component of morality to be considered in this chapter is welfare-provision. I specified this earlier as one that includes the feeling of compassion, and that consists of giving aid to various parties who are not expected to return the favor. Both parts of that definition — the compassion and the non-return — make it hard to defend the idea that welfare-provision evolved biologically, as I shall now explain.

One thing making it difficult to show that compassion in humans evolved biologically is that there is apparently no similar compassion found in other species. (Of course, a human trait need not be found in other animals in order to be innate — many evolved human traits are species-specific to humans, such as the ability to speak. However, it is generally easier to imagine that behavioral traits are innate when they are also seen elsewhere in the animal kingdom.) Some studies of young children seem to indicate that the behavior of sympathy is innate rather than learned (Rheingold and Hay, 1978), but these are not definitive. Reports of findings of sympathy among primates appear contradictory, so I shall not attempt to use them here. It can be said, though, that chimpanzee mothers — like mothers of other mammal species — exhibit great concern for their young.

The trait of compassion in humans may in fact have grown out of such parental nurturance. But compassion is not just love of and caring for the love-object; it is a type of experience of vicarious feeling. When we see someone in pain it hurts *us*. For this reason, I suggest that a possible avenue for the evolution of compassion was by a certain cognitive rather than strictly emotional trait. As Piaget has shown (1975), children at a certain age automatically acquire the ability to see things from another's point of view. It is part of our brain's strategy to form models of experience by placing ourselves in someone else's shoes. This could arouse compassion if the other person happens to be suffering.

A second difficulty in showing that welfare-provision evolved has to do with the fact that welfare is for the good of all, whereas natural selection selects only those traits that are good for the individual and his genes (that is, his relatives). Obviously, many human cultures provide welfare to all members — including the old and disabled who, by definition, cannot repay the favors being done for them. Any instinct for helping such people would, however, have been a losing instinct in evolution. Hence, it is unlikely that we have a pure instinct to work for the good of the group. Again, though, the behavior could possibly be an *extension* of another behavior. We can instinctively work for the good of relatives and the good of persons who can repay us, so why not just decide to help the needy as well?

The word *decide* is crucial here. *Decide* may seem to imply that each person must consciously vote to extend his altruistic efforts to the needy or to some more abstract entity such as "the good of all." But it need not happen that way. As we have seen, traits of human behavior often come to be institutionalized and elaborated in cultural practices. Moral ideas about welfare-provision could come to be articulated into universal principles about the rightness of helping the needy. This would act as propaganda on individuals, coaxing them into voluntary acts of charity. Another important factor is that most persons could recognize, consciously or semiconsciously, that rules about helping the needy amount to insurance protection for themselves.

Conclusion

As we have seen, morality has at least three major components: law and order, judgment, and welfare-provision. Together they call on a number of genetically based traits:

deference to superiors; preference for regularity of behavior, for social order, and for conformity; desire to monitor the moral behavior of others and of oneself; eagerness to settle matters where right and wrong are in dispute; inclination to objectify perceived good and bad; and compassion and vicarious experiencing of another individual's difficulties. My purpose in underlining the *evolved* nature of these things is to try to strengthen my case for claiming that the predisposition toward concern with morality is a fundamental and universal human trait. Clearly we have day-to-day or even hour-to-hour involvement with morality. It is extremely pervasive in our social and psychological life and works so efficiently that we are largely unaware of it.

CHAPTER 10

American Moral Problems

✳ ✳ ✳

This coffee-table book, *A World of Ideas*, is absolute must reading for all Americans — or at least for any who missed the PBS TV series on which it is based. Bill Moyers, an astonishingly thoughtful and provocative interviewer, traveled the country, talking to members of the arts and professions to get their views on contemporary life in the United States. Among these persons are scientists, clergymen, historians, philosophers, educators, novelists, but — perhaps significantly — no elected officials.

Moyers was press secretary to Lyndon Johnson in the 1960s and is obviously a serious student of American history and of the Greek classics. In most of these dialogues he is a full partner. Indeed, one could at times accuse him of "leading the witness," except that these witnesses all seem too sure-footed to be led. No doubt, however, his infectious spirit of inquiry helped the interviewees to speak freely. In the introduction, Moyers remarks: "The chief reward of [doing this series] is the joy of learning, of coming away from each person with a wider angle of vision on the times I live in, on the issues I am expected to act upon, and the choices I can make as father, husband, journalist, and citizen. . . . I have had a career of discovery and feel compelled to share it" (p. viii).

A theme that recurs throughout *A World of Ideas* is that of morality. Hence, in this review I shall concentrate on that topic at the expense of other fascinating themes — such as the richness of cultural diversity in the United States or ideas for public education. (Some of the interviewees' comments about the relationship between morality and politics will surface in Chapter 15.) I shall first let several of the interviewees state

---

Review of Bill Moyers, *A World of Ideas*, edited by Betty Sue Flowers (New York: Doubleday, 1989).

what they consider to be current problem of moral behavior in the United States (the reader should assume that in this chapter all citations of page numbers refer to pages in *A World of Ideas*). Then I shall present what they hold to be the causes — such as the emphasis on individualism over community, the incompatibility of technology and certain values, and, in general, the sad state of moral discourse. At the end, I shall focus on Moyers's direct question, What is a moral life?

The Problem: Current Behavior

It was widely acknowledged in these conversations that "morals" in American life today are not especially impressive. The late Barbara Tuchman, historian, went so far as to tell Bill Moyers that there seems to be "the loss of moral sense, of knowing the difference between right and wrong. . . . We see it all the time [when we] open any morning paper. . . . People go around shooting their colleagues or killing people. How is killing so easy nowadays?" (p. 5). She observed of government life that *false dealing* is now the *prevailing* element in America. "We keep reading about congressmen and municipal officials who are being indicted for one kind of misbehavior or another. . . . Are they not afraid of some kind of punishment, whether social or legal or in conscience?" (p. 6). And what has happened to *outrage?* Tuchman asks. Where is the outrage over the Iran-Contra scandal or over the swindling by the defense industry? Her answer is that "somehow people don't take wrongdoing seriously. Perhaps there's just too much of it. We're not surprised any more" (p. 6). She adds, "We have lost a sense of respect for serious, honest conduct. If we are moved merely by greed, and there's no longer any respect for decent or honest government, then we will suffer the results" (p. 6).

Filmmaker David Puttman states, "I think the totally rampant greed, which somehow the nation seems to have got around to justifying as part and parcel of its heritage, is out of control and is going to do immense damage in the long run" (p. 318). Greed is the theme of further comments by Michael Josephson, founder of the Institute for the Advancement of Ethics. He blames greed in part on the "yuppies" (a term for young upwardly mobile professionals). "The yuppie is the constituency that makes [government scandals] okay. They're the people who applaud success, who allow an Ivan Boesky to say 'Greed is good' and not be hooted down from the stage" (p. 15). Of course, not everybody doing unethical things is motivated by money, but there is a creeping corruption. It is "based on a self-righteous notion of the need to win. . . . Many politicians, for example, treat getting elected as if it were a moral imperative" (p. 15).

Josephson notes that there is a difference between being forced to choose among two or more ethical values and to choose between an ethical value and a nonethical value. Take the oft-cited example of a rapist who asks you if you know where his potential victim is hiding. You lie by saying no; you put the value of protecting the woman ahead of the value of telling the truth. But most of the time those are not the quandaries we face. Rather, Josephson says, "We face simple decisions of self-interest versus doing the right thing. . . . The question is, do we have the strength to do the right thing? Or do we start a rationalizing process that says 'Well, this is really for my family,' . . . or 'If I don't make this money then nobody will have any jobs' " (p. 21).

Various authors in Moyers's book similarly boil the problem of contemporary American life down to a few factors. For instance, it is partly a consequence of the cynicism that followed the assassination of idealistic leaders of the 1960s, such as Bobby Kennedy and Martin Luther King, Jr. There is also a kind of apathy brought about by bureaucracy (Moyers notes "bureaucracies do not summon us to citizenship the way democracy should" [p. 440]). There is a concern with "the pocketbook" now that the economy is in trouble. Besides a loss of outrage, there is little expectation of punishment for wrongdoers if they succeed. There is just too much materialism, which is partly to be blamed on TV commercials. (Historian Henry Steele Commager thinks that commercials have "inspired greed and jealousy and ambition. . . . Children are told to want everything" [p. 229].) Additionally, there are a loss of compassion for the poor and the exclusion of many people from society because they lack money. To Moyers's question "Are we creating a class society?" Commager answers, "We are indeed, for the first time in our history" (p. 229).

Now let us turn to the interviewees' explanations as to the causes of the current problems in our moral behavior.

Individualism Versus Community

Willard Gaylin, psychiatrist, is president of the Hastings Center, which is concerned with bioethics. He believes the most pressing ethical issue of the next decade is the rediscovery of community.

> We're a very individually oriented country, and I love that. I'd rather be more individually oriented than community oriented like the Soviets or the Chinese. But somewhere along the line we've gotten a peculiar idea of what an individual is, what individual pleasure is, what individual purpose is. We see everything in terms of personal autonomy — in terms not only of my rights under law, but also in terms of pleasure, in terms of privilege. I think we have trained a whole generation of people to think in terms of an isolated "I" (p. 119).

Gaylin points out that anyone trained in biology knows that the human being is not like an amoeba. "We're much more like coral, we're interconnected" (p. 119). The fact is we cannot survive without each other, he says: "But now, communities have broken down. In the pursuit of individual liberties we have allowed a corruption of the public space, so that there are areas that are not safe, and where that happens, there is no individual liberty. The people who are living in Harlem, who cannot go out to shop at night because of the crack addicts, are in a prison, and we've helped create the prison by ignoring what community means in this country" (p. 119).

Gaylin observes that people hardly dare to mention the concept of responsibilities, duties, or obligations, thanks to the emphasis on civil liberties. He recalls an article in the *New York Times* that said that individuals in the high-risk categories for AIDS have a right not to know whether they have the disease or not. Thus, they should not be forced to take the test. Gaylin wrote in to agree that they had this right, but that at the same time the ones who exercised such a right were morally obliged to act as if they had been tested positively. "And while I ex-pressed compassion for the victim groups, I said that even being a victim does not allow you the privilege of being a victimizer. The amount of hate mail I received was incredible" (p. 121).

Robert Bellah, sociologist, is a coauthor of *Habits of the Heart*, a study published in 1985 that finds most Americans concerned with personal gratification, even if they pay lip ser-vice to a tradition of community. Bellah, however, hasn't given up on the possibility that this can be modified. His exchange with Moyers went as follows:

> Moyers: There is a case to be made, is there not, that for two hundred years Americans have demonstrated an anticommun-ity, anti-political bias, that we've been on the run for two hundred years from suffocating family ties, from nagging neighbors, from boring civic rituals, that America as a dy-namic, individualistic society is basically anti-community?
>
> Bellah: I think that's a half-truth. For one thing, for the people we talk to, including the most individualistic, "community" is still a good word. They want community. Sometimes one feels it's a little bit superficial, a kind of meeting of the feelings on a momentary basis. But even so, there's a great hunger for community. People don't feel entirely thrilled with the idea of being all alone (p. 228).

Bellah feels that growing consensus about arms control and environmental issues is evidence that we can build community. "We live in a world community. One of our biggest problems is to make that come alive, ethically and politically" (p. 287).

Bellah correctly identifies part of the problem of "individual-ism versus community" as inhering in the fact that caring for self, as a value, diminishes the value or even the concept of caring for others. He notes that the "market model," which is perfectly okay in the economic sphere, is very harmful — and absurd — when it is generalized to all our lives. The maximizing of self-interest makes sense in business, he says, but "you can't have a marriage that works that way. If you're interested only in maximizing your own self-interest, how can you think about the other person to whom you're supposed to be committed?" (p. 282) To Moyers's question "By being good, do you mean thinking of other people?" Bellah, replies "Yes, I do. A public official who thinks only about his or her own interests and not about the entity he or she is supposed to serve is a corrupt official. By the same token, a voter who goes to the polls and asks, Which candidate is best for me? I don't care about which is best for the country, or which is best for other people, just who's best for me? — that is a corrupt voter" (pp. 281–282).

The Incompatibility Between Technology and Certain Values

Besides the very considerable problems for morality caused by Americans' overemphasis on individualism, there are other contributing factors, many having to do with technology. The fact is that technological values are incompatible with certain other values. Sheldon Wolin comments, "Reaganism is a combination of a very strong push toward high technology and a strong state — aggressive foreign policy, strong defense, and the rest of it. But it's also been nostalgic in terms of nineteenth-century, or even eighteenth-century, values about home, church, family, and that sort of thing." These things don't really go together, Wolin believes. "It's that peculiar combination of technological progressivism, in terms of the political state, and a regressive view toward ethics, morality, piety, and family. It's that American proclivity toward wanting to find yourself sanctified by some set of values that you know very well cannot come from what you're actually into" (p. 105).

The historian and Hungarian émigré John Lukacs observes that "an American conservative now is more enamored with *progress* than liberals and progressives were two generations ago" (p. 436). Moyers asked him what kind of progress he was referring to.

> Lukacs: This is a very important question because I think that the great task before all of us and our children, is to rethink the meaning of "progress." Most people think of progress as man's increasing mastery of things. But we have arrived at the point at which man himself becomes a thing. What this world needs is not growth as much as stability. We have to conserve much of the world. We have to conserve much of the past.

Moyers: If you looked at the definition, you'd find that the traditional meaning of progress is moving toward a goal and constantly improving ourselves as we go there. Are you saying we have to change that idea about progress?

Lukacs: But we're not improving ourselves. Progress now means constantly changing the world outside us without really improving ourselves or our minds. The progressive mind denies the existence of sin, of frailty, of the limitations of human nature. These are very life-giving doctrines because the knowledge of our limitations enriches the human mind (p. 436).

Robert Bellah makes a different point — that we foolishly believe that "modern technology will solve all our problems without preventing the individual from doing whatever he or she wants to do. . . . [But] without any guidance or any set of priorities, technological advances can create all kinds of severe problems — the greenhouse effect, for example, or the situations where we can't move in traffic in our major cities" (p. 280). Bellah notes that "Americans have preferred not to think about the . . . realities that link technology to our individual lives." He contends that "we have to recover a more classical notion of politics as the place where we decide together about the things we need to do" (p. 280). Willard Gaylin agrees with Bellah: "What we really prefer is optimism and denial. We don't want to believe there's a problem. For example, no one believes we're running out of anything. I think we're running out of everything. We're running out of 'out.' 'Out' is where my parents threw their garbage. You can't throw the garbage out any more. Out is where your children are going to live, where your grandchildren are going to live. But Americans can't face it [whereas] Europeans can face limitations and shortages" (p. 125).

Environmental scientist Jessica Tuchman Mathews believes there are signs that Americans *are* waking up to crises such as the greenhouse effect. "The question is, will we wake up fast enough to keep up with the problem? This is an issue where politicians will have to lead public opinion," she says, "not follow it. That's hard for elected officials to do" (p. 304).

Moyers: No one thanks you now if the rewards come a generation later.

Mathews: Your children will thank you. We are up against a lot of limits that require us to think ahead and to act in advance of damage, rather than going back to clean it up — because there are some things we can't clean up. . . . We're going to need a new sense of shared destiny. We are the only planet in the universe that we know about where there is life. That is a fact people react to rather strongly and profoundly (p. 304).

The Sad State of Moral Discourse

So far, the conversations have covered the idea that there is a real problem of current moral behavior in the United States, and that there are complicated causes of this, such as the emphasis on individualism over community and the incompatibility of technology with other values. That Moyers's interviewees were able to put this much across in very clear language is a sign, of course, that moral discourse is alive and well. Nevertheless, they themselves identify several areas in which moral language is deficient or troublesome.

The first of these is the familiar complaint that television advertisements are deceptive, including — or especially — those having to do with political campaigns. Moyers notes of 1988, "There was such a growing gap between the rhetoric and the reality. I listened to the candidates but I didn't hear very realistic descriptions of the world out there" (p. 281). Bellah's comment on this is that television "has such a powerful way of presenting immediate images that it tempts the politicians to go for whatever will have the most impact. That [makes the electorate think] about voting only in terms of the most short-term interests or fears" (p. 281).

Sheldon Wolin, a political philosopher, contends that "political language has become increasingly technocratic, dominated by economic modes of understanding" (such as the cost-benefit analysis). "We talk about . . . having to make choices in balancing pollution costs against production costs. That way of thinking . . . leaves no way of talking about what is fundamental in a civic language, which is, why should I contribute, sacrifice, and cooperate in a particular way . . . ?" (p. 109). Wolin's opinion as to why this economic talk is so seductive is that it is talk about things that really concern people today. "A language which seems to be able to make promises about the alleviation of those anxieties then becomes tremendously magnetic and fascinating. People are ready to go along with those who can manipulate that language" (p. 109).

An interesting point about the language of the *law* is made by Mary Ann Glendon, a professor of law. She notes that the way the Supreme Court wrote the decision in the abortion case, *Roe* v. *Wade*, communicated a message about freedom of choice — about the paramountcy of that value. Yet, she believes, there's much more depth and complexity to the way Americans feel about abortion than can be seen in *Roe* v. *Wade*. There are other values involved, but only that one gets mentioned. "As it stands now, it's basically an impoverished moral discourse" (p. 480).

Glendon undertook a comparative study of current European abortion laws and also individual state laws in the United States predating the 1973 *Roe* v. *Wade* decision. She found that the typical solution to the dilemma of "pro choice" versus "pro life" was a compromise of some sort. In most laws, she says, "there was an affirmation of the sanctity of life together with the recognition that there may be some circumstances under which the problem of the woman involved such hardships that abortion ought to be permitted" (p. 473). Many of the European or U.S. state laws protected the rights of the fetus starting as early as the twelfth week of life. The Supreme Court case, however, permits no regulation of abortion in the interest of the fetus until the sixth month — the time of viability. Glendon concludes:

> There is always the danger that if you speak a language that recognizes only individual rights, you will become a people that can think only about individuals. Choices last. Choices that we make as individuals make us into the kinds of people that we are. Choices that we make collectively as a society make us into the kind of society we are. So if you put together a whole lot of legal decisions that give priority to individual rights, and then let them trump everything else, you're contributing in some unquantifiable but nevertheless real way to shaping the society (p. 483).

In *A World of Ideas,* criticisms of moral discourse predictably include those involving patriotism. The Reverend F. Forrester Church, a Unitarian pastor, remarks:

> I listened to Oliver North's testimony before the Senate Committee. He was able to justify every one of his acts according to the highest of virtues — faith, love, hope, fortitude, justice. The testimony was so powerful to the American people because rhetorically and superficially, it represented everything we admire. But for that very reason, it's the more dangerous, because the flip side, the dark side, isn't being seen. We can do tremendous evil in this world in the name of good, in the name of God (p. 419).

Church continues, "When a person wraps him or herself in the American flag and holds the Bible, that person is dangerous, because we respect the American flag and the Bible, and we are likely to follow a person who is wearing the one and brandishing the other. But that person may be leading us right down the wrong road" (p. 419).

The poet Derek Walcott makes a rather different observation — that our leaders speak in a bland language when describing the enemy. The reality is "shielded by the mediocrity of monosyllables that makes the language interchangeable" (p. 433). He notes that Reagan said things like, "I want to do my best for this country" — which says nothing at all. He *should* have been saying, "Let's get rid of the Sandanistas" if that's what he meant. When Hitler said, "We are going to exterminate our enemies," at least you could react, Walcott argues. Reagan *did* want to get rid of the Sandanistas, "but he didn't say it in that language. He said it in a language that is interchangeable with a McDonald's ad. . . . What is bewildering is the fact that the language is ironed out into a uniformity that says nothing on either side" (p. 433).

To me, the most remarkable comments about moral discourse in this book come from Martha Nussbaum, a specialist in the classics. She encourages us to incorporate literature into our moral thinking. The Greek tragedies such as *Antigone* dramatize the real moral conflict of actual lives: we should not pretend that conflicts do not exist. "The stories that we sometimes tell ourselves, that the free will is free no matter what conditions people are living in. . . . Those are evasive and pernicious stories, because they prevent us from looking with . . . compassion at the lives of other people" (p. 453). To Moyers's question "What do you think about the level of our public discourse today?" Nussbaum replies, "We've lost the idea that politics are part of the humanities. We don't expect them to have the contact with literature and the richness of descriptive language that the humanities have always stood for. That's a great loss" (p. 459).

Nussbaum notes that even when the humanities are offered as a central part of curriculum in universities, it is "not with the idea that this is going to improve ethical and public discourse. We see works of literature as amusing or diverting, but not as having a bearing on the most important ethical questions" (p. 459). She remarks:

> This has come about, in part, because of disciplinary separations in the university. People are reading literature in the literature department, which is usually understood to be a place where you pursue questions of form and style without asking about the ethical and social content. We pursue the ethical questions in departments of philosophy and political science, which usually don't read works of literature and so miss the approach to ethical questions that I have tried to characterize (p. 459).

What Is the Moral Life?

In this final section let us look at the replies that Moyers got to his question "What is the moral life?" or related questions. Here I shall not do any analysis or sorting of the replies. I shall simply print the exchange he had with seven interviewees — Leon Kass, a biologist; Forrest McDonald, a historian; and five whom we have already met: ethics lawyer Michael Josephson, clergyman F. Forrester Church, sociologist Robert Bellah, classicist Martha Nussbaum, and historian Barbara Tuchman.

> Moyers to Kass: You once said that we should turn less to science for the answers and should start worrying about leading a moral life. What is your definition of a moral life?

135

Kass: One of its central features is one's aspiration and concern with one's own character and self-command. It extends to those immediate relations that are ours, either by necessity or by choice. . . . It means taking a broader interest in the life of one's community, both locally and nationally, and to some extent even globally. It means to deal with many of the external things that have always made life nasty and short and brutal for too many of our fellow human beings — poverty and pestilence, for example. And it also means holding up the possibility of certain high human peaks of noble action, of generosity, of self-sacrifice, of great beautification of the world through music and the arts (p. 368).

Moyers to Josephson: So what's the mandate for an ethical person . . . ?

Josephson: The mandate is that an ethical person ought to do more than he's required to do and less than he's allowed to do. He must exercise judgment, self-restraint, and conscience. Otherwise, we have a minimalist society where everybody's lawyering everybody else, pushing the world to the limit, and twisting the rules. We need to tell people we can do better. And if it costs us a little bit, so it costs us. It's worth it (p. 27).

Moyers to Nussbaum: I asked you about the moral lesson, and you [talked about] what the tragedies show us. In one sense there is no lesson and no moral, is there? It's simply the revelation of life as seen through the artist, the philosopher, the sufferer, the pilgrim. There's no effort to instruct.

Nussbaum: But you know, sometimes just to see the complexity that's there and see it honestly without flinching and without redescribing it in terms of some excessively simple theory — that is itself progress. It's progress for public life as well as private life, because it's only when we've done that step that we can then ask ourselves, "How can our institutions make it less likely that those conflicts will happen to people? How can we create schemes of child care, for example, that will make this tragic conflict of obligations less of a daily fact of women's lives and perhaps more of a rare and strange occurrence?" (p. 451).

Moyers: What are the essential elements of a good human life?

Nussbaum: One of the essential elements is relationships among people. . . . Another is thinking and reasoning on many different levels, including moral reasoning, because one of the most essential things in the Greek view — and in mine, too — is to become capable of making a plan for the good life. (p. 453).

Moyers to Church: You must pass panhandlers coming up to you. I do, walking to work everyday. What do you do?

Church: Well, you know, morality is a one-on-one operation. Anytime we can provide shelter, anytime we can provide a little food, even perhaps anytime we can provide enough money for a pint of wine to help somebody get through the night, that's okay, as long as we don't *just* do that, as long as at the same time, the members of this congregation and I get radicalized (p. 417).

Moyers to McDonald: You've said through the years that the life-giving principle, not just of our republic but of any republic, is the idea of public virtue. What do you mean by that?

McDonald: I mean what was historically meant, and it goes way back to ancient Greece and Rome. It means simply a devotion to the well-being of the public.

Moyers: — the public interest, over and above individualism. Didn't it also involve the idea that the highest self-realization came through participation in the public enterprise?

McDonald: Yes, man attains his greatest fulfillment through participation in the republic (p. 118).

Moyers to Bellah: You talk about building a moral frame for interdependence, of making technology socially beneficial, of finding a sense of community in solving these problems. But how do we go about that in practical ways?

Bellah: First of all, we have to face the reality, and that means we have to talk about it. People who say we talk too much and that we should act are on the wrong track. The first big job is thinking and understanding, and that means talking together.

Moyers: And this has to be a moral discourse?

Bellah: Yes. When we do that, we may begin to discover more consensus than we think there is. We may agree on certain priorities. Once we see what those priorities are, then we can realize that if each of us does entirely what he or she pleases at all times, none of us will get those priorities answered. So then we have to figure out what are the social arrangements that will allow as many of us as possible to fulfill those perfectly valid individual wants in a way that's supportive of other people rather than destructive to them (p. 280).

Moyers to Tuchman: What do you mean by moral sense?

Tuchman: The sense of what is inherently right and wrong, and of following what you believe is right. [I note that in criticism today] critics of art and drama . . . will accept as great almost any damned thing that they think is funny or that they think will sell or will tickle the art dealers or that's got some attraction that appeals to the mass public, even if it is basically trashy. The acceptance of that kind of thing is an absence of moral sense (p. 6).

   I ask myself, have nations ever declined from a loss of moral sense? . . . I think Germany declined as a result of the loss of a moral sense, which was made evident under the Nazi regime. . . . It happened, for example, to the Turks in the Ottoman Empire. The disappearance of a moral sense, of a moral rule, led to fierce, barbarous oppression and massacres and to the decline of power in the end (p. 5).

Let me try to reduce these seven replies to Moyers's question "What is the moral life?" to one word or phrase each. They are: self-command, self-restraint, compromise, generosity, public virtue, consensus-generation, and maintenance of standards. It is obvious from the wide range of these seven items that morality covers a lot of ground in both private and public life, and that much of the effort needed to improve moral life in the United States has to do with combining private and public morality.

   In conclusion, let me summarize the ideas of the fifteen commentators named above. They look upon the current problem of moral behavior in the United States as including dishonesty, greed, easy killing, low expectations from business and public officials, voter manipulation, and justification of any behavior if it leads to winning. They attribute part of the problem to the emphasis on rights over duties — as in Gaylin's comment about the duties of potential AIDS carriers. Another part of the problem they noted is the incompatibility of technology with other values, both the value of protecting the environment and the intellectual value of recognizing our limitations.

Moyers got many of the interviewees to describe problems of moral language. These included the manipulative language associated with advertising, the emotional language of television images, the wrapping of persons in the flag and Bible-brandishing, the prominence of economic cost-benefit terminology, the blandness of presidential language that does not define the issues, the composing of Supreme Court decisions in a strict language of individual rights, and the divorce of the humanities from political science with attendant separation of the content of great literature from public debate.

Despite all these problems, the tone of voice that comes through (not necessarily in the short excerpts I have furnished) is one of optimism. Indeed, I think that the word that best characterizes Moyers's interviews is *exuberance*. The Americans interviewed are proud of their heritage, particularly of the nation's penchant for problem-solving, of its tolerance and generosity, and of the deep-seated American interest in "being good."

Because I have excluded from this review many of the conversations about ethnic diversity, I have not conveyed a certain subtle point about moral regeneration in America. It is that many of the interviewees seem to believe that the solution lies in people becoming less fearful of neighbors who differ from themselves. It has to do with their belief that what America is all about is sorting out the rights and needs of different groups — and of coming to appreciate their contributions. In short, people are not the problem: they are the solution.

CHAPTER 11

The Elusive Butterfly of Power

✳ ✳ ✳

Power is delightful and absolute power is absolutely delightful.
— Kenneth Tynan

A state that has once been leviathan does not take amiably to the hook.
— Harold Laski

He nothing common did or mean
Upon that memorable Scene:
   But with his keener Eye
   The Axes edge did try.
— Andrew Marvell, *Horatian Ode*

Power is looked upon, in some circles, as the rival of morality or as its logical opposing force. Such relationship as may exist between these two phenomena — power and morality — will be the subject of a later chapter (Chapter 15). In this chapter the goal is specifically *not* to look at their relationship but instead to isolate power as completely as possible from moral considerations. My reason for wanting to present power in a neutral light (some will say I have already taken a position in favor of power by opting to be neutral about it!) is that it will make cleaner the later discussion about the relationship of morality and power.

Many theories or philosophies of power contain implicit or explicit evaluations of power. Conservative, anarchist, and communist philosophies are examples. I shall not analyze those here, as I do not wish to enter into a discussion of whether power-holding is good or bad, whether rulers have a right to rule, and so forth. I prefer to undertake an investigation of power that goes to the essence of the phenomenon of power. This, I admit in advance, may be an impossible or misguided task — there may be no such thing as the essence of power. At the very least, however, I believe I can mount a creditable refutation of the widely held idea that the essence of power can be found in human nature.

This chapter has two parts. Part One consists of a socio-biological search for the human nature of power. I shall go over the evidence from the animal kingdom that suggests that power has something to do with a biological drive and with an ecological circumstance of scarcity of resources. Although the evidence is in some ways compelling, I believe it can be misleading and that a direct analogy to the human situation can be shown to be mistaken. In Part Two, I consider an alternative explanation for the institutionalization of power in complex human society, particularly with reference to the emergence of the state. I offer a "cybernetic theory of the state," arguing that complex systems inherently require things that we associate with power, namely command and control. I hypothesize that the drive for power in the human personality is *incidental* to this.

Before turning to Part One, let me mention that very little illumination comes from defining the word *power*. *The American Heritage Dictionary* offers fourteen definitions. Here are the first six: "1. The ability or capacity to act or perform effectively. 2. A specific capacity, faculty, or aptitude: *his powers of concentration.* 3. Strength or force exerted or capable of being exerted; might. 4. The ability or official capacity to exercise control; authority. 5. A person, group, or nation having great influence or control over others. 6. The might of a nation, political organization, or similar group" (1976, p. 1027). For purposes of this chapter, I intend *power* to mean, roughly, the ability of one individual or group to control another or, as political scientists like to put it, the ability of A to get B to do something that B would otherwise not do. Thus, power is the relationship between two parties.

Part One: A Sociobiological Search for the Human Nature of Power

It is part of the conventional wisdom that power, in the sense of an individual or group of individuals controlling others, is based on human nature. This belief did not originate with sociobiologists in recent decades; it goes back centuries. Thomas Hobbes declared in 1651, "I put for a general inclination of all mankind, a perpetual and restless desire of power after power that ceaseth only in death" (1909, ch. 11). Hans Morgenthau, a very influential twentieth-century theorist of international relations, claimed that "the drives to live, to propagate, and to dominate are common to all men" (1967, p. 31). He quoted approvingly from John of Salisbury to the effect that "if a man can play the tyrant, he will, even in the meanest station" (1967, p. 32).

Sociobiologists may be inclined to think the same way, ostensibly on more scientific grounds. They are aware of such power-related factors in the animal kingdom as aggression and dominance hierarchies and have recently discovered coalition-formation among primates. Let us look at these three clues from the animal kingdom. First I shall describe each one strictly in relation to nonhumans, and then in the following section discuss the human manifestation of these traits. The goal will be to discover if human power structures are determined, ultimately, by genes.

Aggression

The American Heritage Dictionary defines *aggression* (from *ad gradi*, meaning "to step forward") as "the act of commencing hostilities or invasion; an assault." Aggressive behavior is found in species whose members have to compete for resources. The trait is adaptive in that it helps the survival of the individual: he or she gets access to food, water, mates, nesting sites — whatever the scarce resource happens to be. The evolution of aggression thus fits normally into the Darwinian theory of evolution by natural selection. Mutant traits for aggressive behavior, occurring randomly eons ago, would have easily become incorporated into animals' behavioral repertoires because those with the trait would have survived at the expense of nonaggressive individuals.

The aggressive behavior of animals is to a large extent genetically preprogrammed; nevertheless, a cue or releaser from the environment is usually required. Different aspects of aggression no doubt evolved as adaptations to specific environmental exigencies. E. O. Wilson finds eight distinct types of aggression from among numerous species in the animal kingdom (1980, pp. 118–119). These are:

1. *Territorial aggression*, which often consists merely of displays or calls to warn an intruder away from one's home ground.
2. *Dominance aggression*, actions taken to maintain one's place in the social hierarchy.
3. *Sexual aggression*, such as the punitive biting of a female baboon that tries to leave a male's harem, or aggression during actual mating.
4. *Parental disciplinary aggression*, such as to deter the young from entering a danger zone.
5. *Weaning aggression*, used when a mother starts to curtail the offspring's dependence.
6. *Moralistic aggression*, a display of anger towards one who fails to reciprocate an altruistic favor (so far recorded only in humans and in one instance among chimpanzees). (See De Waal, 1982, p. 207.)
7. *Predatory aggression*, either interspecific or cannibalistic.
8. *Antipredatory aggression*, which occurs when defensive action turns into an attack.

From this list it is obvious that aggressive responses are discrete and are related to certain stimuli. Aggression is *not* just a quantity of a force that is stored up in the individual looking for an outlet. Nevertheless, for all these categories of aggression, the body makes use of the same basic physiological response. All mammals have the so-called fight-or-flight response that is called up when the individual is exposed to certain stresses in the environment, in relation to both attack and defense. The endocrine and nervous systems set up the reaction. This involves changes in heart rate, blood pressure, blood sugar, release of substances such as adrenalin, and inhibition of digestive and reproductive functions. It is known that hormones, particularly the male hormone testosterone, play an important role in aggression. For example, castrated male birds may lose certain types of their aggressive behavior, but this can be restored by chemical replacement of testosterone (Wilson, 1980, p. 124). In fact an individual animal, either male or female, if given an experimental dose of testosterone, may go on the attack even when the environmental circumstances do not call for it.

It should be noted here that within a given species, not all animals are equally aggressive. This may be due, first, to slight innate differences, such that a particular individual does not have such a ready physiological response. Second, the difference between two animals may be due to learning, that is, based on experience gained in previous aggressive encounters. Third, there could be situational differences — some individuals happen to be exposed to more conflicts than others. To say that aggressiveness is inherited genetically is merely to suggest that a rather wide range of potential aggressive responses is inherited.

In summary, if there *is* a biological background to power-related behavior, the trait of aggression could reasonably be said to be its primary element. The aggressiveness of one animal in a contest with another may give that individual *power* over the other, specifically the power to control the other's share of the resources. As mentioned above, the original ecological circumstance that elicited the evolution of aggressive behavior was competition over scarce resources. (Note: I am not yet discussing the human species.)

Dominance Hierarchies

The word *dominant* (from the Latin *dominare*, meaning "to be lord and master") is defined as "exercising the most influence or control." Dominance hierarchies are an apparently logical result of the existence, in certain species, of aggressive competition among individuals. Ecologically speaking, dominance is an energy-saving phenomenon: a stable hierarchy allows the members to live in peace for considerable periods of time, as compared with "scramble competition" in which each individual has to fight every day.

Dominance orders are common in both mammals and birds. Sometimes position in the hierarchy is a function of age or size. More often, however, the hierarchies are formed by individuals trying to fight their way to the top. After the initial aggression, the members settle into a pattern, a "pecking order," and do not challenge the status quo for a fairly long period of time. In some species, the top animal, called the alpha, has a way of signaling his dominance, for instance by a self-confident way of walking. Subordinate members, too, have ritualized ways of showing submission. In chimpanzees this includes a greeting in which the subordinate animal bends down and looks up into the face of superiors (Wilson, 1980, p. 270). Typically, once rank is established, the lower animals simply "allow" the higher animals to take the best portion of food, perform the most matings, and so forth.

The evolutionary explanation as to why males, rather than females, are especially aggressive involves the concept that females are a "limiting resource." Males must fight one another for the privilege of reproducing. The females can produce only once per season and are thus tied down by pregnancy; males, conversely, can, and often do, sire myriad offspring. This is part of Darwin's theory of sexual selection that I shall not go into here, but for which there is compelling evidence in mammals (Darwin, 1871; Betzig, 1986).

A pertinent item that should be mentioned here in regard to dominance is that primatologists in recent years have made many new findings about leadership in social species of apes (Smuts et al., 1987). These differ significantly from the stereotype of the dominant animal described above. A chimpanzee leader, for instance, may be one who is helpful and acts "responsibly," such as by breaking up fights (De Waal, 1982), or one who is simply well liked. In this chapter's sociobiological search for the human nature of power, however, I concentrate deliberately on the old stereotype because it is this one that is associated with popular themes of "the human instinct for power" — and is the sterotype I am eager to debunk.

To summarize: as a possible natural antecedent to *power*, the set of animal behaviors associated with hierarchies — dominance and submission — must come in for serious consideration. The formation of a hierarchy fixes the relationship of control among individual animals for a period of time.

Coalition-Formation

A third power-related behavior that we can look at in the animal kingdom is coalition-formation. If hierarchies come about as a logical result of aggression, it seems equally true that coalition-formation arises as a logical result of hierarchies.

The forming of alliances to gain power was once assumed to be an exclusively human tactic. But in 1965 it was observed in baboons by Irven DeVore (in Trivers, 1985, p. 368). He found that besides the *linear hierarchy* of dominance in that species, there is another formation, to which he gave the rather confusing name of *central hierarchy*. Here, for example, a group of baboons gets together and by strength of numbers can overwhelm even the alpha male, by chasing him away from the female that he is attempting to mount. This central hierarchy is not ad hoc: it is an enduring group. One of its members eventually replaces the alpha, and the outgoing alpha may then convene a new group to harass his successor.

Robert Trivers reports an instance he witnessed in a baboon troop in Kenya that was under study by DeVore. The alpha baboon, named Arthur, had just been harrassed by a central hierarchy that included a young male named Rad. After the episode Arthur sent a double-message signal to Rad. "While displaying his canines at Rad (a hostile gesture), Arthur also turned his rear end toward Rad (a gesture of subordination) . . . this threat seemed to say, 'You do this again, and I am going to eat you alive,' while the affiliative gesture seemed to say, 'There is potential for a new hierarchy in [this] group, and if you play your cards right, there could be a special place in it for you.' " Trivers claims that the message could not have been clearer if Arthur had said it in English (Trivers, 1985, p. 370).

Frans De Waal's book *Chimpanzee Politics,* based on intensive long-term observation of one troop of captive chimpanzees (in a seminatural environment), reports many examples of coalition-formation and related behaviors. De Waal claims: "The apes, when carefully studied, reveal themselves to be adept at subtle political manoeuvre. Their social life is full of takeovers, dominance networks, power struggles, alliances, divide-and-rule strategies, coalitions, arbitration, collective leadership, privileges and bargaining. There is hardly anything that occurs in the corridors of power of the human world that cannot found in embryo in the social life of a chimpanzee colony" (1982, p. 14).

It is not clear how much of the behavior of coalition-formation is based on insight and conscious calculation. *Calculated* can mean an action that includes a rational estimate of future consequences, without necessarily being consciously calculated. De Waal points out that even a cat stalking a bird must calculate its pounce: young cats do poorly at estimating, but they improve with experience (p. 28). Perhaps the chimpanzees have some innate tendency for political maneuver but require experience to gain competence at it. This area of study is, unfortunately, only at the speculative stage.

In summary, then, coalition-formation is yet another behavior found in the animal kingdom that may be useful to consider as an antecedent of power.

Manifestations of These Three Traits in Humans

Having sketched the animal evidence of aggression, dominance hierarchies, and coalition-formation, let us now see if there are corresponding behavior patterns in our own species. I acknowledge that if a particular human behavior is found to have a very similar counterpart in animal behavior, this does not prove evolutionary inheritance. Any human trait may be culturally invented rather than innate. Still, it is useful to consider the similarities.

In comparing human with animal behavior, sociobiologists rely on analogy and homology. In cases of *analogy*, one hypothesizes that the human species independently evolved a trait similar to that of another species because they both faced similar environmental exigencies. Thus, for example, humans and dogs share certain behavioral features because they both occupy the ecological niche of group hunter, or social predator. In cases of *homology*, one hypothesizes either that humans share traits with species that are phylogenetically closely related, such as the chimpanzee, or that humans have traits that are very widespread throughout the mammalian class. In the discussion below, the presumptions about the innateness of aggression in humans will be based mainly on homology. Aggression is characteristic of many mammal species, and humans are certainly mammals.

Aggression in Humans

Are humans aggressive? Clearly, there is overwhelming evidence for the manifestation of aggression in our species, from the bullying that occurs on children's playgrounds to the dropping of thousands of tons of TNT onto cities during warfare. That is not to say that all humans are aggressive all the time. In fact, it is noteworthy that we rank rather low on the scale compared to many other species — certainly we are less aggressive than chimpanzees if one merely counts the number of physically violent encounters per hour of social contact per individual. There is also much individual variation. As with animals, this variation may be innate, learned, or situational. Moreover, there is variation in aggressiveness among entire human groups. Conceivably, that variation could be due to a real difference in the gene pools of separate populations. But more likely each person learns his style or degree of aggression from the customs of the group. Pugnacity and gentleness have been cultural themes imposed on whole nations in history — they seem to be arrived at almost as a matter of taste. Undoubtedly, ecological circumstance is influential here as well: plentiful resources could make the society more likely to emphasize nonaggressive behavior.

Is it worthwhile to compare the *occasions* of aggression as shown in humans and animals? Yes. Using Wilson's eight categories, it can be seen that humans meet the full range of types of aggression as do other animals: territorial and dominance aggression; sexual, parental-disciplinary, and weaning aggression; moralistic aggression; and predatory and defensive aggression. Thus there are similarities between aggression in other animals and humans that could be based on a shared evolutionary history. Moreover, an act of aggression by a human involves the same physiology as that of other animals.

The actual *expressions* of aggression, though, are often different for humans, owing to culture and language. For instance, the degree of violence can be greater, thanks to material technology: guns and knives are more destructive than fangs or claws. Humans can consciously reflect on how pain is best caused and thus develop forms of extreme torture, including purely psychological torture. Also, language itself augments aggression since it includes bluff, threat, and intricate modes of deception. (It is worth recalling that Machiavelli virtually equated fraud with force as a method of gaining power.) Furthermore, humans may be *motivated* to use more aggression than other animals since the organization of human society provides greater *rewards* to the successful aggressor. The most a chimpanzee can covet or steal from another is a few bananas, hardly worth a fight to the death. A human, by contrast, may stand to gain enormous wealth by beating his rivals.

Warfare is the best example of organized aggression in the human species, but note that I must omit from the present study warfare and also the type of aggression labeled *communal violence* (such as race rioting). These are not comparable to the types of individual aggression discussed as three clues in the animal kingdom, which showed the relations of power *within* a group. War has rather to do with the members pooling their aggressive strength to fight outsiders. There possibly are "clues" for human warfare in the animal kingdom. Predictably, organized fighting is engaged in by highly social species such as ants, and Jane Goodall (1986) has even recorded warlike activity between two troops of chimpanzees. But this is tangential to our quest for the human power-behavior of individuals. (See Shaw and Wong, 1989 for a discussion of the innate human tendency to make war; see also Maxwell, 1991, ch. 13).

To sum up, aggression is present in the human species as in most mammal species and to some extent accounts for the differential power of individuals.

Dominance Hierarchies in Humans

Do humans have dominance hierarchies? Well, they certainly have hierarchies of some sort. People constantly rank themselves and others according to criteria such as age, strength, intelligence, size, beauty, wealth, and personality. As for dominance hierarchies, in which one individual exerts control over those beneath him or her, these too are very common among humans. They may take place in very small-scale settings, as when one sibling pushes another around, or in a larger group where, say, a factory owner lords it over his employees.

However, before we fall into the trap of saying that humans resemble other animal species in regard to their dominance hierarchies, we must note four important complications. First, in human societies — other than the most primitive ones — the hierarchy often exists in an institutionalized way; newcomers can move into various positions on it by various means, some of which do not involve aggression. For example, in a modern army a university graduate may be given a lieutenant's commission upon enlistment. Another soldier may buy his way into captain status through family influence. A major may get "kicked upstairs" to colonel rank because of some bureaucratic problem. The resulting structure will contain persons who exhibit the proper official relationship of dominance toward one another (the colonel bosses the captain, the captain bosses the lieutenant, and so on), yet they never had to fight their way into those slots by hand-to-hand combat with one another. Indeed, they need not have been judged in comparison with one another on any basis at all.

A second complicating factor is that, owing to the multiplicity of roles in human society, a person may rank high in one hierarchy and low in another. One may be a junior clerk in the office but a respected leader in the church, say, or high in sports but low in some other role. A person may exhibit an aggressive "drive for power" in one area of life but appear meek in another. This certainly does not resemble the typical mammalian arrangement in which the sole alpha is leader in all activities.

A third problem has to do with the fact that human groups do not consist merely of agglomerations of individuals who compete with one another, as is the case in many animal groups. Rather, they form cohesive societies. They cooperate and obey laws and seek collective goals. Their members often suppress their individual aggression on behalf of the group. This is a trait that may have been brought about by the exigencies of fighting off an outside group (Bigelow, 1969; Alexander, 1979). Use of social rules to reduce interpersonal competition could also be a response to the demands of coping with a harsh ecological setting. For instance, it has been noted by anthropologists that Eskimos have an exceptionally cooperative and non-aggressive way of life (Balikci, 1970). (Of course, the mediator of this way of life is the *culture*, the belief system, which instructs individuals on the value of pooled labor and shared food, but the stark necessity of pooling labor and sharing food — the ecological situation — is undoubtedly what first shaped that culture's beliefs.) Examples such as the Eskimo pose a problem for anyone who wants to insist that human nature *must* lead to the formation of dominance hierarchies.

A fourth problem is simply that of inheritance of social rank in human societies. Consider the system of feudalism that covered large areas of the world for long periods of time. For the most part, a person born into the peasantry was destined to remain there; a person born into the nobility was destined to remain there. So one cannot say that the feudal system was based on the human nature of its later-generation members (though of course one might argue that it was based on the human nature of its founders). There is a possible parallel to this in other animals. In at least one species of monkey, the Japanese macaque, social rank is "inherited" through the maternal line. That is, the offspring are treated as though they hold the same hierarchical position as the mother (Wilson, 1980, p. 144).

The above four items complicate the comparison of human and animal hierarchies. Yet a popular belief persists that human political hierarchies *are* a direct reflection of our innate drives. I believe this impression may be based on the fact that humans have a very obvious penchant for rank-formation — a penchant that may well be a legacy of our mammalian past. I propose that what we have inherited from early species may be a sort of package of psychological predispositions related to dominance and submission. That is, humans may inherit a trait for "fitting into a rank" as such. As noted above in the discussion of animal hierarchies, there are frequent aggressive challenges among individuals, but there are also behaviors of which the main purpose seems to be status advertisement. There is a complex of behavior that can be called submissive and a complex called dominant. (No doubt every creature would have to be born with potential equipment for both, because there is no way of knowing what rank it will eventually occupy.)

To summarize the discussion: dominance hierarchies appear frequently in the human species, and these often facilitate the exercise of power by one individual over another. Humans probably have an evolved psychological predisposition for dominant and submissive behaviors and thus find hierarchies comfortable. The formation of those hierarchies, however, is often very different from the simple model in which individuals fight to establish a pecking order.

Coalition-Formation in Humans

And now to the third animal clue concerning the human nature of power: coalition-formation. Do humans practice this trait? Certainly, coalitions are rife in human society, occurring within families, small groups, and political parties and even featuring in geopolitical strategy — such as when the United States "plays the China card" against the USSR. Coalitions of power seem to be the answer to existing hierarchies of power. The discovery by the comparatively weak members of a group that they, when united, have power over their leaders has been important in human history. For example, on the long road that led to English democracy, the events at Runnymede in A.D. 1215 were pivotal. There, the barons saw the vulnerability of the king to their combined power and forced him to sign the Magna Carta. Later, the parliament realized that it could withhold revenue as a way of enhancing its own sovereignty.

The breakup of centralized power has usually been carried out by such limited coalitions as these barons or parliamentarians, perhaps in a manner similar to that of the central hierarchy noted in baboons. This has been true even in Marxist revolutions: it is a vanguard that leads, rather than the entire lower echelon rising up to overwhelm the few rulers at the top. Theoretically, more populous coalitions could be formed, but this seldom occurs. Mutinies, rebellions, and uprisings are relatively rare. The names of a few spring to mind: the Nat Turner revolt of the slaves in Virginia in 1831, the mutiny of Indian soldiers under British command in 1857 or of British sailors subjected to brutal discipline in 1797, the Boxer Rebellion in 1900 directed against foreign domination in China, the Warsaw ghetto uprising against the Nazis in 1943, and so forth.

Most underdogs apparently do not recognize that they have strength in numbers. In ancient Rome, Seneca reported, the Senate voted against a plan to have the million-and-a-half slaves wear special costumes, lest they discover their own numerical strength (Heilbroner, 1962, p. 35). The most important modern cases of broad-based coalitions are trade unions, political parties, and economic boycotts, in which a large group of powerless individuals combine their strength to win on a particular issue.

These are modern phenomena, dependent upon a certain level of education or availability of mass communication.

The summary to this discussion is that humans, like some other primates, form coalitions as a means of upsetting the existing hierarchy of power. The power of numbers can overwhelm even the most formidable ruler, yet the insight into this often takes a long time to arrive at, even by humans: an oppressed majority seldom combines to overcome a tyrant.

Conclusion to Part One

From the foregoing brief sociobiological search for the human nature of power, we can conclude that there are some resemblances between power-related behavior in animals and humans and other animals. The basic animal model is as follows: scarcity of desired resources leads to competition; competition elicits the evolution of aggressive behavior; the differential success of individuals in their aggressive encounters results in the shape of a hierarchy or pecking order; in conjunction with this there is the evolution of various dominant and submissive behaviors.

Humans fit into this model quite well with respect to their simpler power struggles. Human individuals *do* sometimes fight their way into a pecking order. However, it is my contention that the resemblance of larger human power structures to animal dominance hierarchies is superficial and misleading. Above, I listed four ways in which human hierarchies differ from the hierarchies of other animals and refute simple comparisons. These are the ability of an individual to move into high ranks without displaying aggression, the occupation of both high and low roles by one individual, the frequent suppression of aggression for the collective goals of the group, and the inheritance of rank by offspring, especially through social class. I shall argue later that the complex political organizations of humans did not come about (or at least did not *necessarily* come about) through interpersonal aggression and that the animal model does not furnish the essential clue to modern human power.

Part Two: The Institutionalization of Power

It will be the thesis of Part Two that human power behavior is more dependent upon institutionalized roles than upon our instinctive makeup. It is because there are power roles into which individuals may step — particularly in the state — that humans occasionally behave in a spectacularly aggressive way. The structured hierarchies of human society have come about, I propose, not for dominion as such but for cybernetic reasons — for the necessary coordination and centralized control of a complex organization. (The word *cybernetics* comes from the Greek *kubernan*, meaning "to steer, guide, or govern.")

The law of nature that we might look to here is not the law of competition over scarce resources — although that may help to *motivate* the rise of the state — but rather a law concerning the evolution of intelligence. Hundreds of millions of years ago, when the bodies of primitive animals were evolving, a specialization of role or function began to develop, for instance, muscle for locomotion and skin for sensation. These demanded a mechanism of coordination. Nerves supplied the mode of communication, and the nerves' nexus of association, the ganglion, evolved as the protobrain, which became the mode of control. The ganglia of jellyfish and earthworms are early examples.

Human society, over thousands of years, has also proceeded from the simple to the complex, with roles and functions becoming specialized. It has developed characteristics of communication and control not unlike those of the brain itself. The political formation of the state, in its early phase, can be looked upon as a ganglion, a controlling network with an identifiable center. As such it required a hierarchy of control. Let me now offer an ever-so-brief sketch of four stages of human prehistory and history, in which the institutionalization of hierarchical roles of power will be traced. The four stages are those of the hunter-gatherer, the village chiefdom, the early state (kingship), and the modern era.

The Hunter-Gatherer Stage

From the time of the emergence of the modern human, about forty thousand years ago, up to the Neolithic Age, which began ten thousand years ago, the human population consisted of small, isolated bands of hunter-gatherers. Needless to say, no record of their political behavior has been left, but it is reasonable to assume that they did not have a highly structured system. They did not need one for their simple activities.

Looking at contemporary hunter-gatherer societies for evidence of that early way of life is not necessarily reliable but does give some hint of at least the possibility of an egalitarian social organization. Referring to the twentieth-century Bambuti people of Africa, Pierre van den Berghe notes, "They have no chiefs, no slaves, no policemen, no courts, no prisons, no taxes, and no institutionalized rank differences between adult men, other than individual prestige achieved by age and personal qualities" (1981, p. 49). The Bambuti live in loosely structured bands whose compostion frequently shifts.

The very geographical mobility and lack of production of any durable wealth by hunter-gatherers meant that individual members could coordinate their social activities without any structured leadership. Tatu Vanhanen, surveying anthropological literature, found that "the headman, who provides . . . leadership, is dependent on the consent of the members of the group for his actions. He does not usually have much power or many privileges and he has hardly any means of imposing his will on others. . . . Headmanship is not especially desired in those societies, for headmen are as thin as the rest. They have considerable responsibility without any specific rewards" (1984, p. 25).

This hunter-gatherer stage of human social organization, it may be noted, persisted for millennia, in spite of the human instinct for aggression.

Village Chiefdoms

The next stage of political organization, which is more complex than that of hunter-gatherer society but still far less complex than that of kingship or the early state, is that of the village chiefdom. The technological level of society at which the village chiefdom is typically found is that of horticulture, that is, hoe-gardening (as opposed to agriculture, which begins when fields are plowed). Once people settle into villages, some inequalities of power start to appear. In some places the leadership consists of a group of headmen or elders who make decisions on an ad hoc basis; in other societies the leadership may go to warriors or priests; and eventually there may emerge a village chief.

In regard to the rise of a particular individual to the role of village chief, van den Berghe has noted that it may come about through some combination of luck, skill, charisma, or manipulation of the religious function (1981, p. 64). An almost invariant feature, he says, is polygamy. "This occurs long before marked differences in lifestyle, diet, dress, consumption, housing, and so on between ruler and ruled. Even in small-scale societies where the chief lives much like everyone else, he already has more wives" (1981, p. 65). One reason polygamy may have come about is that it was the only type of differential reward available. No luxury goods had been invented, since metals were not yet discovered: even food could not be accumulated because there was little ability to preserve it. The taking on of extra wives was the main way to show one's wealth. But this then *caused* an increase in power. With more wives, brothers-in-law, and associated kin, the chief is automatically stronger than the other males. Such an arrangement, van den Berghe notes, may be the prototype of a "royal family" (1981, p. 65).

At the village chiefdom stage it is proper to speak of there being an *office* of chief. When the incumbent dies, the "chieftainship" will go to someone else. Gerard Lenski points out that there are some peripheral offices as well. In New Guinea, Big Men occupy *positions* of wealth, and among the Iroquois there are *roles* for men skilled in oratory (1966, pp. 127–130). Where military prowess is important, brave warriors may be honored in certain ceremonies, and they may develop warrior societies to consolidate their status. Lenski observes that even as early as the horticultural level of society, positions of inequality become established in a predictable recurring way, that is, they become institutionalized. These positions may include a title and a defined set of responsibilities and privileges. "This development is extremely important since it complicates the relationship between the personal attributes of an individual and his status. . . . Now it becomes possible for an individual to enjoy a reward to which his personal attributes alone would not entitle him" (Lenski, 1966, p. 131).

This institutionalization of prestigious roles is critical to my thesis, but at the village chiefdom level institutionalization does not signify any great need for command or control of society. Rather, I think such routinization of role is merely typical of the way humans inexorably reify their cultural traditions. Once established, a role takes on a reality of its own and becomes a predictable entity in the environment. I would grant, however, that the emergence of formal ranking — even where it is related only to honor and prestige rather than to control of property — could arise from our mammalian background. I am referring to the psychological predispositions for dominance and submissive behavior: these alone may be sufficient to induce the cultural forms to come about.

The Early State

It is with the arrival of despotic kingships that the early state, and the beginning of a command center, can be discerned. This often takes place in advanced horticultural societies, which are distinguished from earlier ones by their metal tools, diversity of crops, irrigation, and much larger population. Here, the leader has a sufficient group of supporters to enable a wider and more vigorous control of society, as in the Incas and many precolonial states of sub-Saharan Africa. In such despotisms, tax collection is a major feature, as is the sudden great separation of the leader — now considered a king — from the common people (Lenski, 1966, pp. 151–157). In Dahomey, according to Herskovits, even the highest ministers of the state had literally to grovel in the dirt when in the king's presence (1938, vol. 1, p. 33). These ministers in turn, when *they* ruled their provinces, expected their subjects to kiss the ground before them. At this stage the king also has even greater access to women — he may have hundreds of wives — and executive power of life and death over his subjects (Lenski, 1966, pp. 154–155; see also Betzig, 1986).

Early kingships, wherever they occur, show a standard cluster of features. George Murdock, in his survey of African despotisms, found that many of them had the following features: divine kingship; eminent domain; insignia of office; royal courts consisting of pages, guards, entertainers, chamberlains, and so on; territorial bureaucracy for collecting taxes, military service, and corvee labor; and "security provisions" such as having the king's brothers blinded or killed to avoid palace revolutions (1959, pp. 32–39). In other words, *rule at the kingly level*, the early state, *compels certain general forms of organization*, although the specific style may be localized.

Despotism, in the sense of arbitrary personal tyranny, is not a necessary feature of kingship: benevolent rule occurs also. However, I have chosen the example of despotic kingship to show that even where there is obvious aggression and apparent "will to power" on the part of the king, it is the *situation* that first demands a concentration of power. The state may, roughly, be said to have arrived when the king rules over a territory larger than that which can be controlled by his relatives. He thus has to appoint nonkin to act as his tax collectors and intermediaries with the people in the hinterland. As K. Oberg notes, the king must therefore give these provincial rulers some rewards, such as the privilege of doubling the tax so they can pocket the difference (cited in Lenski, 1966, p. 176). He must also provide them with a vested interest in his kingdom so that they will support him rather than rival him. In this process, the officials of the state themselves become a ruling class whose interests are selfish, that is, not in harmony with those of the populace.

The point I am driving at is that for a large and complex society to exist, there must be a structure of command and control. It is tempting to view the formation of the state as the expression of human selfishness, avarice, power lust, and so forth and thus to equate political structures with the inevitable low side of human nature. I believe, by contrast, that the low side of human nature is incidental here or at least is theoretically dispensable; the state could exist without it.

The major objection to my view is, I suppose, that the *motive* to form the large state was selfishness, avarice, and power lust. In other words, it is one thing to say that a large state requires a hierarchical structure and another thing to say why one has to advance to a larger state at all. The kings mentioned earlier who "had to" increase their bureaucracy to cover a larger territory could simply have settled for a smaller territory, couldn't they? I cannot deny the likelihood that in many cases it was a characteristic of the individual's personality, rather than the demands of the situation, that led to conquest.

Still, it is worth noting that leaders are often forced to increase their area of control, or lose it altogether. Robert Carneiro's theory of the origin of the state is built on this premise. He holds that the state arose as a result of warfare fought over scarce land (1970, p. 735). Carneiro has shown how, historically, all the arable land in coastal Peru became used up, and the villages had to fight neighboring villages for this scarce resource. The winning village would incorporate the losing one, thus gaining control over those people. Then, having a larger territory to administer, the winning village became more politically organized. But eventually these larger units had to fight other large units, again over land. Through this procedure an entire valley might be unified under its strongest chief. The final two steps were "the formation of multivalley kingdoms through the conquest of weaker valleys by stronger ones . . . and the formation of a single great empire . . . by the Incas" (1970, p. 736).

Not all states arose because of external hostilities, however, so Carneiro's theory does not entirely solve the question. Many other possible explanations for the emergence of the state have to do with technology, trade, military factors, demography, or ecology. For the purpose of my cybernetic theory of the state it does not matter what the particular cause was. Ronald Cohen compared the contending theories of the rise of the state — those based on revenue collection, trade, military service, law, and a generally increased use of communication. He concluded that "to search for specific causes among these developments is in my view a fruitless, even a spurious question. . . . Each of these features [such as trade, technology, military competition, demography] and many more enable the other to emerge and to select from among all possible solutions the centrally organized structure of the state" (1978, p. 37). He argues that no matter how or where the state starts, functional requirements *will force the development of* certain features, and thus "early states are self-limiting in their variance" (1978, p. 37). I agree with Cohen. It is my contention that the state did not come about because of *human nature*, as such, but because of the *functional requirements* of coordinating a large society.

The Modern Era

The modern state has an even greater concentration of power — that is, control over people — than the early state, and decision-making can be very centralized. Even in the ancient period, there was coordination from the top for large systems of public works, military defense, and administration. Modern technology makes it possible for the state to reach into private lives, to supplant civil organizations, to control the media, to forbid religious worship — in short, to be totalitarian.

In the modern era economic structures, too, are more complex and centralized. Before the Industrial Revolution, which began in England around A.D. 1750, the typical human being lived in a self-contained community that produced not only its own food but most other goods as well. After that time, persons in industrializing nations became atomized: they migrated to a city, sold their labor, and bought mass-produced goods. In the nineteenth century, new modes of transport such as the railway allowed a more complicated network of exchange of goods and people. So, just as the command and control center had become necessary in the early state, industries, too, developed the cybernetic wherewithal to coordinate both labor and the market. Concentration of economic power seems, to me, to be inevitable. The merging of businesses was already underway by 1880 in the United States. Robert Heilbroner reports that by 1904, three hundred giants controlled over 40 percent of the nation's industrial capital (1962, p. 115). Six decades later, about half of the corporate wealth of the United States was owned by one hundred firms (1962, pp. 122–123). (It may be noted here that today mergers do not occur simply to rationalize the market, such as by combining similar industries. The *raison d'être* of the megacorporation is to take better advantage of tax laws and accounting procedures and to manipulate the market for the financial advantage of certain parties.)

It is my belief that these internal logics of the system lessen the plausibility of any argument that postulates a simple relationship between human aggression — or greed — and modern political and economic structures. I have no desire to downplay the significance of either aggression or greed in human life;

their significance is manifestly great. But in relation to explaining the hierarchies of power in human society, I think it is important to clear away any extraneous factors and reveal the bare workings of what I call cybernetics. Because of cybernetics, organizations will become hierarchical: this in turn helps them grow in scope and in power.

Conclusion to Part Two

Centralized command and control of a system appears to be something that will develop *irrespective* of certain characteristics of human personality. I acknowledge that it is tempting to see modern political and economic power structures as the institutional expression of power-hunger, aggression, and greed. I acknowledge that it is tempting, also, to think of the example of animal dominance hierarchies as instructive in regard to human politics. But I think we should make the effort to set aside those tempting ideas at least long enough to look at a competing explanation. My own explanation has consisted of noting that there has been, throughout human history, a progression of political structures from the simple to the complex and that these follow a cybernetic imperative: the coordination of a large society requires command and control.

The Ethical Significance of the Cybernetic Theory

Earlier in this chapter I noted that political scientists and philosophers have sometimes linked coercion to human nature. Human beings, they say, have a drive for domination or a will to power. I have used a combination of sociobiological or ethological research and a brief sketch of the origin of state power to demonstrate that the direct link often made between the human individual's aggressive impulse and the development of powerful political structures is false. Now let me speculate on the ethical implications that follow from the finding that this link is false.

My model of the cybernetic theory of the origin of state power is value neutral. It dissociates the fact of power from our normative evaluations about politics. Three implications for political philosophy and ethics that I see here are as follows. First, the value-neutral view is generally less fatalistic than other views of power, so human agency and responsibility find more room here to operate. If power is neither a disembodied force nor an inevitable manifestation of man's evil nature, then perhaps it is something susceptible of human modification.

Second, in a value-free model of power it is easier to make distinctions between the requirements of political institutions and the rightness or wrongness of certain human relationships. Thus, I portrayed the cybernetic requirements of coordination as being intrinsic to any large society, but left aside the evaluation of whether certain arrangements, such as uneven distribution of wealth or decision-making, are just.

Third, the value-neutral view of power, or more specifically the particular evolutionary model that I developed in this chapter, has implications for the question of *the right of rulers to rule.* Since the seventeenth century, that question has been the central issue of political philosophy in the West. Different ethical replies have been provided in answer to it. One such reply is that no-one has the right to rule; it is wrong for people to be governed — hence, anarchy is the preferred system. A second answer to the question of the right to rule is that only the dispossessed have that right — hence, the recommendation for revolution by "the people." A third answer — the conservative one — is that those who have established and maintained the system have perforce demonstrated that they are the best and hence most deserving rulers.

None of those three answers to the problem of the right of rulers to rule would arise from my model. The anarchist answer is seen as ridiculous since the law of cybernetics demands a system of command and control. The communist recommendation for a takeover by the dispossessed is also seen as meaningless since it does not matter which individuals occupy the postions. (Other factors may matter, such as constitutional checks on power or the ability of the public to make demands on their leaders, but substituting persons from a different background would not change the exercise of power.) The conservative ethical answer is likewise thrown out since the cybernetic model challenges the belief that the aristocrats — or anyone — consciously invented the government; a "law of nature" invented it.

So, then, does my model of institutionalized power suggest any particular ethics? No, but by attempting to be value neutral about power (particularly by attempting to deanimate or demystify power) this model allows one better to criticize *particular* political systems. I believe it makes it possible for the observer to concentrate more on the ethical question of all politics: *Cui bono?*

CHAPTER 12

The Genetics of Racism

✳ ✳ ✳

Racism. Ethnocentrism. "Preferring one's own." Fearing (or outrightly hating) the out-group. Are these ubiquitous human traits based on some sort of law of nature? Is there a biological explanation for the ethnic phenomenon? Pierre van den Berghe thinks so. In his startling book, *The Ethnic Phenomenon*, he sets out to explain why "in every age since the recorded history of states, nationalism has inspired masses of people to veritable orgies of emotion and violence" (p. 62) and why "nationalist conflicts are among the most intractable and unamenable to reason and compromise" (p. 62). He investigates the so-called voice of the blood that gives rise to massacres and mutilations, even in the contemporary stage of civilization. Could there, he asks, be something more than immediate political provocation to explain the violence that has occurred recently in such widely dispersed places as Sri Lanka, Lebanon, Ethiopia, El Salvador, and Northern Ireland?

Why do people tolerate exploitation, often without a whimper, when the ruler is a member of their own ethnic group, but unify passionately against domination by outsiders? "On the face of it," van den Berghe says, "it should make little difference whether one is fleeced by people who speak one's own language or a foreign tongue. Yet it clearly [often makes] the difference between passive, reluctant acquiescence and sometimes suicidal rebellion" (p. 62). The short, sociobiological explanation, according to van den Berghe, is that ethnic and racial sentiments are an extension of feelings for one's kin. Such "nepotism" is genetically programmed: it is found in all those species of animal that happen to have a social structure, including humans.

Review of Pierre van den Berghe, *The Ethnic Phenomenon* (Westport, Conn.: Greenwood Press, 1981).

Consider ants and chimpanzees — two highly social species. Each anthill is a complete closed society; each troop of
chimpanzees keeps to itself. Why is it that the members of each
society live peacefully and cooperatively among themselves,
whereas their encounters with other members of the same
species are either indifferent or openly hostile? It is simply
because society depends by definition on cooperation. The altruistic acts that hold the members together are biologically
guided behaviors that evolved via kin selection rather than
natural selection. (See Chapter 5 for an introduction to the
sociobiological theory of altruism.) Individuals can counteract
the Darwinian dictum of selfishness-for-survival if by altruism
they would instead help the survival of relatives. An animal
"shouldn't" risk danger in getting food for the young — because
other, more selfish individuals would have a better rate of
survival. But the family of these unselfish ones has a better rate
of survival, so this trait of altruism is passed down through
genetic inheritance. Kin altruism works for relatives more dis-
tant than offspring, and in fact some social behaviors — such
as defense of a chimpanzee troop — are carried out by adult
male members on behalf of the whole society. This makes sense
because a troop, like an anthill, is basically just an extended
kin group. All the animal need have an instinct for is nepotism.
The mechanism for this may be by a familiar odor or by visual
recognition of individuals.

In humans, the original instinct for recognizing one's fellow
group members would have been personal knowledge of the
whole tribe or use of telltale markers such as costume, facial
scarification, or language dialect. Van den Berghe points out
that even today ethnic groups identify each other by behavioral
customs and by accent. He recounts a macabre incident from
Belgian history: "The Flemings wanted to kill the French army
of occupation in their beds without raising the alarm, so the
problem was how to identify Frenchmen quickly and reliably, in
the dark, in order to slaughter them without fuss. The solution
was to make them repeat a short Flemish phrase 'schilde en de
vriend' . . . that contained phonemes unpronounceable to native speakers of French. History books tell us that the strategem
was devastatingly successful" (p. 34).

Interestingly, van den Berghe believes that although ethnocentrism evolved biologically, by an extension of kin sentiment,

racism did not. The ability to recognize (and hate) outsiders based on sharp differences in appearance did not evolve, as such, for the simple reason that in evolutionary time no group was contiguous to another group that looked very different from itself; intercontinental exchanges of people began only in the colonial era. "Nor am I [saying] that we have an instinctive propensity to stick to people who look like us. Rather, to the extent that we do so, we are 'race conscious' only as a test of common ancestry. The genetic propensity is to favor kin, not to favor those who look like us" (p. 240).

What, then, do we do with this analysis? Sit back and say "ho hum" (or perhaps "three cheers for the voice of the blood")? No. This is where van den Berghe clearly shows that sociobiologists are no purveyors of social Darwinism. He describes the genetics of racism as an "anti-ethic," as it were, and remarks that "the fundamental ethical problem of the industrial age is to find a solution to the tragedy of the commons. Unless we stop behaving naturally — that is, being our selfish, nepotistic, ethnocentric selves — we court collective extinction" (p. xii).

Let me not give the impression, though, that this is a book of platitudes. The author states that "we must know the nature of the beast in us in order to vanquish it" (p. xii), and his way of knowing the beast consists of amalgamating sociobiological research with historical, particularly Marxist, analysis of social structure. Ultimately, he says, ethnic (and race) relations consist of competition for scarce resources. He continues with the animal analogy to sharpen the focus on stratification in human society. Other animals have dominance hierarchies or pecking orders and crude competition among their societies, but humans have more. We have hierarchical *groups* within our societies, that is, social classes, and hierarchies of whole nations over others. In the last analysis, van den Berghe says, "what defines the hierarchy of a group is an order of access to resources" (p. 59), and "there is no hierarchy without underlying coercion" (p. 59). Moreover, "the human capacity for conscious deceit (through ideology, *inter alia*) enhances our species' capacity for group inequality" (p. 160). Socially oppressed groups, he believes, owe their inferior position to technological and/or organizational inferiority in using the means of violence. "Centralized states are almost invariably bolstered by an ideology that disguises the parasitism of the ruling class . . ." (p. 160).

Here again is the difference between foreign domination and that of hierarchical control within a homogenous group: the former rests on naked coercion and is visible and resented; the latter is disguised by social myth — including the myth that people have "contracted" for their role in the division of labor or the myth of paternal benevolence. Van den Berghe states dryly, "The essence of the state is parasitism. . . . No state, whether pre-capitalist, capitalist, or socialist, is a real democracy, however much it may claim that label" (p. 79). He goes further with his dual weapons of sociobiology and Marxism to produce a brilliant comparative history of ethnic relations. His shocking chapters on colonialism, slavery, and assimilationism are not to be missed by anyone seriously concerned with the problem of race. (This part of his book has recently been expanded upon in his edited volume, *State Violence and Ethnicity*, 1990).

Here is a sample of van den Berghe's analysis of one type of ethnic group that he calls "middlemen minorities," who "in the catalogue of human bestiality to man . . . almost invariably appear as victims: Jews in Europe, Armenians in Turkey, Indians in Uganda, the boat people of Vietnam (who are mostly ethnic Chinese), and so forth" (p. 140). What do these people have in common that makes them so vulnerable to literally inhuman treatment? Van den Berghe notes several features of the niche they occupy: middlemen minorities are voluntary immigrants who constitute a tiny minority in the host country where they specialize in the selling of goods or skills. They have strong, authoritarian, extended families; tend to intermarry; and are culturally enclosed in their own ghettos, artisan guilds, religions, and so on. Thus they are slow to assimilate into the host society. They appear as an urban petty bourgeoisie, appreciably better off than the masses but not wealthy like the rulers; they are usually thrifty, hard working, and unostentatious.

Though these middlemen minorities energize the economy and contribute many skills, they are the subject of much hostility both from above and below. Their wealth (known as "weak money") cannot be translated into political power, and often they are subject to special legal discrimination in immigration, officeholding, taxation, and trade. Because of their minority status and their cultural marginality, they are completely vulnerable to attack. Being defined as alien, and therefore not under the protection of the wider ethnic nepotism, they "are often exterminated without a whisper of protest in the general population." A middleman minority can do no right, says van den Berghe. "If it retreats into the protective cocoon of ethnic isolation, it is accused of clannishness. . . . If it attempts to demonstrate its loyalty to the state [as when Indians in Kenya supported black rule], that behavior is ascribed to opportunism. . . . What is good management, fair profit, initiative and free enterprise in the native capitalist becomes greed, usury, unfair competition [etc.] in the pariah capitalist" (p. 140). Moreover, the hostility surrounding them makes middlemen minorities ideal scapegoats for anything that goes wrong. Jews in medieval Europe were accused of poisoning the wells; to the Nazis, the Jews were involved in a worldwide conspiracy that was at once Bolshevik and capitalist. Where such a minority can be implicated, "prejudices are so blinding that no amount of absurdity detracts from credibility" (p. 141).

Van den Berghe tries to show how the social structure of both the host society and the minority and the filling of a particular economic niche lead to an interaction that creates the "typical" middleman minority behavior. This behavior in turn reinforces stereotypes and heightens hostility, "and an almost inescapable vicious circle of ethnic relations ensues." All the behaviors of the minority are shown to be normal human behaviors but narrowed into a particular range of self-defensive reactions. When such broad comparisons as these are made, showing how very diverse cultural groups come finally to act in a very similar way as middleman minorities, then we are at least somewhere on the road to understanding the structural background of some of the monstrous victimizations, sudden expulsions, and even genocides that have taken place in our time. The instinct for nepotism is an irrational force that must be rationally reckoned with. I will quote van den Berghe on the method of human sociobiology: "It seeks to explain behavior in the broadest possible terms, which means at least in pan-human terms, and quite often at an even broader (cross-species) level. Thus sociobiology, through its reductionist strategy of seeking explanations for behavior at the most general level, is the very antithesis of racism or ethnism."

I should not end this review essay without confronting two major misinterpretations that are often made when the word *racism* is uttered in the same breath as the word *sociobiology.*

The first of these has to do with claims that sociobiologists encourage racism or racial discrimination by emphasizing the heritability of traits. True, sociobiology does emphasize the heritability of traits. It is eager to show that social behaviors — whether in humans or other animals — are genetically guided. This in itself has caused many social scientists in the United States to react against sociobiology, mainly by putting a taboo on its study. That is, they prejudge the case, assuming, without knowing what sociobiology actually says, that it must make distinctions between racial groups — or perhaps social classes. They seem to think that sociobiology might say, "You are what you are because of your ethnic ancestry." But in fact sociobiology says, "You are what you are because of your *species* ancestry."

Regional differences in some traits are perhaps culturally induced. Gait, for example, may seem to be a strictly physical characteristic, but humans in different localities may walk differently according to custom, that is, by learning or imitation. Or, they may walk differently according to genetic differences. *Are* there genetic differences among humans? Yes, of course there are, even among children born in the same family. Such genetic differences affect both anatomical and behavioral traits. Are there genetic differences that correlate with different groups or gene pools? Certainly there are. Different populations are known to have different blood groups, different patterns of inherited diseases, different average body size, and so forth. Could these population differences include behavioral traits as well as physical characteristics? Certainly, why not?

Daniel Freedman has studied the differences in activity of infants of different populations a few hours or days after birth. He notes that Chinese babies are more active than Navajo babies (Freedman, 1979, pp. 144–153). Studies of newborns are the least controversial for determining genetically induced differences among humans — whether comparing two brothers or two races — since culture has not yet had its chance to influence the child's behavior. Any studies made later in life may be "contaminated" by learning. (For instance, as is now well known, studies of intelligence are notably untrustworthy when they make proclamations about genetic differences among two groups who have lived different cultural lives.)

In any case, it is not sociobiology's main concern to find differences in genetic traits of *groups* and certainly not its business to make social policy. The fear — hysteria, in some cases — about sociobiology's potential for harming the American policy of equality is perhaps grounded in an unspoken awareness of how easily upset that policy is. The reason a policy of equality is hard to maintain, however, could be the natural racism (not "the natural race differences") of people.

This brings me to my second point, concerning complaints that sociobiology preaches genetic determinism. Sociobiology *does* note that people are racist or ethnocentric or, in the ultimate case, nepotistic. People *do* favor their own, and that favoring is genetically guided. (Genetically guided, of course, does not mean insuperable — numerous societies have chosen, for example, to outlaw nepotism in employment.) Among the many social behaviors that sociobiology has hypothesized to be genetically guided, nepotism is in fact a major one. Thus sociobiology has done a service to equalists by implying that much of the racial discrimination that goes on is probably *not* justified by any real differences but is a manifestation of people favoring their own, fearing intruders, and so forth. Sociobiology performs a similar service to pacifists by encouraging the hope that if we understand the basis of our warlike ethnocentrism, then we may recognize our stupidity and quit the fight.

At first glance it may seem that if sociobiology explains a behavior (racism, polygamy, political hierarchies, and so on) then it excuses it or even endorses it — *tout comprendre c'est tout pardonner.* No doubt this has been a further cause of disgust toward sociobiology among some academics. Clearly van den Berghe does not see it this way, however, nor do I. Sociobiology identifies the behavior but does not tell us if we should choose to practice it, to outlaw it, to enshrine it, or anything else. That is a policy decision to be made by citizens, not scientists.

Discoveries about the biological basis of such habits as racism can in fact lead to action for social justice. Far from reinforcing fatalism about "evil human nature," they show how people can carefully apply their wits and their moral sensibilities to the problems inherent in multiracial societies and in international affairs.

171

CHAPTER 13

The Inevitability of Justice

✳ ✳ ✳

To be a man is to suffer for others.

— Cesar Chavez

The shift from an instinctive altruism based on inclusive fitness to an ethics based on decision-making was perhaps the most important step in humanization.

— Ernst Mayr

Is justice inevitable? From some of the more pessimistic chapters in this book it may appear that a negative answer to that question is warranted. Cruelty, racism, the many traits that contribute to moral inertia, the history of despotism — these do not suggest the inevitability of justice. If anything they imply the impossibility of justice. Yet at least one eminent thinker, Emile Durkheim, has come up with the idea that justice is inevitable. I believe that his fascinating theory has been oddly neglected and wish to give it an airing here.

Emile Durkheim (1858–1917) was a philosopher before he helped to found the discipline of sociology, and he maintained a lifelong concern with the problem of morality. His biographer Georges Davy said in 1920, "Morality was the centre and the end of his work" (quoted in Lukes, 1973, p. 95). Although Durkheim is well known for his work on the ancient origins of morality he is also a brilliant commentator on the role of morality in the modern age. I shall first outline Durkheim's thoughts on the explanation of morality, and then encapsulate his insights about the modern period (and also make references to points of agreement between his theory and sociobiology).

I promise numerous surprises to all but the most dedicated Durkheim exegetes.

The Explanation of Morality

We may begin with a definition of the word *morality* offered recently by the philosopher Alan Gewirth: "Morality is a set of categorically obligatory requirements for action that are addressed at least in part to every actual or prospective agent, and that are concerned with furthering the interests . . . of persons other than or in addition to the agent" (1978, p. 1). Durkheim wanted to account for the two main features of morality alluded to in this definition, namely, the obligatory or imperative nature of moral feeling and the fact that morality works for the good of society rather than for the self-interest of the individual. He was not satisfied by Immanuel Kant's notion that the sense of duty existed a priori — he wanted to explain it.

In Durkheim's chronological explanation of the emergence of human society, *The Elementary Forms of Religious Life,* published in 1912, he arrived at a solution to both of these problems of morality. The solution, as I shall describe below, had the important effect of explaining the *autonomy of the social realm* and the *force that it exerts on the individual.* These, of course, are among the major concerns of his discipline, sociology.

Earlier in this book (particularly in Chapters 5 and 9) I discussed the biological evolution of morality, or protomorality. I also proposed that, in addition to that evolved part of the moral system, humans have invented an externalized moral system — a set of rules, beliefs about the meaning of right and wrong, and institutions, such as courts — to stabilize the practice of morality. I did not, however, try to fill in the blanks as to the exact way in which the moral system got started. Let us consider Durkheim's explanation.

Durkheim claimed that from the beginning humans created society as a sort of "force" over the individual. In *The Elementary Forms of Religious Life* he showed that this happened through the creation of religion (although he emphasized that religion does not necessarily require "God"). In "L'Individualisme et les intellectuels," Durkheim stated, "Once a goal is pursued by a whole people, it acquires, as a result of this unanimous adherence, a sort of moral supremacy which raises it far above private goals and thereby gives it a religious character" (1898, p. 11). That is, social goals are more or less the same as moral goals, and these are, perforce, sacred. The way in which this connects the individual to society in a kind of emotional union has been described as follows by Anthony Giddens, paraphrasing Durkheim:

> The individual member of the collectivity derives his religiosity from the manner in which the sacred force is created. . . . The sentiment of the divine is evoked in collective ceremonial, during which, as a result of the intense emotionality and involvement which is generated, the individual feels himself swamped by the action of an entity superior to himself. Although this force emanates from the collective assembly, it only realizes itself through the consciousness of the individual, *who feels it to be both transcendent over him and yet immanent within him* (emphasis added) (1972, p. 25).

In other words, the group creates external representations of the social good.

My purpose in introducing this chapter with Durkheim's hypothesis is to note two things. First, his "primal scene" accords very well with the sociobiological position that I have been defending in this book. Both the apparent autonomy of the social realm (in this case, the cultural rules of morality) and the force that it exerts on the individual are compatible with Trivers's idea that the moral emotions are the basis of the whole moral enterprise. They also support my contention that people are quick to reify their concepts of right and wrong, making them seem a very objective entity, thus making duty seem like a force.

Second, I present this excerpt from Durkheim's work on primitive religion to tie it in with his theory of social and moral life in the industrial age. I call this his theory of the inevitability of justice. Durkheim devoted his first book, *The Division of Labour in Society* (1984), first published in 1893, to the nineteenth-century problem of moral breakdown, and his book *Suicide*, published in 1897, centered on the problem of *anomie* or normlessness. As Lewis Coser notes (in Durkheim, 1984), it is interesting to compare Durkheim's response to that of other writers of the age who attempted to come to grips with the Industrial Revolution. On the one hand, says Coser, Herbert Spencer and Henry Maine rejoiced in the "gradual decline of social regulation and the emergence of unfettered

175

individualism." On the other hand, Marx saw that the modern style of work "alienated human beings from the products of their labour" (Durkheim, 1984, pp. ix–xiv). Durkheim disagreed with Spencer that the loss of social regulation would be something to rejoice about; in any case he did not think this observation of Spencer's was accurate.

As for Marx's worry about alienation, Durkheim held that this phenomenon was only temporary: it could be dealt with by a "remoralization of industry." Durkheim's own theory of the organization of modern society is original and contains some surprising, or at least counterintuitive, points. Its major themes are about moral individualism and justice, the question of maladjustment, and the rational use of morality; these will now be briefly outlined.

Moral Individualism and Justice

As Anthony Giddens points out, "The main sociological problem with which Durkheim was concerned in all of his major works [was] the theory of moral authority" (1971, p. 478). Durkheim located the moral authority of the modern system at least in part in the idea of "moral individualism." He saw that the development of the individual had come about over time. "It is only by historical forces that he is formed" (Bellah, 1973, p. 150). Paradoxically, the idea of individualism, far from being an expression of people's natural egoism, is a collective idea for which the modern individual is beholden to society. Moreover, moral individualism, or as Durkheim called it, "the cult of the individual," is "founded upon sentiments of sympathy for human suffering [and] a desire for equality and for justice" (Giddens, 1971, p. 481). "It involves not the glorification of self-interest but of the welfare of others" (Giddens, 1971, p. 481).

Continuity in the transition from traditional to modern society can be found, Giddens notes, "in the necessary persistence of moral ideals and codes of conduct which order the functioning of society" (1972, p. 12). So what Durkheim saw in the nineteenth century was not the emancipation of the individual from all moral bonds but simply a new type of moral bonding. This new type was attributable to the division of labor

176

itself. "The division of labour gives rise to rules ensuring peaceful and regular cooperation between the functions that have been divided up" (Durkheim, 1984, p. 338). The term *organic solidarity* that Durkheim used to describe the bonds of modern society was a biological reference to the way in which the parts of the body function interdependently. He noted that "if the division of labour produces solidarity, it is not only because it makes each individual an agent of exchange, to use the language of the economists. It is because it creates between men a whole system of rights and duties joining them in a lasting way to one another" (1984, pp. 337–338).

Here then is the crucial point: the cohesion of modern society is based on a moral understanding among people. That understanding contains both the ideal of moral individualism (for example, the value of freedom and the value of fulfilling one's special talents) *and* an acceptance of justice as the correct regulator of social interaction. For Durkheim, the source of moral authority in modern times, as I read it, lies in *the legitimation that the practice of social justice confers on individualism*. Unlike the natural-rights theorists, such as Locke, who saw the right to freedom and pursuit of happiness as contained intrinsically within the individual's own nature, Durkheim implies that we are entitled to rights because we extend them to others. Individualism is moral because it applies to all: we have to care about everyone's dignity and worth, not just our own.

It seems that once humans had acquired an advanced, complex social organization, an appropriate moral code *had* to be found. Just as in traditional society myths sprang up to explain the individual's obligations and adherence to group norms, so, too, in modern society myths of justice and equality sprang up. As Durkheim shows, such beliefs are thought to be indisputably true, even sacred. An interesting point about the modern moral code of individualism and justice is that it has no real competitors: we can speculate that this is the only "logical" moral code for modern people. Granted, one major ideology, liberalism, stresses individualism over justice; the other, socialism, stresses justice over individualism; but these two more or less exhaust the "respectable" possibilities of the twentieth century. I suspect that the narrowness of choices reflects our evolutionary makeup, that is, we are prone to set up equitable systems. (I shall refer to E. O. Wilson's theory of this in Chapter 15.)

Maladjustment and the Rational Use of Morality

The second important contribution that Durkheim makes to an understanding of the role of morality in the modern age concerns an interpretation of modern times as a temporary period of maladjustment. The reason why it is temporary is that morality can become better organized and more rational. Durkheim wanted more economic *and moral* regulation of the factors that have resulted from the division of labor, such as more careful delineation of the obligations and relationships among the parts. In *Le Socialisme*, published in 1928, he noted: "In the most advanced societies of present-day Europe, production appears to be unrelated to consumption needs, . . . industrial centralisation seems to have given birth to enterprises too large for society to ignore. . . . [It places the worker] in a state of inferiority which prevents him from concluding equitable contracts" (quoted in Giddens, 1972, pp. 13–14).

Carmen Sirianni notes of *The Division of Labour in Society* that "the conclusion of the entire work is that more justice is the solution to the crisis in the division of labour" (1984, p. 454). Some of the specific suggestions Durkheim made seem unsuitable today. For example, he advocated the formation of "corporations," somewhat like medieval guilds, to guide the relationship among occupations. However, what is important is his general idea that we can actively create morality. In "La conception sociale de la religion," in 1914, he wrote: "The old ideals and the divinities which incarnate them are dying because they no longer respond sufficiently to the new aspirations of our day; and the new ideals which are necessary to orient our life are not yet born. Thus we find ourselves in an intermediate period, a period of moral cold" (quoted in Bellah, 1973, p. xlvii). Yet, he assures us, there is a "warmth" in the depths of society of new moral ideas seeking to come forth. These aspirations and agitations will "one day or another reach a clearer self-consciousness and translate themselves into definite formulas around which men will rally" (quoted in Bellah, 1973, p. xlvii).

Although primitive society may have created its morality unconsciously, Durkheim sees no reason why this cannot be done consciously. The closing paragraph of *The Division of Labour in Society* states: "In short, our first duty at the present time is to fashion a morality for ourselves. It can arise only of its own volition, gradually, and under the pressure of internal causes that render it necessary. What reflection can and must do is prescribe the goal that must be attained" (1984, p. 340).

Durkheim was willing to give this role to the state. The division of labor "must be infused with *moral* centres and these must be under the general moral guidance of the state" (Giddens, 1971, p. 481). Durkheim often referred to the state as the brain of society that gives direction to inchoate forces. In "Lecons de sociologie" (published in 1950), he wrote that "the state . . . is and must be a centre of new and original ideas which must put the society in a position to conduct itself with greater intelligence than when it is swayed merely by diffuse sentiments working on it" (quoted in Giddens, 1972, p. 21).

I suspect that the relative lack of attention paid to Durkheim's ideas on the rational remoralization of society may have to do with his uncritical faith in the state. Much political and social science writing in the twentieth century has identified the state as the cause of, rather than the solution to, society's woes, and the experience of totalitarianism has not done much to suggest that state officials can be entrusted with the "moral guidance" of society. In fact, though, the democratic state has been the focus for the articulation of social policy, and the welfare state is the main allocator of economic justice today. In any case, Durkheim's theory of the rational organization of morality need not depend on the state: "remoralization" could be in the hands of clergypersons, civic leaders, or any other interested social group.

Sociobiology and Rational Morality

As suggested earlier, there are parallels between Durkheim's theory of the origin and nature of morality and that of sociobiology. I believe that Durkheim's view of the role of morality in the modern age is also one that finds support in sociobiology. Three major points of *The Division of Labour in Society* were summarized above: (1) Social cohesion in modern society, that is, organic solidarity, depends on the presence of moral authority; (2) "justice" is the social morality invented by free, modern persons; it demands respect for the welfare of all individuals; and (3) in times of maladjustment, morality can become more rational in order to give direction to social life. The reasons why a sociobiologist can endorse these are as follows. First, since we evolved with a strong attachment to moral authority, it is likely that we would not have shed the relevant psychological traits in the modern age. (Indeed our susceptibility to fanaticism may be evidence of this, even whilst we pride ourselves on being critical of authority.) Second, given a society that divides its labor and has complex systems of exchange, and given our evolved sense of monitoring reciprocity, justice seems to be the most likely system for our cultures to develop: there are no obvious alternatives.

Third, the sociobiologist would predict the inevitability of maladjustments: we evolved in a very simple environment, but many of our cultural institutions have their own dynamics (for example, the dynamics of technology, of bureaucracy, or of capitalism) that complicate human social organization. In times of maladjustment why should morality not come to the fore as a guiding system, since its principal function is to channel the relationships among individuals?

If I were asked to name the one most exciting scientific discovery of this century, it would be the sociobiological discovery of the nature of morality. If I were asked to name the one most profound implication of this discovery, it would be — as Durkheim anticipated — that the moral organization of modern society is the self-conscious task of responsible individuals.

CHAPTER 14

What Has Mortality to Do With Morality?

✳ ✳ ✳

Imannuel Kant exclaims, "Duty! Wondrous thought . . . by holding up thy naked Law in the soul, and so extorting for thyself always reverence, if not obedience . . . whence thy original?" With that quotation, Charles Darwin, in *The Descent of Man* (1877, p. 97), opened his discussion of "the moral sense," a subject that he said "no one has approached . . . exclusively from the side of natural history" (1877, pp. 97–98). In this new book, *The Biology of Moral Systems*, Richard Alexander approaches the subject of the moral sense from the side of natural history — in no uncertain terms. In particular he applies William Hamilton's theory of inclusive fitness. This theory, the linchpin of sociobiology, holds that an individual's ultimate fitness in evolution is measured by how many of his genes are included in future generations (Hamilton, 1964).

Alexander believes that sociobiological theory proves the ethical philosophy of utilitarianism to be mistaken. If the human moral sense is innate, it had to have evolved by strict principles of natural selection. Natural selection always acts on the individual and his genes; hence, the moral sense could not have evolved for the good of the group. John Stuart Mill's principle of "the greatest happiness for the greatest number of people" is thus no reflection of the true motives of moral actors. According to Alexander, such *indiscriminate beneficence* could never be a product of evolution. He thus recommends contractarianism, in place of utilitarianism, as the best available ethics (p. 80).

Review of: Richard Alexander, *The Biology of Moral Systems* (Hawthorne, New York: Aldine de Gruyter, 1987).

Lamenting that Roscoe Pound's call for a general theory of interests has gone unheeded for decades by philosophers (Pound, 1941), Alexander takes up the task himself. He sets the stage by defining *conscience* as "the still small voice that tells us how far we can go in serving our own interests without incurring intolerable risks" (p. 102). He traces the development of moral behavior from original acts of altruism, directed only at one's kin, to the reciprocal type of altruism based on exchange of favors with any individual, up to the full moral systems in which society as a whole administers the rewards and punishments for altruism and selfishness, respectively (Trivers, 1985). Throughout this long process what is occurring is not some kind of gradual human enlightenment about goodness. Rather, according to Alexander, it is the evolution of moral strategies in which Ego is always out to win at the expense of his neighbor. Morality is a game of interests.

One of Alexander's primary ideas is that the human psyche itself evolved largely under the selective pressure of one individual trying to outwit another. "Social behavior evolves as a succession of ploys and counterploys" (p. 9). "Self-awareness is a way of seeing ourselves as others see us so that we can cause them to see us as we would like them to" (p. 107). This is true even of moral behavior, according to Alexander. For instance, he argues that a person who acts altruistically, with seeming disinterest, may stand to gain something intangible such as enhanced reputation. "Who among us is not a little humble in the presence of someone who has casually noted that he just came back from giving blood?" (p. 157) Participation in idealized systems of ethics, too, can be shown to be ultimately to Ego's advantage: it allows Ego to moralize about others. "Pressure is applied by each individual so as to cause his neighbor, if possible, to be a little more moral than himself" (p. 102).

So it may seem that Alexander is a cynical realist in the mold of Machiavelli. But Machiavelli at least gave the individual credit for calculating his own benefit! In Alexander's view, all that can ever count is *reproductive success* — that is, the representation of one's genes in future generations. Alexander, a professor of zoology at the University of Michigan, was one of the first to develop human sociobiology (although, to date, he has eschewed the word *sociobiology*) (Alexander, 1979, 1987).

He, along with various colleagues from such other disciplines as psychology and anthropology, attempts to find ultimate genetic explanations for human behavior and social structure. They carry out field studies that almost totally ignore the conscious motivation of persons or the history of culture (for example, Daly and Wilson, 1988; Chagnon and Irons, 1979; Betzig, 1986). (See also my book, *The Sociobiological Imagination,* 1991.)

The emphasis of this particular school of sociobiology is always on showing how behaviors, including altruism, are adaptive in the Darwinian sense, since they cause the gene for the respective behavior to proliferate. An individual need never be aware of his true motive for altruism. To read the journal articles of these researchers is to see the words *reproductive success* and *fitness maximization* on almost every page. This may seem patently ridiculous in an age when men are queuing up for vasectomies. However, the point is that it does not matter whether or not modern humans care to have children. What counts is that Nature has already selected certain behaviors because they originally helped the inclusive fitness of the individuals who practiced them. Altruism, as we have seen, is one of those behaviors.

Being acquainted with the methodology of this school, I approached Alexander's book with considerable skepticism as well as a general resistance to the selfish-gene idea of Richard Dawkins (1976). However, I found myself quite persuaded by the opening chapter. In it, Alexander extensively covers G. C. Williams's theory of senescence, pointing out that individuals must die so that the gene can get on with its proliferation (Williams, 1957). Why do we not live to be two thousand years old — a biological feat that could easily be accomplished, as in the case of California redwoods? Alas, we are mortal — for the gene's sake.

This idea is so radical that we must pause here to think about it. Williams, Dawkins, and Alexander are all saying that the gene is what evolution is all about. Other entities, such as anatomical traits, species, societies, length of life, even individuals themselves, are in some sense incidental. The power of the gene to direct evolution is indeed so difficult to contemplate that Dawkins had to resort to an anthropomorphic device. He spoke of "the selfish gene" as if a gene had a mind, or a will, or desires. As far as I know, Dawkins does not believe the gene to possess any such faculties — it is just a way of explaining the effect that a gene can have.

Members of the public may be under the impression that the term *selfish genes* means "genes that make humans behave selfishly." Not at all. It is the gene that is being selfish — for itself. And its selfishness may, paradoxically, cause its owner to do some very unselfish things. The genes selfishly want to get into future generations, and they know, so to speak, that one good way to do this is to promote altruism toward kin. In the case of the bee described by Hamilton (1964, p. 28; see Chapter 5), it was said that she, the bee, would "rather" help the family than go and start a new nest. I do not pretend to know what individual bees really want to do, if anything, but the party that would "rather" that the bee help the family was really the genes of the bee, not the individual bee. (Of course, individuals that have to carry out what the genes dictate often appear as if *they* very much want that thing, too.)

If this selfish-gene metaphor is too taxing, one can just go back to the straight way of saying it. The mathematics of reproduction in Hymenopteran insects showed that bees that help the family do end up having more of their genes in future generations than those that go off and start a new nest. That is all there is to it. More genes result later, so Dawkins animates the gene and shows that it is as if the gene personally and deliberately (and selfishly) made it happen. The reader may take it or leave it!

To get back to *The Biology of Moral Systems*, one disappointment of Alexander's new treatise is that it does not mention the current controversy over group selection. His previous work (1979) had emphasized the idea that in-group cooperation evolved under the pressure of out-group hostility. And so it would be interesting to see him take on the critics of this position. Another disappointment is that Alexander makes only a passing allusion to *sympathy*, so important in Darwin's, not to say Hume's, understanding of the moral sense. Nor at any point does he acknowledge that the transition to more generalized systems of morality and law could be the outcome of a purely intellectual trait — that of the universalizing of principles. Still, this book goes far beyond what anyone would expect from a biologist (one, in fact, whose principal species of study has been crickets!). It contains cogent criticism of many contemporary works of philosophy, such as those of Richard Brandt, Kurt Baier, John Rawls, and Peter Singer. Alexander sums up his review of ethical philosophies with this remark: "I do not expect that moral and ethical arguments can ever be finally resolved because conflicts of interest cannot be finally or ultimately resolved. Compromises and contracts, then, are (at least currently) the only real solutions. . . . This is why moral and ethical decisions must arise out of decisions of the collective of affected individuals; there is no single source of right and wrong" (p. 191).

Let us consider an example of the relationship between conflicting interests and moral rules. Alexander cites a work in medical ethics by C. Strong that deals with respective rights of infants, parents, and physicians (in this case, neonatologists). Obviously, the right of a defective newborn to receive "heroic" treatment may conflict with the right of the parent, if the care of that child would require a huge sacrifice of time or money. Alexander notes that whilst the ethical discussion is underway, participants (or observers) may try to appeal to some general rules involved. One such rule is the physician's responsibility to "put the patient first." But where did this rule come from?

It came from a mutual need. The patient who puts his fate in the hands of a stranger needs to feel assured that that person is committed to do the right thing. The doctor similarly needs to have his patients' trust, or they will not come back again. He is motivated to do the right thing, for his reputation's sake at the very least. But today this situation has changed. Alexander says:

> I suggest that the forcing apart of physicians' and their patients' interests by the impersonality and non-repetitiveness of physician-patient interactions in modern urban society is a principal reason for the rise in dissatisfaction, litigation, and the expenses of medical care. For example, excessive use of diagnostic procedures (that are often risky to the patient) are carried out to protect the interests of physicians and hospitals because, I believe, physicians and hospitals have lost the ability to convince patients that they have indeed assumed the medical interests of the patients as if they were their own (p. 92).

By contrast he notes that the old-style family doctor, who had a stable population of patients with whom he interacted regularly, was seldom subject to litigation. "Patients had other ways . . . to reciprocate inferior treatment, and more reasons to believe they were obtaining the best care the physician could give" (p. 92).

To return to the case of the neonatologists, Alexander and Strong recognize that an entire medical subspecialty has developed to care for impaired newborns. Thus, an additional interest — one that puts pressure on the parents — must now be considered. It may strike them as a moral pressure but in fact it is an interest pressure. Throughout his book, Alexander is at pains to correct philosophers' errors. He shows, for instance, that philosophers often talk as if matters of conflicting interests arise *because we operate under moral systems*. But the opposite, he says, is true: we operate under moral systems (or invent them in the first place) because there are conflicting interests. I repeat Alexander's essential ethical advice: "Moral and ethical decisions must arise out of the decisions of the collective of affected individuals" (p. 19). Practical solutions to moral questions, he believes, can be devised that will lessen the social and political problems of the world (p. xvi).

Another theme of *The Biology of Moral Systems* — one that I cannot develop at length here — is that of deception, particularly self-deception. Deception is basic in animal evolution. "Organisms resulting from the long-term cumulative effects of [natural selection] are expected to resist efforts to reveal their interests fully to others" (p. xv). The cases in which individuals are totally honest in their signals to one another are the rarities, Alexander notes, such as in the communication of honeybees. These have a mutual interest in "telling the truth" to one another with respect to food sources or danger to the hive. But this situation, surprisingly, is unlike that for the majority of animal signals — as Richard Dawkins and J. R. Krebs have shown, for example, in their article "Animal Signals: Information or Manipulation?" (1978).

Alexander admits that "humans are not accustomed to dealing with their own strategies of life as if they had been tuned by natural selection" (p. 19). But he is persuaded that the effort should be made to see it this way, and he believes that "evolutionary understanding *changes attitudes*" (p. xvi). "I expect collective interests to be better served when decisions are made with more information [such as about what the interests really are] and by a larger proportion of the people involved, and . . . I expect deception to be more difficult as knowledge about morality is enhanced" (p. 13).

Significantly, in the Library of Congress system, this book is cataloged as a work of ethics, not of biology. One hopes that philosophers will welcome this earnest, if iconoclastic, contribution to their field. At the very least, I believe, Alexander demonstrates that it makes a profound difference when the would-be philosopher of morals has first attempted to tackle seriously the question, Whence thy original?

CHAPTER 15

The Relationship Between Morality and Power

✳ ✳ ✳

From each according to his agility, to each according to his greed.
— Ali Mazrui

The cry of liberation of this people is a cry that reaches up to God, and one that nothing and no one can stop.
— the late Archbishop Oscar Romero of El Salvador

A slave who dies of natural causes will not balance two dead flies on the scales of eternity.
— Eldridge Cleaver

In this chapter I shall specifically focus on the way morality in human society relates to another phenomenon, namely, power. In Chapter 11, I gave a rather idiosyncratic view of power: my concern there was to "denature" it. I argued that political structures develop in human society to meet certain cybernetic requirements, rather than to give expression to a power-hungry human nature. But here I shall revert to the more usual understanding of the word *power*. I mean it to conjure up that range of behaviors that political scientists usually study. Thus, *power* will include official control of people by governments or other institutions and will also include more subtle ways that people have of controlling one another through economic status, through propaganda, and so forth.

The question before us is, What is the relationship between morality and power? From my reading of the relevant literature I discern three quite distinct answers to that question. Let me call them the academic approach, the Thrasymachean approach, and the traditional approach.

The Academic Approach

The academic approach, for want of a better name, is the one that says *there is no relationship* between morality and power. Morality is one thing, power is quite another, and they are simply not related. Sometimes this distinction is said to reflect a lack of meeting ground between power and morality in the persons of their respective practitioners. Michael Howard observes that "the grammar of power, so intricate, so compelling, becomes for those who operate it a universe in itself — as indeed for the moralist and the reformer, the ethical objective can become an exclusive obsession which makes him disdain the tedious and murky problem of how to attain it" (1983, p. 63).

What I call the academic approach to the relationship between morality and power, however, is one that figures most prominently in the field of international relations, especially in the writings of the realist school. The realist endeavors to dissociate himself from all idealist, or as E. H. Carr calls them, utopian ideas (1958, p. 5). (*Utopian* in this context does not mean dream-building perfectibilism, but includes any moral schemes based on a rationalist approach to politics.) The realist, in contrast to the idealist, wants to be hardheaded about the interactions among states, the national-interest motives behind all foreign policy, and so forth.

Most international relations theorists would probably agree that morality and power do have some relationship in domestic society. Stanley Hoffman notes, for example, that "within the state, power, whether it is exercised by political leaders or by social groups, is often at the service of common ideals; this restricts the scope of power politics and indeed the essence of the polity is — ideally — the prevalence of cooperation over conflict. The opposite is true in world affairs" (1978, p. 107). In drawing up a dichotomy between morality and power in the global arena, the realists have, in my opinion, made it prestigious to think that the two areas really can be separated. I have contended that this is nonsense, in my book, *Morality among Nations* (1990), and shall not attempt to rehearse the argument here. Indeed I shall not discuss the academic approach any further in this chapter, other than to say that it is academic. It has mainly to do with the professional need of political scientists and international relations theorists to isolate a particular phenomenon, power, in order to give it their undivided attention.

The two other answers to the question What is the relationship between morality and power? can be stated succinctly as follows. The Thrasymachean approach says *power determines morality;* the traditional approach says *morality curtails power.* Let me now briefly defend the Thrasymachean approach, that power determines morality.

The Thrasymachean Approach

I take the name, of course, from Thrasymachus in the Socratic dialogues, who claimed that "justice is the right of the stronger." The slave-owner can justly overwork the slave because that is the nature of the relationship. The thief justly owns what he has stolen since he succeeded in stealing it. *Might* makes the status quo *right.* A major criticism of this extreme view is that it calls for collapsing the definition of morality into the definition of power: it equates good with strength or success. Surely, however, *good* or *right* must mean something else.

There is a second and more useful interpretation of the claim that power determines morality. It is expressed in E. H. Carr's remark, "Power goes far to create the morality convenient to itself" (1958, p. 229). This involves a sociology-of-knowledge interpretation of morality. It is largely associated with Karl Marx's insights about a society's laws and politics being mere superstructure on the economic relations of the day. The powerful create the myth about what is right and just in a way that argues for the rightfulness of their activities. To this end they use public relations efforts, co-optation, inducements, or any means at their disposal to cover up the true relationship of exploitation.

Carr offers two examples of the way in which power creates the morality convenient to itself. The first is the myth of the "harmony of interests." The liberal comes to believe that each individual, by acting to promote his own interest (however ruthlessly), will contribute to the good of the community (1958, p. 80). The second myth is that of "the indivisibility of peace."

Toynbee, for example, declared that "international law and order were in the true interests of the whole of mankind . . . whereas the desire to perpetuate violence in international affairs was an antisocial desire" (quoted in Carr, 1958, p. 83). That, of course, is the argument that did duty in every strike in the early days of the British and American labor movements, Carr says. It led "employers, supported by the whole capitalist press, to denounce the antisocial attitude of trade union leaders . . . and to declare that the true and ultimate interests of workers lay in peaceful cooperation with the employers" (1958, p. 83).

The view that power controls morality in this way is, I believe, quite accurate. The powerful do indeed have the lion's share of control over ideas and communication and thus over the construction of a conservative ideology. There is even some merit in Nietzsche's suggestion that Christianity is a slave morality. "Blessed are the meek" encourages powerless people to remain powerless — on moral grounds.

The Traditional Approach

We now turn to the third answer to the question What is the relationship between morality and power? — namely, the traditional approach, which holds that morality curtails power. As Alan Gewirth observed, the chief concern of political philosophy in the West has been the moral criticism of politics (1965, p. 1). Leo Strauss wrote, "Pain, suffering, injustice, and their prevention, these are the eternal problems of public morals — the agenda of public policy (as Bentham would have said!)" (1968, p. 237). Such remarks imply that the possession of some moral standards — that is, ideas as to what is right and what is wrong — gives people a weapon against power holders. Writing during the French Enlightenment, Charles Duclos commented, "Of all empires, that of the intellectuals, though invisible, is the widest spread. Those in power command, but the intellectuals govern, because in the end they form public opinion, which sooner or later subdues or upsets all despotisms" (quoted in Passmore, 1970, p. 192).

I personally would not wax quite so lyrical about the empire of the intellectuals; nevertheless, a reasonable case can be made that morality does curtail power. Morality — or moral ideas — tends to become universalized. What starts in the individual as a sense of fairness concerning one-to-one reciprocal transactions does lead eventually to notions of equality and the belief that all people deserve fair treatment. This goes against power structures in which persons receive very differential treatment according to how much power they wield. Let me offer a very brief historical sketch to defend that argument. I shall show that the Stoic idea of equality made its way into Christianity, which in turn helped to bring about modern democracy and even modern communism.

Equality: From Stoicism to Communism

As described in Chapter 5, the Stoic philosophers, beginning with Zeno in the third century B.C., constructed the idea of human equality out of a cosmological scheme. They saw the universe as run by natural law: humans through reason followed this natural law, and this sharing of reason made human beings equal. The idea passed into Christian thought, for example, through Christ's disciple, Paul, who was Greek educated. A central idea that developed in Christian doctrine was the equality of all souls before God. Stoicism also passed into the West through Roman law; Cicero was its major exponent.

This equality tenet of Christian metaphysics also sowed the seed for the idea of natural rights that appeared in the seventeenth century in the writings of John Locke. Still, the intervening Middle Ages were times of feudal hierarchy. During this period, by concentrating on the inner spiritual life and downplaying the importance of material welfare or political activity, the Christian myth largely abetted the political status quo. Indeed, the Church and the state became entwined in many ways, with sons of noblemen becoming bishops and cardinals (not to mention vice versa). There may have been plenty of democratic propaganda in the New Testament, but fortunately for the elite, peasants were unlikely to find out about it, since Latin literacy was restricted to the clergy.

The Reformation was the turning point. Righteous anger over church abuses, such as the selling of indulgences, caused Martin Luther to criticize ecclesiastical corruption. Later he went further; he attacked the very authority of the Church and emphasized *individual responsibility* for interpreting the Word of God. The Reformation spread very rapidly throughout Europe; the movement was aided by the humanistic influences that had grown out of the Renaissance, and the Vulgate translations of the Bible now made widely available by the printing press. Various religious leaders began to preach a radical egalitarianism in the sixteenth century. This went furthest with Ulrich Zwingli in Switzerland and John Knox in Scotland.

In the seventeenth century, the Puritans in England contributed to the moral attack on state power and on hierarchies in general. Among their radical groups were the Levellers, who recommended the heretofore inconceivable idea of a universal male franchise. In 1647, Thomas Rainsborough made the astonishing statement: "For really I think that the poorest he that is in England hath a life to live as the greatest he; and therefore truly, sir, I think it's clear, that every man that is to live under a government ought first by his own consent to put himself under that government" (quoted in Woodhouse, 1938, p. 53). Such were the fast-moving developments over the next century, in ideas concerning equality, freedom, and natural rights, that by 1776 Thomas Jefferson was moved to claim — what could hardly be further from the truth — that it is *self-evident* that all men are created equal.

In our century, Mao Tse-tung no doubt went further than anyone had ever gone in "putting down the mighty from their seat and exalting the humble" in the 1949 communist revolution in China. He later carried the theory of equality to macabre extremes in the Cultural Revolution. Although it would be inaccurate to say that Mao had ever absorbed Christian or Stoic thought, he did get his basic idea of communist revolution from Karl Marx, who was an inhabitant of the Christian West. Marx in turn got his ideas of socialist equality from Jean Baptiste Fourier, Pierre Proudhon, and others who were in turn influenced by earlier thinkers (Corcoran, 1983b).

It would be wrong, of course, to claim that a moral idea, that of equality, was the sole factor leading to the broadening of the power base. Economic factors were crucial, such as the rise of the merchant classes in Europe or the availability of vast tracts of free land in North America. Even in regard to the success of the Reformation, it can be pointed out that all was not due to rebellion from below. Many princes found that opposition to the Roman church gave them quite a convenient excuse to establish state religions and that in doing so they got to expropriate the land and other local wealth of the Church.

I believe that Tatu Vanhanen has arrived at an interesting compromise between the two views (of ideational versus economic influence). His wide survey of democracies has yielded the conclusion that "democracy will emerge under conditions where power resources have become so widely distributed that no group is any longer able to suppress its competitors or to maintain its hegemony" (1984, p. 25). Vanhanen considers the two main *power resources* in this definition to be wealth and knowledge. Knowledge includes knowledge of moral ideas, as happened when the peasants found out what was in the Bible, thanks to the Vulgate translations. It is interesting to note that Vanhanen wrote in 1984 that the prospects for an increase in the number of democracies today is good, since those prerequisites of democracy are spreading. "Modern technology has made inevitable the diffusion and growth of intellectual power resources as well as the more equal distribution of economic and other power resources" (1984, p. 26).

The Sociobiological View

So far in this chapter, I have dismissed the academic approach that says there is no relationship between morality and power and basically defended both the Thrasymachean view ("power determines morality") and the traditional view ("morality curtails power"). Thinking back to material from earlier chapters, particularly Chapter 9 on the evolved components of morality and Chapter 11 on the explanation of power, it may now be worthwhile to ask whether there could be a sociobiological view on the relationship between morality and power.

I believe three points are worth making. First, there can be no sociobiological view that stems from evidence of a relationship between morality and power in the animal kingdom, because among nonhuman species *there is no morality*. True, there is some antecedent of human cooperative behavior in animal altruism but virtually no development of a sense of right and wrong. (I say "virtually" because the evidence is not yet clear about a possible protomoral sense in primates; see Ellis, 1990.) Such altruism as does exist in nonhuman animals has never reached the stage at which it could be turned into externalized rules, beliefs, religions, philosophies of equality, and so forth. Therefore altruism cannot reach out to have any effect on the structure of power. Altruism and power are simply two unrelated phenomena. (I might therefore magnanimously allow that the academic approach is correct with respect to the animal kingdom: there is no relationship, there, between morality and power!)

The second point is that sociobiology offers some support to the Thrasymachean position that power determines morality. Recall my proposal in Chapter 9 that morality has three components: law and order, welfare-provision, and judgment. Reciprocal altruism, the moral emotions, and the sense of right and wrong are the likely antecedents to the judgment component, but participation in mammalian hierarchies is the likely background to the human penchant for law and order. Humans are willing to obey rules: they even seek rules. Those rules may cover a range of subjects — predictably every society will prohibit such antisocial acts as killing and stealing, for example. But a portion of the rules is usually devoted to enkindling respect for authority as such. I see that endorsement of authority as merely a moral overlay on a set of social relations that would normally exist anyway due to power structures. Thus, sociobiology does give some aid and comfort to the Thrasymachean view that power is there first, and it determines the morality that eventuates. Similarly, I believe that the realist position on law, which E. H. Carr has expressed as follows, would seem credible to sociobiologists: "Once it is understood that law is a function of a given political order, whose existence alone can make it binding, we see the fallacy of the phrase 'rule of law' or 'government of laws and not of men.' . . . The law is not an abstraction. It cannot be understood independently of the political foundation on which it rests and of the political interests which it serves" (1958, p. 178).

Sociobiology, however, offers an interesting challenge to the conspiracy theory that power determines morality by conspiring to create a myth in its own support. Granted, most cultures do invent a myth to show why the present system is just or how injustice in this life will be compensated for in the next. Marxists imply that such myths are created by the powerful to maintain their hegemony, but it has always been difficult to prove that they do this with conscious intent. The fact is that the *powerless* are just as likely to invent these myths. Ironically, we might note that Stoicism itself — despite the fact that it later came to be a weapon against hierarchies — was first developed as a philosophy of resignation. It recommended that persons "fit in" with the system, that they act "stoically" — with a lowercase s. Edward Zeller noted of the period, "The chief value of philosophy [was] that it provided men with a refuge against the miseries of life" (1886, pp. 228–229).

The third point is that the sociobiological view offers considerable support for the traditional approach, which holds that morality curtails power. By "sociobiological view" here I refer to the overall picture I painted in earlier chapters regarding the development of ethical principles out of a basic evolutionary heritage of moral emotions. People feel that there is a rightness and wrongness about certain social relationships, and they seek to make those relationships conform to principles. Animals who are low on social hierarchies may dislike the treatment they get but they do not have a standard of fairness, an ethical principle, to use on their own behalf, as a means of demanding better treatment. Humans do. They can even use the principle of equality to obliterate hierarchies, at least for limited periods of time.

As a further point about the sociobiological view of this subject, I should note that E. O. Wilson has made the fascinating suggestion that the contemporary movement for universal human rights is the expression of a "mammalian imperative." He says:

> Our societies are based on the mammalian plan: the individual strives for personal reproductive success foremost and that of his immediate kin secondarily; further grudging cooperation represents a compromise struck in order to enjoy the benefits of group membership. . . . We will accede to universal

rights because power is too fluid in advanced technological societies to circumvent this mammalian imperative; the long term consequences of inequity will always be visibly dangerous to its temporary beneficiaries (1978, p. 199).

He concludes that "this is the true reason for the universal rights movement and that an understanding of its raw biological causation will be more compelling in the end than any rationalization contrived by culture to reinforce and euphemize it" (1978, p. 199).

I am not sure that Wilson is entirely correct, insofar as people do, for very long periods of time, submit to social structures that maintain inequality — even caste systems. However, once people happen to see that morality can be used to curtail power, the powerful are indeed in trouble.

The Democratic Experiment

In my school days I was taught that in the democratic system of the United States any citizen could run for office, that his election or defeat would depend upon where he stood on the issues, and that once elected he would vote to please his constituents and/or to please his conscience. I do not recall hearing a word about the independent agenda of government bureaucracies, the power of small lobbies, the buying of candidates (to be fair, PACs — political action commitees — did not exist then), or indeed anything about the corruptibility of democracy in the United States. I was also certainly unaware that the structural problems of democracy had been well debated by the ancient Greeks. For us, the high point of political sophistication consisted of reading George Orwell's *1984* in high school and realizing what dangers totalitarianism posed to the human mind.

My innocence came to a rather abrupt halt in the late 1960s. At that time prejudice quickly moved in the other direction — at least on university campuses — toward indictment of all government (or perhaps all governments except that of "Uncle Ho" in North Vietnam). At that point, it became "known" to all intellectuals that the U.S. system was one big lie, that the military-industrial complex was in charge, that "the people" had no power (except flower power, the power of lettuce boycotts, and so forth), that dissidents were being bugged and would be persecuted, and that bribery was the norm in national as well as local politics.

Why do I bring this up here in a chapter on the relationship between morality and power? I do so to introduce the idea that morality has now gone further in curtailing power than merely establishing the principles of equality and rights. It inquires about morality within government, even "good" government. Political scientists and many journalists concern themselves with the problems posed both by human nature and by various structures in government. There is great emphasis today on accountability. Researchers constantly make use — wittingly or unwittingly — of moral ideas, for instance, about honesty, to test democracy. They assume that morality can be brought to bear as a corrective on power (that is, on "abuses" of power).

I have entitled this section "The Democratic Experiment" to underscore the fact that modern democracy is still at an experimental stage. Alexander Hamilton wrote in *The Federalist* in 1787, "It seems to have been reserved to the people of this country . . . to decide the important question whether societies of men are really capable or not of establishing good government from reflection and thought" (1961, p. 1). Judith Shklar points out that the philosophers of the late eighteenth century were "a great deal more radical . . . than later social revolutionaries for they did not regard men as the agents of historical destiny, but as the free creators of society" (1957, p. 5).

Liberalism, notably through the work of John Locke in the late seventeenth century, had made government the servant of the people. It showed that values could be stated first, such as the value of freedom or the value of happiness, and then the political and economic (in those days, not so much the economic) arrangements organized accordingly. The question today is whether this can really be done. There is even the question of whether Americans really have a democracy. To Bill Moyers's question "Do we have a democracy now?" the political philosopher Sheldon Wolin replied, "I think we don't. The idea of democracy and the idea of a strong, centralized state, inherently bureaucratic . . . are not compatible notions. Democracy implies involvement, shared power, and above all, a significant equality. State power means the opposite of those" (Moyers, 1989, p. 99).

The definition of *democracy* given by *The American Heritage Dictionary* is "government by the people, exercised either directly or through elected representatives." Obviously most people do not exercise government directly, and there is even much question of how freely and consciously they choose their elected representatives. Michael Josephson notes that "ninety-eight percent of the incumbents running for Congress won last year [1988]. That's the same percentage as in Russia. So we don't have any proof that there really are serious, open elections or that this money makes any difference. Incumbents get money by a fifteen-to-one ratio because money follows incumbency, not ideology" (quoted in Moyers, 1989, p. 26). Noam Chomsky adds that elective office is being moved away from popular control by the fairly new procedure of stage-managed, public-relations-organized campaigns. "Candidates decide what to say on the basis of tests that determine what the effect will be across the population. Somehow people don't see how profoundly contemptuous that is of democracy" (quoted in Moyers, 1989, p. 45).

The flaws in our system are now being revealed, of course, so there is room for change. Karl Popper, a philosopher of science, believes on the grounds of philosophy of science that democracy is the best system. Just as science is an open system in which errors can be discovered by anyone and new, more correct ideas can take over, so a form of government can be the same. Popper wrote: "I use the word rationalism to indicate, roughly, an attitude that seeks to solve as many problems as possible by an appeal to reason, that is, to clear thought and experience rather than by an appeal to emotions and passions" (1945, p. 224).

The important thing is that there be an open society in which rational debate can occur. "Authoritarianism and rationalism . . . cannot be reconciled, since argument, which includes criticism and the art of listening to criticism, is the basis of reasonableness" (Popper, 1945, p. 226). Popper wrote his book, *The Open Society*, in 1945 as a criticism of various closed societies in Europe at that time. However, the book's central idea is useful for building confidence in democracy's future prospects. Henry Steel Commager states the case positively as follows: "I cheerfully confess an abiding faith in democracy. . . . I believe in freedom as a method of arriving at truth and avoiding error" (quoted in Moyers, 1989, p. 221).

Summary

Let me now summarize the foregoing thoughts about the relationship between morality and power and recall other chapters in this book that were concerned with this subject. In Chapter 8, I investigated the relationship between cruelty and power in the case of the Rum Corps and the Australian convicts. There it appeared that raw, animal-like power was in effect: those with superior power were able to crush — in a straightforwardly violent way — the bodies (and spirits) of those of inferior power. I noted that one factor accounting for this barbarism was isolation of the victims from society's protection. That is, the morality of civilization was not able to curtail this power because it wasn't visible. In the end, though, Bishop Willson did at least get the sadist John Price removed from Norfolk Island. As for Price's own end, incidentally, it was as much a case of power against power as morality against power. On March 26, 1857, Price went to the quarry at Williamstown where a gang of convicts was laboring. Robert Hughes writes:

> With his usual bravado, he walked straight into the midst of them, escorted only by a small party of guards. A hundred prisoners watched him marching up the tramway that bore the quarried stone from the cutting-face to the jetty. Quietly they surrounded Price, and their circle began to close. . . . The guards fled; Price turned and began to run down the tramway when a stone . . . caught him between the shoulder blades and pitched him forward on his face. Then, nothing could be seen except a mass of struggling men, . . . and the irregular flailing of stone-hammers and crowbars (1988, pp. 550–551).

In Chapter 3, I claimed that moral ideas form an important part of the power struggle between ethnic groups; I also proffered a ten commandments of interethnic relations that called on moral principle to modify sheer power, such as in the case of protecting vulnerable minorities and of avoiding bloodshed through compromise. In Chapter 4, I outlined Max Stackhouse's calm proposal that church people — both laity and clergy — should take control, at least intellectual control, of decisions that are made by powerful economic institutions. (Why? Because civilizations need moral rudders and because Christianity offers a valid anthropology about our material and spiritual needs and inclinations.)

In Chapter 2, I quoted Sissela Bok on the reasons why society should act to curtail the power of government in its practice of secrecy. Her reasons were, on one level, because it is right to do so, but on another level, because it is necessary to do so — if we would avoid social collapse. In Chapter 11, which inquired into the human nature of power, I argued against construing the manifestations of state power as the result of a human urge to control others (even if parallels to the Rum Corps abound) and argued in favor of a cybernetic imperative. My agenda in that research, however, included the fact that denaturing power structures thusly gives us a better ability to criticize their performance according to our moral standards.

The two chapters preceding this one — Chapter 13 on Durkheim's theory of justice, and Chapter 14 on Alexander's theory of interests, contained complex and somewhat incompatible views on the relationship between morality and power. Durkheim believed that both in the prehistoric and the modern setting people grant a legitimacy to certain social arrangements, including power arrangements, by imbuing them with moral meaning. The modern power arrangement includes much equality and this — he says — gets its moral legitimacy from people's willingness to act justly toward one another. For Alexander, interest is everything. The striving of individuals to take care of their biological interests can explain, he claims, not only the evolution of advanced moral systems but the very evolution of the human psyche. I may not have done justice to the pungency of Alexander's theory in Chapter 14 and recommend that anyone wanting to think in a radically new way about the relationship between morality and power read his book, *The Biology of Moral Systems.*

Finally, in this chapter I pooh-poohed the academic approach that denigrates any effort to think simultaneously about issues of morality and power. I then gave what I hope was an evenhanded treatment of the Thrasymachean approach (power determines morality) and the traditional approach (morality curtails power). The sociobiological viewpoint on the relationship between morality and power was presented as giving a boost to both. It supports the former by showing that many rules are a moral overlay on the existing social relations and the latter by showing that moral ideas about equality often bring about a leveling of hierarchical relationships.

I concluded with a section on the democratic experiment, endorsing Popper's belief that in an open society *criticism* keeps the play of forces between morality and power ever on the move. I should let Reinhold Niebuhr have the last word since his is one of the most famous remarks on the subject of the relationship between morality and power. In his book, *Moral Man and Immoral Society* (1932), he wrote, "Politics will, to the end of history, be an area where conscience and power meet, where the ethical and coercive factors of human life will interpenetrate and work out their tentative and uneasy compromises" (p. 4).

CHAPTER 16

Nuclear Democracy

✳ ✳ ✳

Had not Barbara Tuchman already made claim to the title "The March of Folly," any of these three books could have used it appropriately. The development of the U.S. nuclear arsenal is treated by these authors from three different and quite original perspectives, but folly is never far from their theme. The stunning contribution of Clarfield, Wiecek, Kaplan, and Ford consists of clarifying the chain of events, apportioning the responsibility, drawing out the human dimensions of each nuclear decision, and generally rubbing the reader's nose in it. All three books deal with the American side of the problem; they take up their case pretty much without regard to "the evil empire," but in the end this seems justified: one almost feels that the factors that lead America to do its nuclear thing could operate in the absence of a real enemy. (Which is not to say that there was not a real enemy.) Not the whining variety of ingrates living in a privileged free society, these authors weep over the lack of overall perspective inherent in democracy and argue for more intelligent coordination of goals, values, and costs. They succeed in making myopic politics look contemptible and outmoded.

Nuclear America, a forty-year history, opens with Enrico Fermi working in an empty squash court at the University of Chicago in 1942, achieving the first sustained chain reaction. (A later vignette has Fermi at the Trinity test site at Los Alamos taking bets, just before the explosion, as to whether it might ignite an atmospheric chain reaction and incinerate the planet.) This book consists of highlighting the various turning points in

---

Review of Gerald Clarfield and William Wiecek, *Nuclear America* (New York: Harper and Row, 1984); Fred Kaplan, *The Wizards of Armageddon* (New York: Simon and Schuster, 1983); and Daniel Ford, *The Button* (London: Allen and Unwin, 1985).

the atomic age, the events that narrowed the choices for subsequent decisions. Here I shall mention only two early ones. The first was the decision to use the atom bomb, a weapon of awesome destruction, at Hiroshima. It could have been argued that, in the long tradition of "the just war," such indiscriminate killing of civilians was illegal and unethical. Had the United States stayed its hand, perhaps the use of atomic warfare could have been outlawed in the same way as biological warfare. Of course, the German air onslaught had helped to harden the public conscience, and furthermore, in the opinion of Clarfield and Wiecek, President Harry Truman was confident that the American people would back his decision because of the widespread hope for revenge against the Japanese.

It is true that the American people were not consulted (and it is true that scientists and religious leaders did argue against the atom bomb) but one can believe, from reading this book, that public opinion tends to drag down, not drag up, the principles of leaders. General Leslie Groves is noted as worrying, probably rightly, that he would catch hell from the taxpayers if they found out that he had spent two billion dollars to produce a bomb and then not used it.

The second turning point was that of the proposed international control of nuclear weapons — a plan put forward by David Lilienthal, Dean Acheson, Robert Oppenheimer, and others. Under this plan, in the early days of U.S. nuclear monopoly, an international authority would have owned all uranium mines, processing plants, and so on. If a country seized control of these facilities, it would give a year's warning that it had war in mind. It might have worked. But Truman unwittingly allowed Bernard Baruch, whom Clarfield and Wiecek call self-promoting, to take charge, and he quickly changed the plan to one that would be unacceptable to Stalin. Foreshadowing later arms control efforts, this plan was geared to domestic consumption: it was ridiculously one-sided. For one thing, "Baruch and his banker friends found the idea that the Authority should own and operate mines . . . dangerously socialistic" (Clarfield and Wiecek, p. 96). Moreover, and here legislators and the news media were his allies, Baruch capitalized on Americans' fear of losing the country's "atomic secrets." I was a child in the United States at the time (during the Rosenberg trial hysteria) and have always believed that we owned some atomic secrets. It has only recently been driven home to me, partly through Clarfield and Wiecek's book, that given the internationalism of the knowledge of physics, there is no such thing as an atomic secret.

The Wizards of Armageddon also starts in the 1940s, opening with a chapter on Bernard Brodie and the influences of Yale, Princeton, and the University of Chicago on his intellectual formation. Here was a civilian who had specialized in military theory, who would set out personally to convince the U.S. government of the folly of "national suicide" implicit in the strategy of atomic retaliation. Using Leo Szilard's idea of limited war (nuclear battles between military forces, rather than the bombing of cities), he helped establish the doctrine of counter-force in the RAND Corporation. RAND was a consulting firm whose only customer was the U.S. Air Force; it had an enormous behind-the-scenes influence that increased in the 1970s and 1980s, and Kaplan in this book does his best to reveal all. Kaplan was instrumental in having John Knowlton of the Library of Congress declassify hundreds of Air Force memos under the Freedom of Information Act — an act whose date of passage may one day be celebrated in the United States with as much significance as the Fourth of July.

The leading villain in Kaplan's book is interservice rivalry. For example, around 1960, the Army and Navy disputed the Air Force's highly specious missile-gap figures. In reply, SAC (Strategic Air Command) men General George Keegan and General James Walsh gave the Pentagon officials a series of briefings, complete with the new satellite photography — to prove that the Soviets were hiding their ICBMs (intercontinental ballistic missiles). "Photos of mediaeval towers, agricultural silos, a Crimean War memorial were depicted as cleverly disguised missile silos" (Kaplan, 1983, p. 288). In another instance, the Navy denounced the bombing of cities as immoral and uncivilized, since bombing was the Air Force's job. However, once the Navy got *Polaris*, with its submarine-launched missiles, they glorified this assignment. An interesting subplot of Kaplan's book is that the RAND men — the country's top war theorists — could not recommend the buildup of ground troops, even when that was the best policy for avoiding nuclear war — because RAND's paymaster was the Air Force. I have not captured here the cynicism of the brass, but Kaplan does so convincingly: the "good of the country" is always of lower priority — if it features at all — than the good of the service.

Kaplan's man is Ike. Kaplan sees Eisenhower as the only leader with enough prestige and common sense to have held the military at bay, the one who always kept sight of the "great equation," which consisted of how to protect the national security without wrecking society in the process (p. 178). Eisenhower presciently claimed that "a bankrupt America is more a Soviet goal than an America conquered on the field of battle" (p. 176). But even that president had less control over SAC than was realized. Kaplan describes a scene in 1957 in which Robert Sprague was trying to find out what Air Force General Curtis E. Le May was doing to protect the United States against Soviet nuclear attack. (Sprague, a layman, had been commissioned to investigate the possibility of a Soviet surprise attack.) Le May took Sprague into his "secret office," showing him that espionage data, such as that from Soviet military radio transmissions, would provide six hours' warning of any attack. The general said, "If I see that the Russians are amassing their plans for an attack, I'm going to knock the shit out of them before they take off the ground." "But that's not national policy," Sprague replied, flabbergasted. "I don't care," Le May rejoined. "It's my policy" (p. 134).

The Button takes up this problem of military control in the United States in much more frightening depth. Whereas almost every American believes that his nation would never strike first, Ford shows that today's military takes a U.S. preemptive strike for granted. This book, by a former director of the Union of Concerned Scientists, is a strange combination of two kinds of information, each well documented and each shocking. The first concerns the very poor command, control, and communications (C^3) system of the United States — an idea Ford got from Desmond Ball, the Australian defense specialist. The second concerns the wide delegation of the authority to shoot: the word *button* in the title is a come-on; in fact, there is no button by which a president can control the starting of a war.

Of interest to Australians, and serving as a typical example of the vulnerability of the U.S. early-warning system, is the fact that the station at Nurrungar (300 miles northwest of Adelaide) can be readily disabled by a small team of saboteurs (Ford, 1985, p. 66). The purpose of the Nurrungar facility is as follows.

Should the Soviets launch an ICBM, the flame during the rocket-boost phase would be detected by an infrared telescope on a certain U.S. satellite known as DSP-East that constantly monitors the Eastern Hemisphere. This satellite, however, could not send its data directly back to NORAD (North American Air Defense Command) because it is on the other side of the globe. It must instead transmit to a readout station, and the only place in the world geared for this is Nurrungar. Australia then forwards the information by cable to the United States. Ford notes that not only is the ground station at Nurrungar vulnerable to having its antenna wrecked by conventional explosives, but the cable could be cut anywhere it comes to shore, namely Sydney, Wellington, Hawaii, or San Francisco (1985, pp. 67–68).

It is also noteworthy that there are only three radio transmitters in the world that broadcast very low frequency (VLF) messages to U.S. submarines; they are in Maine, Washington, and Northwest Cape, Western Australia. One of the startling items in Ford's book is that U.S. Navy submarines that have lost contact with the continuously broadcast "we're happy" message (which indicates peacetime) are allowed to make a decision on their own to fire nuclear missiles. Now! Today! Ford thinks that this probably won't happen accidentally, though, since the Navy — which has much more nuclear firepower than the Air Force — does not have the Air Force's "use it or lose it" mentality. Ford notes that it is because SAC must launch its missiles from its silos "on warning" that the problems brought out in this book — the dangers of hair-trigger policy — are of extreme importance.

Here, the message is that the military is quite aware of the poor quality of the C^3 system but doesn't care to do much about it. The reason is that since it is understood that communications will collapse soon after a war begins (and Ford discovered that 94 percent of U.S. military transmissions depend on commercial telephone lines!), the Air Force looks upon first-strike as the only intelligent response if the Soviets start to get itchy. Ford believes that it is the weapons, the hardware, not the doctrines of public policy, that will guide events. He says, "Once the MX and D-5 are deployed . . . they will create an inescapable temptation for the United States, in a dire crisis, to use them before the Soviets use their SS-18s" (p. 235). Ford's work seems so out of line with received wisdom that one might be curious about the official reaction to it. I asked Ford if there had been any serious rebuttal by the government. He said that Defense Secretary Caspar Weinberger wrote to Congress saying that *The Button* was all wrong, that there was no problem, "and that if there were, it was being corrected" (personal communication, August 1986).

There is not too much repetition among these three books, and I would recommend that they be taken as a trilogy. Although written somewhat in the exposé style (which gives them their humor and their punch), they are not out to paint good guys and bad guys. The shenanigans of Congressmen, the rabble-rousing of news editors, the childishness of military chiefs are served up fairly sympathetically as problems of democracy that should be dealt with intelligently, not ignored. High technology is not depicted as awesome or even much worthy of respect: Kaplan denigrates the inbredness of the think tanks, such as RAND, with their weird, mathematical view of reality; Ford makes the big machines look sloppy, useless, and dangerous. Ethical problems are seen as having been left out of consideration by accident (perhaps because there is no bureaucracy to promote them?) rather than because of any evil inherent in human nature.

In short, these four authors observe that the nation is not a unified system like the human body, with a brain and a heart that work in some balanced way. The social system has "little logics" of its own: these spew out problems that then have to be dealt with by the thinking brains and feeling hearts of the members of society. The nuclear problem is but the most critical instance of this phenomenon. Because of its enormity, the nuclear issue may be the one on which citizens refuse to continue in their passive, complacent fatalism. We are in the habit of looking for big solutions to big problems; but this big problem is the result of many little problems, as defined in these books. The only solution, then, is the confronting of myriad, tedious little problems, for example, by restructuring the reward system in the military in order to diminish inter-service rivalry. "Let a thousand solutions bloom."

In general, this complex new literature makes the nuclear problem seem quite secondary to the issue of democratic control. Citizen responsibility, rather than aggrieved protest, is the new theme. Peace movement, take note.

CHAPTER 17

The Social Homunculus

Our remedies oft within ourselves do lie.
— William Shakespeare, *As You Like It*

No man is an island, entire of it self . . .
And therefore never send to know for whom the bell tolls.
It tolls for thee.
— John Donne, *Devotions*

The Brain as a Homunculus

In the last few decades, much has become known about how the human brain works. Through experiments with perception, memory, and reasoning; through postmortem examinations of the brain; through developmental studies of children; and through observation of patients' reaction to psychiatric medication; scientists have been able to come up with a lot of information about the human mind. Things that were once considered spiritual properties have now been found under the microscope. It is still not known, however, how the various systems of the brain work together. Specifically, it is not known how decisions are made. How does an individual sum up past experiences, innate preferences, cultural learning, and immediate urges in order to make a decision? We do not know, but certainly there is some dependable, intricate mechanism by which this is done: people can and do make appropriate decisions almost instantly when choices are presented. Almost equally instantly their brains send instructions to nerves and muscles to take the required action to carry out the decision.

Sometimes it is claimed that there is a tiny person ("a little green man") — a homunculus — in the brain who organizes all of this. That is not literally true, of course. The alleged homunculus is the whole brain, or even the whole body. At best we can say that people have a unified sense of self. (Even the rare split personalities do not coexist at the same moment — they take over in sequence.) This whole self is what organizes input and output. And if it commands the wrong output — such as telling a person to walk out of the house into the snow without boots — it will soon receive feedback (cold wet feet!) advising it to reassess the situation.

The Social Homunculus

I bring all of this up in order to introduce an idea about society, namely, that it lacks a central coordinator. Society has no built-in homunculus. (I shall use that word in this chapter since there is no real word to designate quite what I mean.) Naturally I do not claim that society is entirely lacking in coordination. A very small human society, say a group of five persons living on a desert island, can communicate directly with one another. They can report individual perceptions to each other ("The fish are on this side of the island today") and so achieve a unified knowledge through the medium of lan- guage. They can also organize themselves, voluntarily or by force, into a chain of command so that decisions made in the brain of one individual would be carried out by all. ("You get the coconuts.") I must say, even very large societies appear to be well coordinated. One speaks of "what China is doing this week" — or this generation — as though there were a single organism called China.

Yet there is no biological system that is responsible for the coordination of a society's members or their activities. In ant society there is such a homunculus. There is constant chemical communication among all members of an ant colony. Messages received chemically can, for example, inform the society that one caste (such as the caste of soldiers or foragers) is depleted in numbers, and action will be taken to create more of that caste (Hölldobler and Wilson, 1990). Among humans, one part of the group could be ailing, and other parts would not neces- sarily respond. They may respond, if some conscious decision is taken to so do, but we cannot depend on this happening in any automatic fashion.

Almost certainly such response is not controlled by Nature, but by people acting individually or collectively. The homunculus, or coordinator, in "society's brain" is thus not a fixed thing. It changes all the time according to degree of communication among people, the accuracy of their perception, and the institutional mechanisms they have set up for overall guidance of society.

Morality as Social Homunculus

I propose that *morality* plays a major role in such overall guidance of society. As depicted in earlier chapters, morality has two parts. It has the evolved biological apparatus, such as the conscience and moral emotions of individuals, and it has the externalized, invented part, consisting of rules, beliefs, principles, punishment systems, and so forth. As claimed by Richard Alexander and by others, human society could not have become complex in the first place if morality had not been available to coordinate personal interactions beyond one-to-one type of exchanges. Morality is thus a very important basis of social organization. I believe we take morality for granted and hardly notice its ubiquitous presence. We interact with one another with our moral monitor always tuned in to pick up signals of good and bad behavior. Also, we act, on a daily basis, as if we were obeying unseen commands — namely, the commands of the laws that we ourselves have culturally invented. ("Walk on the right side of the sidewalk.")

Besides the particular rules, there is also the general background that Emile Durkheim (1915) labels "the moral understanding." Religions and ideologies provide us with a world view that determines the overall rightness and wrongness of things and give us a sense of what constitutes a good and desirable life and what constitutes an objectionable life. Until recently, religion was perhaps the social homunculus par excellence. It guided a person through the social order, even through the whole universe. Religion saturated the environment with a myth that gave a why and wherefore to the individual's every action. It also coordinated the good of the group, allocating resources — or altruism — from one part to another.

In the contemporary stage, where revealed religion is not accepted by many people, the efficacy of what I am calling this social homunculus has obviously declined. Things fall apart, as artists of this century have reflected. Society appears to run amok: no one is coordinating it responsibly. There are two logical reactions to this state of affairs. One is *a sense of fatalism.* As John Lukacs says, "What is taught in our schools and universities all over the world is that we don't have control of our destiny, that we are programmed by genes or hormones or psychology or society or environment. We are more and more destitute of the sense of free will. This is part of technological development and the mind-set of an age at its very end. It is not life-giving. It is really a very despairing view of human nature and of its capacities" (quoted in Moyers, 1989, p. 437). The other reaction to the gap in social coordination is an invigorated *sense of agency.* Here, people recognize that they have something to contribute to social decisions. Consider this comment by the novelist and political activist Tom Wolfe, concerning the successful protest by citizens against the Westway Project in New York City. "Block politics *do* work. . . . Every financial interest you can think of was behind Westway, this colossal project not only to rebuild the West Side Highway, but to build gigantic real estate complexes through half of Manhattan down to the Battery. There were billions — *billions* — of dollars at stake, a lot of it already committed. And it was stopped! It was stopped rather easily by a coalition of neighborhood groups, who are against gigantism. . . ." (quoted in Moyers, 1989, p. 70).

Thus, people can perceive if something is going wrong, if one part of society is getting out of control, and can communicate with one another to organize a protest. Individuals can and do perform the role of social homunculus. They use morality to do this, insofar as a major feature of morality is judgment or evaluation. So, morality itself can be said to be a homunculus — a little green man helping to coordinate society. I do not think it is too farfetched to make an analogy with the ants again. The ants, as a society, have a mechanism for evaluating trouble in their society and for taking corrective action. In human society, morality is a powerful mechanism for performing that function.

This book has reported the writings of numerous authors who today use morality as a social homunculus or coordinator. They have analyzed what is wrong and what is "ailing" and have made various specific recommendations. We have heard, for example, such exhortations as "restore great literature to political debate," "demand honesty in government," "draw connections between the responsibility of the consumer and the activities of the corporation," "own up to the fact that technology is incompatible with certain other values," "revitalize the Christian concept of stewardship," "be critical of trashy art," and "find racism's breeding grounds and act preventively." Besides these specific correctives we have heard advice from many sources on how to understand our — may I say it again? — our social homunculus.

Recapitulation

Let me now sum up the material of the preceding sixteen chapters, and then offer a final comment.

Chapter 1, " 'Design Errors' in the Human Moral System," found four "errors" in the original design of the moral system. These are the option of deviance (a drug dealer can choose to ruin society for personal gain), demographic limitations (moral enforcement originally required face-to-face contact), tribalism (the rules of humane treatment often terminate at the country's border), and the arbitrariness of values (humans can invent values, and sometimes invent unhealthy ones). Three other flaws in the human moral system, related specifically to modern life, were identified as the diffusion of responsibility (it is hard to apportion blame when interactions between two parties are very indirect), the moral immunity of officeholders and group persons (including the nation and the corporation), and the coexistence of voluntarism and structuralism (which confuses people about whether they can or cannot be moral agents). I suggested that the modern flaws create a discomfort in the basic moral emotions that may eventually be sufficiently irritant to demand corrective action.

Chapter 2, "The Trickle-up of Trust," suggested that a main danger today is the climate of distrust. Sissela Bok noted a two-way street: dishonesty at high levels corrupts society in general, but it is up to individuals to reassert fundamental moral values. She developed a critique of government secrecy by using Kant's theory that four moral principles are essential to social life: restraint on violence, restraint on deception, restraint on betrayal of one's word, and restraint on excessive state secrecy. Secrecy, in particular, renders ordinary citizens powerless because it keeps from them information they need to influence policy. Bok recommends that Clausewitzian strategy be used in a "war against war," since she believes that it is no longer possible for war to be sane. Persons opposed to war, hatred, and violence need to make long-term plans and to coordinate their efforts.

Chapter 3, "Ten Commandments of Interethnic Relations," focused on interethnic conflicts, showing that they are usually conflicts among values. Five values isolated were: the value of cultures themselves, the functioning units of society, modernization, national pride, and the human being. I argued that articulation of these values is especially needed because ethnic relations is an area where fuzziness about values creates an atmosphere that is easily exploited. I recommended that social scientists be forthright in discussing these values instead of pretending that they can talk exclusively about the facts. We should admit that the area of interethnic relations is loaded with moral ideas.

The ten commandments of interethnic relations I proposed were (1) protect minorities (because they are vulnerable), (2) protect cultures (as each is unique), (3) encourage compromise, (4) call a demagogue a demagogue, (5) eschew the double standard (whites are not the sole proprietors of racism), (6) rate the effects on individuals (such as the cost of refugeeism), (7) expose outside interests, (8) recognize the advanced forms of nationalism (such as tariff barriers), (9) identify racism's breeding grounds, and (10) be aware of the politicization of the United Nations. (That organization often cannot act on behalf of humanity, since it represents states.)

Chapter 4, "Christianity: The Voluntary Society," argued in favor of giving conscious moral direction to political economy. Max Stackhouse noted the need for a public theology and pointed out that the absence of one today is exceptional. He argued that Christian theology provides a very valid anthropology: it shows that body and soul are united and that people are naturally social and willing to make voluntary sacrifices. He quoted Shailer Mathews, "To disregard the promptings and needs of the social part of the personality is to invite an intellectual and moral death whose earliest symptoms are sin and abnormality of all sorts" (Stackhouse, 1987, p. 54). Stackhouse maintained that industry should not be based on the desire for individual profit, but should be conducted for the service of the community. He recommended looking for ways in which corporations can be stimulated to act more morally.

Chapter 5, "Natural Law, Social Contract, and Sociobiological Theory," recalled the main philosophical questions about human society. What is the underlying basis of the social order? What motivates people to cooperate? Is human nature compassionate and self-sacrificing, or is it driven to self-aggrandizement? I noted that the two major Western theories replying to those questions are those of natural law and social contract. The former imagines a conscience by which people innately know right from wrong and a system in which people want to "agree with God." The latter alleges a social contract made by prehistoric people as their means of achieving a modicum of social harmony.

I then showed that social cooperation has now been explained biologically, in the case of nonhuman animals, through the theories of kin altruism (William Hamilton's formula of inclusive fitness) and reciprocal altruism. I sketched E. O. Wilson's four pinnacles of social evolution (corals, ants, some mammals, humans) and argued that humans never had a presocial phase, since their hominid forebears were already social. I outlined the fossil evidence from *Australopithecus* to *Homo sapiens neanderthalis* to Cro-Magnon man and then presented Robert Trivers's theory of the evolution of reciprocal altruism. I suggested that once moral emotions gave individuals a sense of right and wrong this laid the groundwork for the development of morality, of law, and ethics.

Chapter 6, "Green Ideas and the Ethics of Hunger," dealt first with such ways of mixing ethics and economics as through "socially conscious investing" and "investing for social change." Examples of projects such as LETS and GRI were furnished as part of Susan Meeker-Lowry's strategy to play up the successes of citizens' attempts to make their economy more responsive. Onora O'Neill's critique of the philosophy of rights was presented; it showed the inadequacy of the concept of rights to stimulate redress of the problem of world hunger and poverty. She recommended a (maverick) Kantian theory of obligation that would consider the context in which economic decisions are made. It would concentrate on human autonomy and material needs and identify social structures that coerce or deceive. I noted that the factor of sympathy as a motivator had been underemphasized in the ethics of hunger.

Chapter 7, "Moral Inertia: Contributing Factors," asked why it is that people do not act against massive evils, such as the evils of torture, of irreversible pollution, of extreme poverty, or of the arms race. I suggested that our inertia is not only due to the human-nature reasons often given — such as laziness, selfishness, or cowardice — but is also caused by numerous less dramatic factors. These include the following cognitive traits: perceptual selectivity (if we are not trained to see evil, we ignore it), the proclivity toward optimism, the Emperor's New Clothes syndrome (one doubts one's own senses if they are not in accord with the majority's), dichotomization (which suggests that the alternative to a particular evil may be an equally great evil), solutionism (the belief that there is a perfect solution to every problem), and the numbing effect of statistics.

Language problems were also identified as the contributors to moral inertia. Three result from emotions connected with religion, authority, and patriotism. I called them the realm of the sacred (words or concepts that restrict further thought), the force of authority, and the logic of nationalism (my group is automatically right and good). Five other language problems noted were sloganeering (oversimplifying the issues), Nuke-speak (overcomplicating the issues), Orwellian euphemism, the open-endedness of language itself (allowing, for example, two incompatible values to be endorsed simultaneously), and the unavailability of words to express certain moral relationships. Finally, I listed problems inherent in two major ideologies. Liberalism overemphasizes individualism and legality; Marxism overemphasizes economic determinism at the expense of political criticism, and concentrates too much on the virtue of the future system.

Chapter 8, "Is Cruelty Okay?", inquired into the causes of cruelty. I began by noting that most people assume that there are no particular causes (except, say, aberrant personality) and that suffering will somehow work its way to justice in the long run. A review of three books detailing historical examples of cruelty showed a range of contributing causes. Robert Hughes's Australian study included desire for money, status reinforcement, group rivalry, sadism, and isolation from the protection of society. M. Scott Peck's analysis of the MyLai massacre came up with group dynamics such as dependency on the leader, group narcissism, specialization, and intellectual laziness. Edward Peters's study of the history of torture blamed rationality, logic, professionalization, nationalism, devotion to philosophy, and a technological anthropology. From this long list I identified two things, the "herring factor" and intellectual laziness, as the major maintainers of cruelty. I asked "Is cruelty okay?" and showed that the answer could be "yes." I suggested that it would take a strong conviction that cruelty is not okay to combat routine economic cruelties. I blamed bystanders for not acting against cruelty.

Chapter 9, "Three Major Components of Morality," broke the broad concept of morality into three parts: judgment, law and order, and welfare-provision. Various biological explanations were given for the evolution of each of these. Judgment arises from the moral emotions, which evolved thanks to reciprocal altruism and the threat posed by cheaters. The human penchant for law and order may not only be related to sensing of right and wrong but may have to do with hierarchies: individuals need to know where they stand, so that life will be predictable. The trait of conformity may reinforce this from another source.

It was noted that the welfare-provision component of human morality has a less direct biological explanation. The trait of compassion is species-specific to humans and may have developed in some way from maternal nurturance. It is probably related also to our mental capacity for vicarious experience: seeing another person hurt, hurts *us*. One thing we know is that an instinct to look out for absolutely everybody could not have evolved as such, because natural selection cannot work for the good of all. Most likely, humans, after they had fully evolved, used their compassion and their vicarious feelings to concoct welfare systems. This would easily have been aided by the brain's tendency to universalize rules and by religion's tendency to specify exactly what God wants us to do ("Love thy neighbor as thyself"). Welfare-provision was no doubt motivated by enlightened self-interest as well.

Chapter 10, "American Moral Problems," presented the thoughts of various people interviewed by Bill Moyers on the subject of moral life in the United States today. Among their complaints about current behavior, they listed dishonesty, greed, easy killing, voter manipulation, low expectations of public officials, and the ethos that anything is acceptable if it leads to winning. They noted various causes of the problem, which I boiled down to the emphasis on individualism over community, the incompatibility of technology and other values, and problems of moral language. These last include the deceptiveness of language used in television ads, especially those of political campaigns; the trick by which people wrap themselves in the flag or brandish the Bible; the blandness of presidential language that conceals foreign policy; and the sequestering of major literary ideas about human life from public discussion. Moyers's question "What is the moral life?" yielded a rich range of answers that I condensed to self-command, self-restraint, compromise, generosity, public virtue, consensus-generation, and the maintenance of standards.

Chapter 11, "The Elusive Butterfly of Power," attempted to refute the notion that modern political power structures are an expression of human nature's drive for power. I conducted a sociobiological search for the biological antecedents of human power and noted that aggression, dominance, and coalition-formation in the animal kingdom have some obvious correlates in human behavior. However, I stated that irrespective of those things, a cybernetic imperative is involved in the organization of complex society. Hierarchical structures are required for communication and control when the number of individuals involved in an enterprise is large or when they are geographically spread out.

A brief sketch of prehistory showed that institutionalized roles of power began to develop at the horticultural stage and that administrative networks always accompanied the formation of the state. Such offices may be filled by power-hungry types — and often are — but they *need* not be. I showed that the cybernetic theory of the state is useful for separating out the value-neutral aspects of political structures from our moral evaluation of them. We may, for example, decide ethically that unequal distribution of goods is unfair, but in the cybernetic model that would not call for the withering away of the state, since the state is necessary for coordination of any complex society.

Chapter 12, "The Genetics of Racism," used the theory of inclusive fitness to argue that the human tendency toward nepotism and toward protection of "one's own people" is a natural instinct. Pierre van den Berghe pointed out that mistreatment of minorities is a symptom of the failure to extend the umbrella of altruism to cover strangers. It was suggested that such knowledge of the basis of our racist habits puts the onus on us to ameliorate the effects of that behavior or to find ways to discourage the behavior.

Chapter 13, "The Inevitability of Justice," argued that the modern system of the division of labor requires "moral warmth" just as did the earlier, more communal style of production. Emile Durkheim believed that this warmth would be found. He also believed that the moral authority of the modern system derived at least in part from the idea of moral individualism. This individualism is paradoxically not an expression of egoism but is a collective idea. It is founded upon sentiments of sympathy for human suffering and a desire of equality and justice for everyone. As I understand it from Durkheim, the practice of social justice confers a legitimacy on individualism. We are entitled to rights because we extend them to others, and this is the main moral code by which we moderns operate. Nevertheless, this is not enough to make things right: conscious attention is needed to remoralize the economy. "What reflection can and must do is prescribe the goal that must be attained" (Durkheim, 1984, p. 340).

Chapter 14, "What has Mortality to Do With Morality?" showed that mortality can be used to buttress the argument that the so-called selfish gene directs evolution. We age and die not because living bodies are incapable of enduring more than a century — redwood trees last for millennia. Rather, we undergo senescence because the gene wants to get on with it. From this argument, Richard Alexander developed the notion that altruism evolved "to please the gene," as it were. Humans should understand, he said, that our moral sense is basically something that operates in the interest of our inclusive fitness. Moreover, we should recognize that moral transactions and moral rules have all got something to do with the competition among interests. Because of this, the best morality of which we are probably capable is that of contract and of compromise. He recommended that we turn our attention away from philosophical mysteries of morality, these mysteries having now been solved.

Chapter 15, "The Relationship Between Morality and Power," inquired as to whether these two respective phenomena have any connection with each other. The academic approach says they do not, but that, I claim, is because some political scientists want to isolate power to study it exclusively. The Thrasymachean approach says that the two are related, insofar as power determines morality. The traditional approach holds that morality curtails power. I defended both of these views and then offered sociobiological support for each one. Power does determine morality to some extent — a clue to this being the fact that deference to authority is itself a universally found moral rule. Yet morality curtails power, too, since morality's sense of right and wrong can be extended to the wrongness of unequal treatment. I outlined the career of the idea of equality from stoicism up to communism and considered E. O. Wilson's claim that universal human rights is a mammalian imperative. Finally, I discussed the democratic experiment, showing that moral criticism of politics comes into play on an ongoing basis in the open society.

Chapter 16, "Nuclear Democracy," identified a number of specific problems that contribute to the arms race, such as interservice rivalry, the inbredness of think tanks such as RAND, and the U.S. military's assumption that it may be pushed into a first-strike attack. An underlying theme of this chapter was *drift*, as seen, for example, in the way the United States drifted into the use of the first atomic bomb at Hiroshima. It was pointed out that there were other reasonable options to a nuclear arms race, such as international control of all uranium, but these options were not given much hearing. I concluded that efforts toward nuclear peace must be multilevel and must include dealing with the prosaic problems of bureaucracy.

Three Top Priorities

To return to the theme of this chapter, there is no little green man in society who coordinates all social relationships or acts to make life just. Feedback in our social system has to be made through multitudes of individual, thinking persons. As I implied in Chapter 1, many people fail to realize that their moral sensibilities are useful for solving social problems. They feel as though they are watching a film, and no matter how vital the events may be, they cannot touch the people in the film or change the course of historical developments. I have tried in this book, especially in the review essays, to marshal evidence that people can influence events by applying their moral power to social problems. They can do the work of the social homunculus.

As a conclusion, since such a plethora of moral suggestions has been made in this book, I would like to narrow the field down to three. These top priorities are merely my own preferences. The reader can pick out any set of three — or other number!

The first priority in my scheme would be, as Judith Shklar says, to "put cruelty first" (1984, p. 8). If we could lay out all our ideas about "bad things" on the table at one time, I think the cruel bad things could be given some special place. Cruel bad things would, at a minimum, include physical violence, torture, starvation, extreme economic exploitation, and the persecution of minorities. Putting cruelty first would mean giving a higher priority to the rescue of particular victims and would also mean such intellectual things as articulating a clearer philosophy of ethics concerning persons in need. It would mean breaking the silence that allows cruelty to flourish and imposing discipline from outside. I defend the reasonableness of "putting cruelty first" by presuming that if any of us were the victims, we would wish it to be first!

My second recommended priority would be to "tame the tigers." The "tigers" consist of such daunting entities as the nation and the corporation. By "taming" them I mean to insist on recognizing their humble origins and purposes. As Max Stackhouse says, the purpose of industry is to serve the community. By "taming" them I also mean to deprive them of what Thomas Nagel calls their moral immunity. It does not make sense for group persons, such as corporations and nations, to be exempt from accountability, and it makes only limited sense for officeholders to be similarly exempt. At the very least, the effects of corporate and national actors must be carefully observed, and responsibility assigned to someone. It is absurd for us to remain blind to these effects and to try to escape all responsibility ourselves. As M. Scott Peck noted in his analysis of the ladder of collective responsibility, the buck stops at the top. If the whole society sponsors an evil program, all those who participate in that society share some personal responsibility. The lack of articulation of this fact has been perhaps the biggest gap in our moral language.

My third priority would be to "bring morality down to earth." As Richard Alexander says, we need to realize that rules have to do with the resolving of conflicts, that is, with competing interests. The poet Ogden Nash asks (in his "Kind of an Ode to Duty"):

O Duty!
Why has thou not the visage of a sweetie or a cutie?

The answer is obvious from sociobiology. Duty cannot be a sweetie or a cutie because it is necessarily painful. Duty involves self-restraint, sacrifice, and generally suppressing the instinct to follow one's interests. For this reason, we should recognize that the making of new rules cannot please everyone — there is always a price to be paid by some party. Certainly this is true when the issue concerns the economy or the environment.

On the same note, we should admit that the source of the "rightness" of these rules (such as the rule "put cruelty first") is simply ourselves. A rule becomes right because people agree to it. People talk about a problem, study it, apply precedents or principles to it, consult their highest beliefs and traditions, and then decide what is right. What other source of right could there possibly be?

Bibliography

Alexander, Richard (1979) *Darwinism and Human Affairs*. Seattle, Wash.: University of Washington Press.

—— (1987) *The Biology of Moral Systems*. Hawthorne, N.Y.: Aldine de Gruyter.

Alston, P., and K. Tomasevski, eds. (1984) *The Right to Food*. Dordrecht: Nijhoff.

The American Heritage Dictionary of the English Language: New College Edition (1976). Boston: Houghton Mifflin.

Arblaster, Anthony (1984) *The Rise and Decline of Western Liberalism*. Oxford: Blackwell.

Arnold, E. Vernon (1911) *Roman Stoicism*. Cambridge: Cambridge University Press.

Balikci, A. (1970) *The Netsilik Eskimo*. Garden City, N.J.: Natural History Press.

Beitz, Charles R. (1988) "Recent International Thought." *International Journal* H3:183–204.

Bellah, Robert N. (1973) *Emile Durkheim on Morality and Society*. Chicago: University of Chicago Press.

Berelson, Bernard, and Gary Steiner (1964) *Human Behavior: An Inventory of Scientific Findings*. New York: Harcourt, Brace, and World.

Berlin, Isaiah (1980) *Against the Current*. Edited by Henry Hardy. New York: Penguin.

Betzig, Laura (1986) *Despotism and Differential Reproduction*. Hawthorne, N.Y.: Aldine de Gruyter.

Bigelow, Robert (1969) *The Dawn Warriors: Man's Evolution Towards Peace*. Boston: Little, Brown.

Bok, Sissela (1985) "Distrust, Secrecy, and the Arms Race." *Ethics* 95:712–727.

—— (1989) *A Strategy for Peace: Human Values and the Threat of War*. New York: Pantheon.

Brenkert, George (1983) *Marx's Ethics of Freedom*. London: Routledge and Kegan Paul.

Bull, Hedley (1984) *Interventions in World Politics*. Oxford: Clarendon Press.

Carneiro, Robert (1970) "A Theory of the Origin of the State." *Science* 196: 733–738.

Carr, E. H. (1958) *The Twenty Years' Crisis: 1919–1939*. London: Macmillan.

Cela-Conde, Camilo (1987) *On Genes, Gods and Tyrants: The Biological Causation of Morality*. Hingham, Mass.: Kluwer.

225

Chagnon, Napoleon, and William Irons, eds. (1979) *Evolutionary Biology and Human Social Behavior: An Anthropological Perspective.* North Scituate, Mass.: Duxbury Press.

Cherfas, Jeremy, and John Gribbin (1982) *The Monkey Puzzle.* New York: Pantheon.

Claessen, Henry J.M., and Peter Skalnik, eds. (1976) *The Early State.* The Hague: Mouton.

Clarfield, Gerald, and William Wiecek (1984) *Nuclear America.* New York: Harper and Row.

Cohen, Marshall (1984) "Moral Skepticism and International Relations." *Philosophy and Public Affairs* 13:299–346.

Cohen, Ronald (1978) "State Origins: A Reappraisal." In *The Early State,* edited by Henry J.M. Claessen and Peter Skalnik. The Hague: Mouton.

Colletti, Lucio (1977) "A Political and Philosophical Interview." In *Western Marxism, a Critical Reader,* edited by staff of *New Left Review.* London: New Left Books.

Connor, Richard C., and Kenneth S. Norris (1982) "Are Dolphins and Whales Reciprocal Altruists?" *American Naturalist* 119:358–374.

Corcoran, Paul (1983a) "The Limits of Democratic Theory." In *Democratic Theory and Practice,* edited by Graeme Duncan. Cambridge: Cambridge University Press.

—— (1983b) *Before Marx: Socialism and Communism in France, 1830–48.* London: Macmillan.

Daly, Martin, and Margo Wilson (1988) *Homicide.* Hawthorne, N.Y.: Aldine de Gruyter.

Darwin, Charles (1877) *The Descent of Man and Selection in Relation to Sex,* 2d ed. London: Murray.

Davy, Georges (1920) "Emile Durkheim: L'ouvre." *Revue de Metaphysique et de Morale* 27:71–112.

Dawkins, Richard (1976) *The Selfish Gene.* Oxford: Oxford University Press.

Dawkins, Richard, and J. R. Krebs (1978) "Animal Signals: Information or Manipulation?" In *Behavioral Ecology,* edited by J. R. Krebs and N. B. Davies, pp. 282–309. Oxford: Blackwell Scientific Publications.

De Waal, Frans (1982) *Chimpanzee Politics.* New York: Harper and Row.

Diggins, John Patrick, and Mark Kann, eds. (1981) *The Problem of Authority in America.* Philadelphia: Temple University Press.

Donelan, Michael (1982) "The Community of Mankind." In *The Community of States,* edited by James Mayall, pp. 140–157. London: Allen and Unwin.

Dunbar, Robin (1988) *Primate Social Systems.* Ithaca, N.Y.: Cornell University Press.

Dunn, John (1979) *Political Theory in the Face of the Future.* Cambridge: Cambridge University Press.

Durkheim, Emile (1898) "L'individualisme et les intellectuels." *Revue Bleue* 10:7–13. A full translation appears in Steven Lukes (1969) "Durkheim's Individualism and the Intellectuals." *Political Studies* 17:19–30.

——— (1910) Contribution to discussions of "La Notion d'egalite sociale," seance du 30 decembre 1909, in *Bulletin de la Societe francaise de philosophie*, 10:59–63, 65–67, 69–70.

——— (1915) *The Elementary Forms of the Religious Life*, translation of 1912 edition by J. W. Swain. London: Allen and Unwin.

——— (1984) *The Division of Labour in Society*. Introduction by Lewis Coser. Translated by W. D. Halls. London: Macmillan.

Elliot, W. A. (1986) *Us and Them.* Aberdeen: University of Aberdeen Press.

Ellis, Lee (1990) "The Evolution of Collective Counterstrategy of Crime: From the Primate Control Role to the Civil Justice System." In *Crime in Biological, Social, and Moral Contexts*, edited by L. Ellis and H. Hoffman. New York: Praeger.

Etzioni-Halevy, Eva (1983) *Bureaucracy and Democracy*. London: Routledge and Kegan Paul.

——— (1989) *Fragile Democracy*. New Brunswick, N.J.: Transaction Books.

Falk, Richard (1981) *Human Rights and State Sovereignty*. New York: Holmes and Maier.

Ford, Daniel (1985) *The Button*. London: Allen and Unwin.

Freedman, Daniel (1979) *Human Sociobiology*. New York: Free Press.

Fromm, Erich (1968) *The Revolution of Hope*. New York: Harper and Row, Perennial Library.

Gauthier, David (1986) *Morals by Agreement.* Oxford: Clarendon.

George, Susan (1984) *Ill Fares the Land*. London: Writers and Readers Cooperative.

Gewirth, Alan (1965) *Political Philosophy*. New York: Macmillan.

——— (1973) "Ethics." *The New Encyclopaedia Britannica*, 15th ed.

——— (1978) *Of Reason and Morality*. Chicago: University of Chicago Press.

Giddens, Anthony (1971) "Durkheim's Political Sociology." *The Sociological Review*, new series, 19:477–519.

——— (1972) *Emile Durkheim: Selected Writings*. Cambridge: Cambridge University Press.

Goodall, Jane (1972) *In the Shadow of Man*. London: Collins.

——— (1982) "Order Without Law." *Journal of Social and Biological Structures* 5:353–360.

——— (1986) *The Chimpanzees of Gombe*. Cambridge: Harvard University Press.

Gough, J. W. (1957) *The Social Contract: A Critical Study of Its Development*, 2d ed. Oxford: Clarendon.

Hamilton, Alexander, James Madison, and John Jay (1961) (Reprint from 1787) *The Federalist*. Introduced by W. R. Brock. London: Dent.

Hamilton, William D. (1964) "The Genetical Theory of Social Behaviour, I, II." *Journal of Theoretical Biology* 7:1–16, 17–52.

Hanson, Russell (1985) *The Democratic Imagination in America*. Princeton, N.J.: Princeton University Press.

Bibliography

Hardin, Garrett (1968) "The Tragedy of the Commons." *Science* 162:1243–1248.

Hardin, Garrett J., and John Baden, eds. (1977) *Managing the Commons*. San Francisco: W. H. Freeman, 1977.

Harris, Marvin (1974) *Cows, Pigs, and Witches*. New York: Vintage.

Heilbroner, Robert (1962) *The Making of Economic Society*, 6th ed. Englewood Cliffs, N.J.: Prentice-Hall.

Herman, Edward (1982) *The Real Terror Network*. Boston: The South End Press.

Herskovits, Melville (1938) *Dahomey, an Ancient West African Kingdom*. Locust Valley, N.Y.: Augustin Press.

Hesse, P. (1987) "Stereotypes Mask Feelings of Fear." *Media and Values* 39:5–6.

Hobbes, Thomas (1909) (Reprint from 1651 with an essay by W. G. Pogson Smith.) *Leviathan*. Oxford: Clarendon.

Hoffman, John (1984) *The Gramscian Challenge*. Oxford: Blackwell.

Hoffman, Stanley (1978) *Primacy or World Order*. New York: McGraw-Hill.

—— (1982) *Duties Beyond Borders*. Syracuse, N.Y.: Syracuse University Press.

Hölldobler, Bert, and E. O. Wilson (1990) *The Ants*. Cambridge: Harvard University Press.

Howard, Michael (1983) *The Causes of Wars and Other Essays*. London: Unwin.

Hughes, Robert (1988) *The Fatal Shore*. London: Pan.

Isaac, Glynn (1979) "The Food Sharing Behavior of Protohuman Hominids." In *Human Ancestors: Readings from Scientific American*, edited by Glynn Isaac and Richard Leakey. San Francisco: W. H. Freeman.

Izard, Carroll (1978) "Emotions as Motivations: An Evolutionary-Developmental Perspective." *Nebraska Symposium on Motivation* 26:163–200.

Jackall, Robert (1988) *Moral Mazes: The World of Corporate Managers*. New York: Oxford University Press.

Kamenka, Eugene (1986) "Why Was the Bolshevik Terror Wrong?" (A review of Steven Lukes, *Marxism and Morality*, *The New York Times Book Review* (February 2) p. 20.

Kaplan, Fred (1983) *The Wizards of Armageddon*. New York: Simon and Schuster.

Keal, Paul (1983) *Unspoken Rules and Superpower Dominance*. London: Macmillan.

Keith, Arthur (1948) *A New Theory of Human Evolution*. London: Watts.

Kozol, Jonathan (1980) *The Night Is Dark and I Am Far from Home*. New York: Continuum.

Kuper, Leo (1981) *Genocide*. New York: Penguin.

—— (1985) *The Prevention of Genocide*. New Haven, Conn.: Yale University Press.

Lenski, Gerhard E. (1966) *Power and Privilege*. New York: McGraw-Hill.

Luban, David (1986) "The Legacy of Nuremberg." *QQ: Report from the Center for Philosophy and Public Policy*, College Park, Md.: University of Maryland, p. 6.

Lukes, Steven (1973) *Emile Durkheim: His Life and Work.* London: Allen Lane.

———— (1977) "Power and Structure." In *Essays in Social Theory.* London: Macmillan.

———— (1985) *Marxism and Morality.* Oxford: Clarendon.

Lumsden, Charles J., and E.O. Wilson (1981) *Genes, Mind and Culture: The Coevolutionary Process.* Cambridge: Harvard University Press.

McGuinness, Diane (1987) *Dominance, Aggression and War.* New York: Paragon.

MacIntyre, Alasdair (1966) *A Short History of Ethics.* New York: Macmillan.

Mack, John E. (1988) "The Enemy System." *The Lancet* 2:385–387.

McNaughton, David (1988) *Moral Vision.* Oxford: Blackwell.

Macridis, Roy (1986) *Modern Political Regimes.* Boston: Little, Brown.

Mathews, Shailer (1897) *The Social Teachings of Jesus.* New York: Macmillan.

Maxwell, Mary (1984) *Human Evolution: A Philosophical Anthropology.* New York: Columbia University Press.

———— (1990) *Morality among Nations.* Albany: State University of New York Press.

Maxwell, Mary, ed., (1991) *The Sociobiological Imagination.* Albany: State University of New York Press.

Maynard Smith, John (1964) "Kin Selection and Group Selection." *Nature* 201:1145–1147.

Meeker-Lowry, Susan (1988) *Economics as If the Earth Really Mattered.* Philadelphia: New Society Publishers.

Michels, Robert (1958) *Political Parties.* Glencoe, Ill.: Free Press.

Morgenthau, Hans (1967) *Politics Among Nations.* New York: Knopf.

Moscowitz, Moses (1968) *Human Rights.* New York: Oceana Publications.

Moyers, Bill (1989) *A World of Ideas,* edited by Betty Sue Flowers. New York: Doubleday.

Murdock, George (1959) *Africa: Its Peoples, Their Culture, and History.* New York: McGraw-Hill.

Nagel, Thomas (1978) "Ruthlessness in Public Life." In *Public and Private Morality,* edited by Stuart Hampshire. Cambridge: Cambridge University Press.

Niebuhr, Reinhold (1932) *Moral Man and Immoral Society.* New York: Scribners.

———— (1941) *The Nature and Destiny of Man.* New York: Scribners.

O'Neill, Onora (1986) *Faces of Hunger.* London: Allen and Unwin.

Orwell, George (1950) *Nineteen Eighty-Four: A Novel.* London: Secker and Warburg.

Packer, Craig (1977) "Reciprocal Altruism in *Papio anubis.*" *Nature* 265:441–443.

Passmore, John (1970) *The Perfectibility of Man.* New York: Scribners.

Peck, M. Scott (1983) *People of the Lie.* New York: Simon and Schuster.

Peters, Edward (1985) *Torture.* Oxford: Blackwell.

Bibliography

Pettman, Ralph, ed., (1986) *Teaching for Human Rights.* Vol I: *Preschool and Grades 1–4.* Vol II: *Grades 5–10.* Canberra: Australian Government Publishing Service.

Piaget, Jean (1975) *The Child's Conception of the World.* London: Littlefield.

Popper, Karl (1945) *The Open Society.* Vol 2: *Hegel to Marx.* London: Routledge and Kegan Paul.

Pugh, George Edgin (1978) *The Biological Origin of Human Values.* London: Routledge and Kegan Paul.

Ralston, Holmes III (1988) *Environmental Ethics.* Philadelphia: Temple University Press.

Reader, John (1981) *Missing Links: The Hunt for Earliest Man.* London: Collins.

Reynolds, Vernon, Vincent Falger, and Ian Vine, eds. (1987) *The Sociobiology of Ethnocentrism: Evolutionary Dimensions of Xenophobia, Discrimination, Racism and Nationalism.* London: Croom Helm.

Rheingold, H. L., and D. F. Hay (1978) "Prosocial Behavior of the Very Young." In *Morality as a Biological Phenomenon,,* edited by Gunther Stent. New York: Springer-Verlag.

Richards, Graham (1987) *Human Evolution.* London: Routledge.

Rousseau, Jean-Jacques (1984) (Reprint from 1754) *A Discourse on Inequality.* Translated and with introduction by Maurice Cranston. New York: Penguin.

Ruse, Michael, and E. O. Wilson (1986) "Moral Philosophy as Applied Science." *Philosophy* 61:173–192.

Sandel, Michael (1982) *Liberalism and the Limits of Justice.* Cambridge: Cambridge University Press.

Scruton, Roger (1982) *A Dictionary of Political Thought.* London: Pan.

Sen, Amartya K. (1984) "The Right Not to Be Hungry." In *The Right to Food,* edited by P. Alston and K. Tomasevski. Dordrecht: Nijhoff.

Sherif, Muzafer (1956) "Experiments in Group Conflict." *Scientific American* 196:54–58.

Shklar, Judith (1957) *After Utopia.* Princeton, N.J.: Princeton University Press.

——— (1984) *Ordinary Vices.* Cambridge: Belknap/Harvard University Press.

Shue, Henry (1980) *Basic Rights.* Princeton, N.J.: Princeton University Press.

——— (1984) "The Interdependence of Duties." In *The Right to Food,* edited by P. Alston and K. Tomasevski. Dordrecht: Nijhoff.

Singer, Peter (1981) *The Expanding Circle: Ethics and Sociobiology.* New York: Farrar, Straus, and Giroux.

——— (1984) "Ethics and Sociobiology." *Zygon: Journal of Religion and Science* 19:141–158.

Sirianni, Carmen J. (1984) "Justice and the Division of Labour: A Reconsideration of Durkheim's Division of Labour in Society." *The Sociological Review* 32:449–470.

Smart, J.J.C. (1989) *Our Place in the Universe.* Oxford: Blackwell.

Smuts, Barbara B., Dorothy L. Cheney, Robert M. Seyfarth, Richard W. Wrangham, and Thomas T. Struhsaker, eds. (1987) *Primate Societies.* Chicago: University of Chicago Press.

Solzhenitsyn, Alexandr (1975) *The Gulag Archipelago.* Translated by Thomas P. Whitney. London: Fontana/Collins.

—— (1978) Speech at Harvard University Commencement, Cambridge, Mass.

Stackhouse, Max (1984) *Creeds, Society, and Human Rights.* Grand Rapids, Mich.: Eerdmans.

—— (1987) *Public Theology and Political Economy.* Grand Rapids, Mich.: Eerdmans.

Strauss, Leo (1968) *Liberalism: Ancient and Modern.* New York: Basic.

Thigpen, Robert (1972) *Liberty and Community: The Political Philosophy of William Ernest Hocking.* The Hague: Martinus Nijhoff.

Tiger, Lionel (1979) *Optimism: the Biology of Hope.* New York: Simon and Schuster.

Trinkhaus, Erik, and William W. Howells (1979) "The Neanderthals." *Scientific American* 241:94–105.

Trivers, Robert (1971) "The Evolution of Reciprocal Altruism." *Quarterly Review of Biology* 46:35–57.

—— (1985) *Social Evolution.* Menlo Park, Calif.: Benjamin/Cummings.

Tuan, Yi-Fri (1989) *Morality and Imagination.* Madison: University of Wisconsin Press.

van den Berghe, Pierre (1981) *The Ethnic Phenomenon.* Westport, Conn.: Greenwood Press.

—— (1989) *Stranger in Their Midst.* Niwot, Colo.: University Press of Colorado.

van den Berghe, Pierre, ed. (1990) *State Violence and Ethnicity.* Niwot, Colo.: University Press of Colorado.

Vanhanen, Tatu (1984) *The Emergence of Democracy, a Comparative Study of 119 States, 1850–1979.* Helsinki: The Finnish Society of Science and Letters.

Vincent, J. R. (1986) *Human Rights and International Relations.* Cambridge: Cambridge University Press.

Walzer, Michael (1978) "Teaching Morality." *The New Republic* 178:11–12.

Wilkinson, Gerald (1984) "Reciprocal Food Sharing in the Vampire Bat." *Nature* 308:181–184.

Williams, George C. (1957) "Pleiotropy, Natural Selection, and the Evolution of Senescence." *Evolution* 11:398–411.

—— (1966) *Adaptation and Natural Selection.* Princeton, N.J.: Princeton University Press.

Wilson, E. O. (1978) *On Human Nature.* New York: Bantam.

—— (1980) *Sociobiology: The Abridged Edition.* Cambridge: Harvard University Press.

Wong, David B. (1984) *Moral Relativity.* Berkeley: University of California Press.

Bibliography

Woodhouse, A.S.P., ed. (1983) *Puritanism and Liberty, Being the Army Debates 1647–49.* London: Dent.

World Commission on Environment and Development (1987) *Our Common Future.* Oxford: Oxford University Press.

Wright, Peter (1987) *Spycatcher.* New York: Dell.

Wrong, Dennis H. (1979) *Power: Its Forms, Bases, and Uses.* Oxford: Blackwell.

Zeller, Edward (1886) *Outlines of the History of Greek Philosophy.* Translated by Sarah Frances Alleyne and Evelyn Abbott. London: Longmans, Green, and Co.

Index

Abortion, 133
Academic approach, 190–91, 202–3
Africa: Bambuti, 156; despotisms, 158–59
Agency, moral, 11, 13, 14, 16; regarding power, 163; sense of, 214
Aggression: in animals, 143–45; defined, 143; in humans, 148–50; physiology of, 144–45; and political structures, 161; types of, 144
Alexander, Richard, 9, 181–87; on conscience, 182; on groups, 151, 202; on interests, 182–84, 224; on mortality, 183–85, 221; on utilitarianism, 181
Alston, P., 65
Altruism, 49–53, 118, 183; kin, 151–52, 166; and power, 196
American moral problems, 126–35, 220
Analogy, 148
Anarchy, 163
Anthropology, 115; Christian, 39–40; evidence of human evolution, 47–49; and torture, 104, 107
Arbitrariness of values, 9, 15
Australian penal colony, 87–94
Australopithecus, 47–48
Authority: dislike for, 80; in Durkheim, 176–77; force of, 175; necessity of, 81

Baboon, 50, 52, 147
Baier, Kurt, 185
Ball, Desmond, 208
Bambuti, 156
Bat, vampire, 52
Beitz, Charles, 84
Bellah, Robert, 129–30, 131, 137–38, 178
Benedict, Ruth, 63
Berelson, Bernard, 72
Berlin, Isaiah, 73
Betzig, Laura, 146, 183

Bible, 42; brandishing of, 134, 220; in the Reformation, 194–95
Bigelow, Robert, 9, 151
Big Men, 157
Bok, Sissela, 17–22, 202, 216
Borsodi, Ralph, 60
Brain: evolution of, 47–49; as homunculus, 211–12; and right and wrong, 118; tendency to universalize rules, 220; and thinking about groups, 29; value guidance, 10
Brandt, Richard, 185
Brenkert, George, 82
Bull, Hedley, 33

Capitalism, 40, 81, 83, 192
Carneiro, Robert, 160
Carr, E. H., 190–92, 196
Chagnon, Napoleon, 111–12, 183
Cheating, 53, 118
Chiefdom, 156–58
Chimpanzee: closed society, 166; cooperate socially, 44; evolution of, 47; politics of, 147; sympathy in, 121; warfare in, 150
Chomsky, Noam, 200
Christian: anthropology, 39–40; on ends and means, 84; ideas about equality, 193–94; way of social living, 37–42, 216–17
Church, F. Forrester, 134, 137
Church, the, 37; investing, 58; and Reformation, 193–94; and torture, 103–4, 112
Clarfield, Gerard, 205–07
Class, social, 33, 154, 167–68; in United States, 127
Classics, 134–35
Clausewitz, Carl von, 18–20, 216
Coalition-formation: in animals, 146–48; in humans, 153–54
Cognitive traits, 72–74
Cohen, Marshall, 73

233

Index

234

Index